CRITICAL THEORY IN INTERNATIONAL RELATIONS AND SECURITY STUDIES

This book provides an assessment of the legacy, challenges and future directions of Critical Theory in the fields of International Relations and Security Studies.

It provides 'first-hand' interviews with some of the pioneers of Critical Theory in the fields of International Relations Theory and Security Studies. The interviews are combined innovatively with reflective essays to create an engaging and accessible discussion of the legacy and challenges of critical thinking. A unique forum that combines first-person discussion and secondary commentary on a variety of theoretical positions, the book explores in detail the interaction between different theories and approaches, including postcolonialism, feminism and poststructuralism. Scholars from a variety of theoretical backgrounds reflect on the strengths and problems of critical theory, recasting the theoretical discussion about critical theory in the study of world politics and examining the future of the discipline.

Both an introduction and an advanced engagement with theoretical developments over the past three decades, *Critical Theory in International Relations and Security Studies* will be of interest to students and scholars of international politics, security studies and philosophy.

Shannon Brincat is a University of Queensland Postdoctoral Research Fellow.

Laura Lima has recently submitted her doctoral thesis at the Department of International Politics, Aberystwyth University.

João Nunes is a Postdoctoral Fellow at the University of Warwick.

CRITICAL THEORY IN INTERNATIONAL RELATIONS AND SECURITY STUDIES

Interviews and reflections

Edited by Shannon Brincat, Laura Lima and João Nunes

Routledge
Taylor & Francis Group

LONDON AND NEW YORK

First published 2012
by Routledge
2 Park Square, Milton Park, Abingdon, Oxon OX14 4RN

Simultaneously published in the USA and Canada
by Routledge
711 Third Avenue, New York, NY 10017

Routledge is an imprint of the Taylor & Francis Group, an informa business

British Library Cataloguing in Publication Data
A catalogue record for this book is available from the British Library

Library of Congress Cataloging in Publication Data
Critical theory in international relations and security studies : interviews
and reflections / edited by Laura Lima, João Nunes and Shannon Brincat.
       p. cm.
    Includes bibliographical references and index. 1. International
relations—Research. 2. Security, International—Research. 3. Critical
theory. I. Lima, Laura, 1979– II. Nunes, João, 1981– III. Brincat,
Shannon, 1979–
JZ1234.C75 2012
327.101—dc23

                                                              2011026003

ISBN: 978-0-415-60157-3 (hbk)
ISBN: 978-0-415-60158-0 (pbk)
ISBN: 978-0-203-14549-4 (ebk)

Typeset in Bembo
by RefineCatch Limited, Bungay, Suffolk

Printed and bound in Great Britain by
TJ International Ltd, Padstow, Cornwall

CONTENTS

CONTRIBUTORS

Brooke Ackerly is Associate Professor of Political Science at Vanderbilt University, Nashville.

Pinar Bilgin is Associate Professor in the Department of International Relations at Bilkent University, Ankara.

Ken Booth is Senior Research Associate and Director of the David Davies Memorial Institute of International Studies at the Department of International Politics, Aberystwyth University.

Shannon Brincat is a University of Queensland Postdoctoral Research Fellow in the School of Political Science and International Studies.

Robert W. Cox is Professor Emeritus of Political Science at York University, Toronto.

Richard Devetak is Senior Lecturer in the School of Political Science and International Studies, University of Queensland.

John M. Hobson is Professor of Politics and International Relations at the University of Sheffield.

Kimberly Hutchings is Professor in the Department of International Relations at the London School of Economics.

Laura Lima is a PhD candidate at the Department of International Politics, Aberystwyth University.

Andrew Linklater is Woodrow Wilson Professor at the Department of International Politics, Aberystwyth University.

Mark Neufeld is Professor in the Department of Politics and Deputy Director of the Centre for the Study of Global Power and Politics at Trent University, Ontario.

João Nunes is Postdoctoral Fellow in the Department of Politics and International Studies, University of Warwick.

Mustapha Kamal Pasha is Chair in International Relations in the Department of Politics and International Relations, University of Aberdeen.

Jacqui True is Professor in the School of Political and Social Inquiry at Monash University, Melbourne, Australia.

Martin Weber is Senior Lecturer in the School of Political Science and International Studies, University of Queensland.

Michael C. Williams is Professor in the Graduate School of Public and International Affairs, University of Ottawa.

Richard Wyn Jones is Professor and Director of the Wales Governance Centre, Cardiff University.

ACKNOWLEDGEMENTS

The project of this book started taking shape in the beginning of 2009 in Aberystwyth, Wales. We were then PhD candidates whose interest in critical theory and Critical Security Studies had taken us from our native Australia (Shannon Brincat), Brazil (Laura Lima), and Portugal (João Nunes) to the 'Inter-Pol' department at 'Aber'. The lively postgraduate culture of the department allowed us to engage in interesting discussions with our colleagues, as well as with some of those who have been giving shape to critical debates in IR in the past decades. It was out of these experiences that the idea first came about of engaging with critical theory through the lives and professional experiences of theorists.

We are very appreciative of the enthusiasm and time generously extended to us by the four interviewees of this book – Robert W. Cox, Andrew Linklater, Ken Booth and Richard Wyn Jones. We thank them for their careful consideration of the questions asked, as well as for their commitment to providing thorough responses. We are also very thankful to the ten scholars who agreed to join this conversation, and who took the time to engage with the interviews in such a thoughtful way: Brooke Ackerly, Pinar Bilgin, Richard Devetak, John Hobson, Kimberly Hutchings, Mark Neufeld, Mustapha Pasha, Jacqui True, Martin Weber and Michael C. Williams.

At Routledge, we thank Heidi Bagtazo, Hannah Shakespeare and Alexander Quayle for believing in this project and supporting it until its final stages. We would also like to thank the journal *Global Discourse* for giving permission to re-publish part of the interview with Andrew Linklater.

Shannon Brincat would like to thank the University of Queensland for the award of a Graduate School Research Travel Grant and Mid-Year PhD Scholarship, without which this volume would not have been possible, and also the ongoing love and support of Bree Rhodes. Laura Lima would like to thank the *Comissão de Aperfeiçoamento de Pessoal de Nível Superior* (CAPES) in Brazil for providing her with a PhD scholarship, and Pieter and Carla Vandersteen for their love and friendship. João Nunes gratefully acknowledges the support of an Economic and Social Research Council Postdoctoral Fellowship.

1

INTRODUCTION

Shannon Brincat, Laura Lima and João Nunes

The idea for this volume came out of a desire to assess the trajectory of critical thinking in the study of world politics. We saw critical theory as having reached an impasse, after the highly successful period in which its popularity surged – almost to the point of becoming 'mainstream' or common sense in some parts of the academic world. We the editors are part of a generation of researchers for whom the word 'critical' has become, to a great extent, a household name. The proliferation of 'critical approaches' led us to ask a number of questions. Does it still make sense to use the 'critical' label to designate an approach or methodology? Is there an emerging 'critical orthodoxy'? What has the critical literature achieved? Where has it failed or remained silent? What are its limits and challenges? How can critical thinking be pushed forward? Finally, what has happened to 'traditional' ('uncritical') thinking? We set out to provide a fresh perspective upon the 'critical turn' in International Relations and Security Studies – one that would revisit its origins, celebrate its eclecticism, consider its limitations and open doors to future developments.

Critical theory in world politics has been surveyed and assessed on a few occasions.[1] The perspective adopted in this book is different in three important ways. To begin with, our starting point was the strand of critical theory reaching back to Kant, Hegel, Marx and the Frankfurt School. This choice is justified by our own intellectual background – when this project was firstly discussed, we had ongoing research projects that applied insights from this strand of critical thinking – and also by the fact that we had been working in proximity with authors who made important contributions to the fields of International Relations and Security Studies by drawing on this form of critical theory. Importantly, however, and while this lineage would remain a reference point throughout the project, we did not envision a 'balance-sheet' of a specific body of work or a theoretical tradition. Rather, we used this understanding of critical theory as an entry-point into a broader discussion about the different meanings of critical thinking. We started with critical theory as a range of authors and texts, and sought to explore the ways in which critical thinking can be seen as a broader attitude of thought, a disposition towards the world, a lens through which to grapple with the diversity of social life. On another level, we started within a 'circle of proximity' – shared research interests among us editors, a number of authors we were familiar with – and set out to explore the limits of what we knew by confronting the familiar with some difficult questions, by probing into its shortcomings, by opening up this body of work to scrutiny and criticism.

The second way in which this volume differs from its predecessors is closely interlinked with these intellectual motivations. The format we chose for the book was determined by the objective of exploring the breadth and reach of critique by taking the standpoint of a particular strand of critical thinking. Relying once again on our 'circle of proximity', we interviewed four scholars who we saw as important figures in the use of critical theory in the study of world politics. We considered that the work and life of these four scholars could prompt different kinds of reflections. We thus asked a number of scholars from diverse critical persuasions to comment on these interviews. Our selection of interviewees and commentators was not driven by a desire to follow or establish a canon, but by the objective of promoting self-reflection and a dialogue that was as open as possible. This volume does not claim to provide a definitive account of what critical theory is or a truthful narrative of its origins and development. We are well aware that the way in which this volume has been organized, and its participants selected, is in itself a particular narrative – which necessarily entails drawing certain boundaries and even some exclusions. Different ways of addressing the critical turn in world politics would yield different results.[2] Those are the necessary limitations of a project of this nature – but we have sought to minimize any bias by opening the discussion to contributors from a broad range of backgrounds and critical orientations.

We have refrained from establishing a common understanding of 'critical theory' and even from imposing a common designation. As the reader will immediately notice, our contributors have different things in mind when they write 'critical theory': some prefer to stick to the Critical Theory of the Frankfurt School, others to its broader Marxist meaning, and still others use critical theory to denote a variety of critical approaches, including post-colonialism, feminism and post-structuralism. Although the format of the book was conceived as dialogical, the conversation we envisaged never aspired to a consensus or a common denominator between the authors; rather, the objective was to showcase the variety of ways in which critique has been pursued in the study of world politics, and to open the floor to a discussion about some of its most important themes and challenges. At the same time, however, we endeavoured to prevent the discussion from turning into a cacophony – in this context, having the interviews as reference points proved immensely useful.

Ultimately, the dialogical format followed in this book reflects more adequately what 'doing critique' is: to be open to the world, to engage with others and to confront the limits of one's own thinking. The format breathed life into what is often seen as a dry, abstract and impersonal process. As has been shown elsewhere, interviews can provide valuable opportunities for illuminating the human dimension of scholarship.[3] At the same time, interviews are windows that reveal how intellectual work is at once personal, social and political – thereby requiring different kinds of negotiations between the three. This is particularly important in the case of critical thinking, which has always emphasized the way in which knowledge is socially embedded and driven by interests. In this context, doing critique means also exploring the ways in which personal experiences, ways of seeing the world and ways of acting in the world are interconnected. The interviews and reflections in this volume show that critical enquiry is not merely an intellectual process of reason alone. Rather, critique is a lived experience, which feeds on the cross-fertilization between different areas of activity, academic and non-academic (as the interview with Robert Cox illustrates). At the same time, critique often involves complex negotiations between the ethical, the political and the historical (Andrew Linklater); or between the academic and the personal (Ken Booth). It may involve the interplay of academic work and political activism and struggle (Richard Wyn Jones). The idea of critique as a lived experience is present, in different ways, in some of the responses to the interviews: for Jacqui True, for example, the congruence between the way in which critique is 'preached' and 'practiced' is central when assessing the merits of a work that claims to be critical; as Mark Neufeld suggests, critical thinking must be given new life through the reinjection of a passionate commitment; Kimberly Hutchings speaks of the necessity of 'turning towards the world'. In sum, this volume shows that critique must be lived as well as theorized.

The third way in which this volume is distinctive is its dual focus on International Relations and Security Studies. Although we consider both fields to fall under the general rubric of world politics, we found it important to specify them. To begin with, a great number of the contributors to this volume have been important figures on both fields. Secondly, the field of Security Studies has recently witnessed extremely dynamic theoretical debates, to the extent that it is no longer possible to talk of it as a subfield of International Relations. Rather, we think that the birth of Critical Security Studies and the growing popularity of critical approaches to security have altered the traditional relationship between the two fields of study.[4] Instead of Security Studies being subsidiary of International Relations, we are now witnessing a more intensive cross-fertilization between the two – and, very often, the field of security leading the way in terms of theoretical innovation. This volume displays some of the synergies that can be created by bringing together these two areas of enquiry.

How the volume is organized

The volume is divided into two parts. The first (Part I), features four interviews conducted with Robert W. Cox, Andrew Linklater, Ken Booth and Richard Wyn Jones. Our objective as interviewers was to provide the opportunity for these scholars to reflect about the development of critical theory in their work, to gauge their views on the impact of their work and to discuss the challenges and possible directions for future research. While taking into account differences in research interests, methods and subject-fields between the four interviewees, we organized our questions around five common areas of enquiry:

1. their initial engagement with critical theorizing;
2. the importance of a commitment to emancipatory change in their work;
3. the impact of their work on the discipline(s);
4. the practical implications of their work and of critical thinking more generally; and
5. their thoughts on the challenges and future developments of critical thinking.

The interviews were mostly conducted through various face-to-face meetings (with the exception of Wyn Jones's, which resulted from electronic exchanges), and were digitally recorded. The interviewees were involved in editing the transcripts of the interviews, and thus had the opportunity to change and elaborate their views.

The second half of the volume (Parts II–IV) includes commentaries on these interviews, penned by a number of scholars from various theoretical, normative and interpretive backgrounds – united by their engagement with critical thinking in International Relations and/or Security Studies. Here, our objective was to provide a forum in which different debates surrounding critical thinking could be developed, and in which a diverse range of voices could be heard. The commentators were asked to use the interviews in Part I as a starting point for reflections on the legacy, shortcomings and future of critical theory. The degree of engagement with the interview material varies, but, all of the reflections can be seen as responses to the interviews in Part I or as broader responses to critical thinking as a whole. We have divided these ten commentaries in three parts – Origins (Part II), Limits (Part III) and Future Directions (Part IV). This division is merely an indication of what we considered the most important theme of each chapter. In fact, most (if not all) of the chapters can be seen as addressing these three themes, or at least as having important implications for each of them.

We have deliberately steered away from adding a concluding chapter. Although some of the main themes coming out of this dialogue will be highlighted below, and even though we will go so far as to venture some ideas as to what this might mean for critical thinking, we are very reluctant to engage in the exercise of closure that a conclusion would imply. It is best to let the contributions speak for themselves and to allow the readers to draw their own conclusions. We believe that the primary contribution of this volume is the way it shows the extraordinary diversity of critical theorizing as applied to the study of world politics and, more importantly, the way it seeks to strengthen the critical field as a site of permanent contestation, questioning and self-reflection. We believe that the critical spirit is stifled when one attempts to encapsulate it into formulas or common denominators; in contrast, it thrives when one seeks to learn instead from its example of permanent unrest.

Origins ... and departures

Thinking about origins is important when assessing a theoretical approach. This project began with a particular narrative of the origins of critical theory in the study of world politics: we observed that 2011 marked the thirtieth anniversary of the publication of Robert Cox's 'Social Forces, States, and World Orders – Beyond IR Theory' (1981) and of Richard Ashley's 'Political Realism and Human Interests' (1981). These two articles are indeed significant in that they signalled the moment in which insights from critical theory were self-consciously applied to the study of world politics. These two articles were not scattered efforts; in fact, they reflected a broader movement in the discipline. At about the same time, Andrew Linklater's book *Men and Citizens in the Theory of International Relations* (1982) contributed to setting the agenda of a critical-theoretical approach to International Relations theory; not long afterwards, Ken Booth's (1991) 'Security and Emancipation' showed how critical thinking could be used to radically rethink understandings and transform practices of international security.

In these works, one can witness the formation of a critical approach to IR theory. But that is not the same thing as saying that critical theory in the study of world politics originated with these works – or that a line of intellectual influence can be drawn from the thought of Kant, Marx, the Frankfurt School, up to the contributions of these authors. Whilst conducting the interviews and observing the debate that they sparked, we realized that our initial assumptions regarding the 'intellectual tradition' of critical theory in world politics were somewhat misplaced – or at least that they needed to take into account a broader perspective. The reality of intellectual life is messier than we originally thought, and critique – as an attitude of thought and a lived experience – cannot be neatly summarized into a coherent narrative.

For example, it was particularly illuminating to learn that Robert Cox was heavily influenced by the thought of Edmund Burke, one of the founding figures of modern conservatism, and that he does not see the Frankfurt School as being part of his intellectual inheritance. Andrew Linklater, on the other hand, while explicitly drawing on the Frankfurt School, cannot be considered a 'follower' in that he has used in creative ways the historical sociology of Norbert Elias – who, as Linklater suggests, can be seen as one of the 'flag-bearers' of the critical tradition. Ken Booth reveals how he encountered 'critical theory' almost by chance, and how it helped him bring together a series of notions about world politics he had developed through other means.[5]

The responses to the interviews go even further in complicating the narrative about the origins of critical theory. Mustapha Pasha's analysis of the subject of critical international theory explores the origins of critical thinking within a particular Protestant cosmology, and shows how the 'logic of Western Reason' underlies the emancipatory commitment. In his contribution, Richard Devetak provides an in-depth investigation of the intellectual heritages of Cox and Linklater. Focusing on how these two authors have mobilized the views of history of Vico and Kant, respectively, Devetak's chapter is a prime example of how revisiting the origins can give cause for re-evaluating the trajectory and future possibilities of critical theory. Yet another example of the usefulness of taking a fresh perspective on origins is the chapter by Michael C. Williams. Williams writes about the context of the Frankfurt School in exile in the United States, and argues that the strict separation between the School and American positivist political science is both erroneous and detrimental to the critical purposes.

Limits …

As mentioned above, this volume sets out to provide a forum in which the short-comings of, and challenges to, critical theory in the study of world politics could be discussed in a lively and constructive way. In this respect, this book can be seen as an exercise in self-reflection – an indispensable feature of any intellectual endeavour that purports to be critical. Once again, the format of the volume proved its usefulness: the interviews constituted moments of introspection, in which the authors reflected about the development of their thinking, their hesitations and changes of opinion. Linklater provides a fascinating overview of thirty years of work, in which he constantly struggled with the shortcomings of some of the founding fathers of the critical tradition. Although demonstrating important lines of continuity – such as the interest in the expansion of the horizons of moral community – his intellectual journey is also animated by acknowledging the limits of Kant, Marx and Habermas, which he has sought to overcome by engaging with theorists outside the 'canon' of critical theory.

Booth has shown in his work that he takes seriously the feminist injunction to see the personal as political, by reflecting in a candid way about his own intellectual trajectory and the way he came to recognize earlier mistakes.[6] He goes further by exploring the shortcomings of pure thought when confronted with events in the political world – he admits, for example, the difficulty in sustaining a pacifist position in the messy realm of political affairs; at the same time, however, he reveals his own hesitations about the merits of intervention. Wyn Jones is also very forthright in confronting the limits of his own thinking: he shows, for instance, how his recent work on Welsh politics has impacted upon his views of critique and contributed to changing his opinion about the role of quantitative Political Science. Also, looking back at his earlier works, he admits to having been mistaken when equating security with emancipation.

Unsurprisingly, the responses to the interviews engage in depth with various limitations of critical theory. In fact, as Brooke Ackerly argues in her chapter, the recognition of limits must be in-built into the very act of thinking critically about the world. Thus, she frames critique within a broader disposition characterized by both skepticism and humility: the former leads critical thinking to revisit and challenge accepted meanings, while the latter renders its approach collaborative and permanently open to questioning. Even though Ackerly identifies elements of skepticism and humility in the words of the four interviewees, she still finds many problematic elements in the version of critical theory they uphold. One of her main concerns is the concept of emancipation, a 'totalizing' term which, in her opinion, sidelines concrete claims for empowerment and rights.[7]

Other commentators use a variety of strategies to engage with the limits of critical theory. Jacqui True, for example, examines the interviews against a set of criteria: engagement with other theories and theorists; self-reflexivity about the interviewees' own work; and the identification and practice of emancipatory possibilities. Deploying these criteria, she detects blind spots in the critical theory presented in the interviews (and in the questions that we, the interviewers, failed to ask). As a result, she argues that the version of critique put forward by the interviewees ultimately fails to live up to its own claims. John Hobson's contribution also seeks to turn the critical gaze on critical International Relations theory itself. He appraises the trajectory of critical theory from the standpoint of subaltern and Eastern agency, and argues that critical theory has fulfilled only half of its mandate: while it has revealed structures of power in the world, it has not yet analysed the agency of subaltern and non-Western actors in global politics and economics.

On a different note, Martin Weber asks critical theory to reflect on the nature of its engagement with other theoretical approaches. Seeking to 'make uncomfortable' this theoretical tradition, he observes that all too often different critical approaches talk past each other, preferring to remain at the level of what he terms an 'external' form of critique, which usually dispenses with appreciative engagement. An obvious conclusion from Weber's reflection is that critical theory needs to take theoretical dialogue more seriously. While Weber gives most of his attention to dialogue between different critical approaches, Williams' reflection about the 'American-positivist-realist other' of critical theory also serves as a cautionary note against overplaying the difference between 'critical' and 'traditional' theory. Booth and Wyn Jones also comment on the pitfalls of building 'straw-men' for justifying one's own position, arguing that realism is actually much more complex – and closer to critical thinking – than the picture normally provided by critical theorists.

Amidst all the criticisms, a dissonant voice is introduced by Pinar Bilgin's defence of Critical Security Studies against accusations of Eurocentrism. For Bilgin, the way in which critical theory has been used by authors like Booth and Wyn Jones has considerably broadened the scope and reach of Security Studies. Her reflection is particularly interesting in the context of the debate carried out in this volume, in that she argues that accusations of Eurocentrism must be turned against those who accuse critical theory of being Eurocentric. In sum, the contributions to this volume depict an immensely rich picture of the multiple challenges facing critical theory today and the vibrant debates surrounding it.

... and opportunities

Lest the reader think that the book does not have anything positive to say about the future of critical theory in the study of world politics, we hasten to add that all contributions offer important clues as to how critical thinking – and critical practice – can be developed. This is true even for the more pessimistic views: Ackerly, for example, suggests that the version of critical theory put forward by the four interviewees is exhausted; nonetheless, she argues for another version of critical theorizing, one that is predicated upon the methodologies of feminist theory (True also places emphasis on the importance of feminist methods for doing critique).

This book thus contains a number of future directions for critical theory: more attention to historical change and difference, more openness to dialogue and a more sustained engagement with the complexities of world politics. Cox wishes critical theory to develop as an 'historical mode of thinking' (this volume, 20). Theories arise out of historical situations, experiences and dilemmas, and the role of critique is to examine the historical elements that are likely to bring about structural change. As a result, critical theory must strengthen its historical methodologies. Echoing Cox's remarks about the crucial importance of historical thinking, Linklater's work shows how critical theory can benefit from an engagement with historical sociology – to help critical theorists adopt a long-term view of complex historical processes in world politics.

In addition to strengthening the historical awareness of critical theory, the contributions to this volume overwhelmingly point towards the necessity of developing a sensibility to difference. These calls should be taken in conjunction with Devetak's genealogy of the thought of Cox and Linklater, and with Pasha's analysis of the cosmological assumptions underlying critical theory – given that, after all, the engagement with difference cannot be dissociated from self-reflexivity. In what concerns the ways in which critical theory can engage with complexity and multivocality, Hobson makes the case for a critical theory that not only offers a critique of power and social inequality, but also paints a picture of subaltern agency and resistance. This vision can be seen as an important rejoinder to Cox's idea of a cosmopolitanism predicated upon transcivilizational dialogue and upon the recognition of fluidity and difference. An important contribution in this context – and a promising direction for critical theory – is Neufeld's analysis of Edward Said's 'contrapuntal reading', which, he argues, allows for dissonant voices to be considered without the compulsion to establish a unified meaning or a harmonious whole. Contrapuntality can thus become an important critical method for the analysis of difference and pluralism. The calls for more pluralism are echoed by Hutchings, who argues for a more sustained engagement with feminist, post-colonial and green arguments in what she terms a 'democratization of critique' (this volume, 213). The desire for more pluralism also underlies Williams' engagement with what has often been seen as the 'other' of critical theory.

As Ackerly shows in her contribution, openness towards difference is an important step in a more sustained engagement with world politics. In this context, she stresses the importance of feminist methodologies, which in her view must be central components of any form of theory that claims to be critical. In the field of Security Studies, the approach to security put forward by Booth and Wyn Jones has distinguished itself from most of its critical counterparts by arguing for a more comprehensive engagement with the real conditions of insecurity experienced by 'real people in real places' (in the words of Wyn Jones). In their interviews, they emphasize this point once again, with Wyn Jones going so far as to argue that the ability to engage with the world of practice is the ultimate test for the validity of a critical theory. For Wyn Jones, this means, among other things, that critical theory must go beyond anti-statism and engage with state practices and with the functioning of political institutions.[8] Neufeld's contribution is also important in this regard, in that he argues for the necessity of 'transformative intellectuals' to engage with politics and praxis in specific historical communities. For Hutchings, the question of practice means that critique must 'run towards the world'. Downplaying the importance of arguments about, for example, the philosophical foundations of critique, she claims that the 'authority' of critique must be transferred towards the world in its complexity and in its multiple temporalities.

In sum, the contributions to this volume show how critical thinking can be developed through the deepening of its historical awareness, the broadening of its scope so as to account for plurality and difference, and the reinforcement of its engagement with the subject matter of world politics. These contributions identify gaps and opportunities, putting forward concrete measures for pushing critical theory beyond its current limitations.

The life of critique

The contributions to this volume provide important insights as to the origins, current state, challenges and future directions of critical thinking in world politics. Engaging in a dialogic and self-reflective exercise, they showcase the vibrancy of intellectual exchanges within the critical field. While demonstrating the importance of preserving theoretical heterogeneity, the contributions also show that there are common concerns, that conversations can take place, that disagreement is almost always fruitful for the critical enterprise and that areas of convergence can be found.

In addition to demonstrating the vitality of the critical field, the voices in this volume illuminate different aspects of the 'life of critique'. To begin with, they provide important clues for a reassessment of its origins and genealogy. Critical thinking cannot be circumscribed to the works of philosophers – or contained in edited volumes such as this one – because its development is supported by the interplay of deeply ingrained ideas (as Pasha shows) and intimately connected with struggles that occur daily on a multiplicity of sites. Critique must thus be seen as an organic phenomenon, always in motion and always restless – as Cox states in his interview, it must be fluid and 'non-scholastic'. The contributions also show that critique must see itself as an intervention within an ever-evolving social and political life – Hutchings refers to this as the 'turn towards the world'. They show that critique is more than just a theory: it is a lived experience, an attitude, a form of practice – in Booth's words, a 'way of life'.

Finally, this volume demonstrates the crucial importance of critique for living and acting in the world. On the one hand, the ideas and methods that fall under the critical banner – historical, sociological, feminist, subaltern, among others –

are important tools for thinking about, and addressing, the multiple situations of exclusion and oppression in the world today. On the other hand, critical theory offers important clues as to how we might live in order to minimize the reproduction of these forms of exclusion and oppression. As Cox argues in this volume, critique implies a change in the way we think about ourselves and about our relationship to the world. In times of global interconnectedness, global injustices and global dangers, the first and foremost lesson of critical theory may just be an injunction to personal transformation.

Notes

1 The trajectory of the critical literature in International Relations can be accompanied in Hoffman (1987), Linklater (1996), as well as in the contributions to Wyn Jones (2001) and Rengger and Thirkell-White (2007). The intersection between critical thinking and post-positivism is one of the common themes of the contributions to Booth, Smith and Zalewski (1996). A useful reader is Roach (2007).
2 A different take into this question was provided in Edkins and Vaughan-Williams (2009).
3 See in this regard Munck and Snyder (2007).
4 The seminal volume of Critical Security Studies is Krause and Williams (1997). Recent surveys of the different critical approaches to security are C.A.S.E. collective (2006) and Peoples and Vaughan-Williams (2010). Also useful are Booth (2005) and Fierke (2007).
5 In his recent book *Theory of World Security*, Booth explains in detail his theoretical influences and his own approach to theory-building as 'pearl-fishing' from several sources – see Booth (2007: 37–91). This approach resonates with Cox's remarks about being a 'non-conformist' who does not belong to a school or doctrine (this volume, 17).
6 See Booth (1997).
7 Interestingly, in his interview Cox also reveals some dissatisfaction with concepts such as 'emancipation' and 'progress'.
8 The challenge of engaging with the world of political institutions from a critical-theoretical perspective has recently been taken up in Roach (2010).

Bibliography

Ashley, R.K. (1981) 'Political Realism and Human Interests', *International Studies Quarterly* 25(2): 204–36.
Booth, K. (1991) 'Security and Emancipation', *Review of International Studies* 17: 313–26.
_____ (1997) 'Security and Self: Reflections of a Fallen Realist' in K. Krause and M.C. Williams (eds) *Critical Security Studies: Concepts and Cases*, London: UCL Press.
_____ (ed.) (2005) *Critical Security Studies and World Politics*, London and Boulder: Lynne Rienner Publishers.
_____ (2007) *Theory of World Security*, Cambridge: Cambridge University Press.
Booth, K., Smith, S. and Zalewski, M. (eds) (1996) *International Theory: Positivism and Beyond*, Cambridge: Cambridge University Press.
C.A.S.E. collective (2006) 'Critical Approaches to Security in Europe: A Networked Manifesto,' *Security Dialogue* 37(4): 443–87.
Cox, R.W. (1981) 'Social Forces, States and World Orders: Beyond International Relations Theory', *Millennium* 10(2): 126–55.
Edkins, J. and Vaughan-Williams, N. (eds) (2009) *Critical Theorists and International Relations*, London: Routledge.

Fierke, K.M. (2007) *Critical Approaches to International Security*, Cambridge: Polity.

Hoffman, M. (1987) 'Critical Theory and the Inter-Paradigm Debate', *Millennium* 16(2): 231–49.

Krause, K. and Williams, M.C. (eds) (1997) *Critical Security Studies: Concepts and Cases*, London: UCL Press.

Linklater, A. (1982) *Men and Citizens in the Theory of International Relations*, London: Macmillan.

_____ (1996) 'The Achievements of Critical Theory' in S. Smith, K. Booth and M. Zalewski (eds) *International Theory: Positivism and Beyond*, Cambridge: Cambridge University Press.

Munck, G.L. and Snyder, R. (eds) (2007) *Passion, Craft, and Method in Comparative Politics*, Baltimore: Johns Hopkins University Press.

Peoples, C. and Vaughan-Williams, N. (2010) *Critical Security Studies: An Introduction*, Abingdon: Routledge.

Rengger, N. and Thirkell-White, B. (eds) (2007) *Critical International Relations Theory After 25 Years*, Cambridge: Cambridge University Press.

Roach, S.C. (ed.) (2007) *Critical Theory and International Relations: A Reader*, London: Routledge.

_____ (2010) *Critical Theory of International Politics: Complementarity, Justice and Governance*, Abingdon: Routledge.

Wyn Jones, R. (ed.) (2001) *Critical Theory and World Politics*, London and Boulder: Lynne Rienner Publishers.

PART I
Interviews

2

FOR SOMEONE AND *FOR* SOME PURPOSE

An interview with Robert W. Cox

Robert W. Cox is widely regarded as one of the leading critical theorists in the study of world politics. Spanning International Relations Theory and International Political Economy, his work has been hugely influential since the publication of his two articles 'Social Forces, States and World Orders' (1981) and 'Gramsci, Hegemony and International Relations' (1983). Cox was born in 1926 in Montreal, Canada, and worked for 20 years at the International Labour Organization – an experience that inspired his first book (co-authored with Harold Jacobson), *The Anatomy of Influence: Decision-Making in International Organization* (1974). He then turned to the academia and taught at Columbia University and York University, Toronto. His most recent book, co-authored with Michael Schechter, *The Political Economy of a Plural World: Critical Reflections on Power, Morals and Civilization* (2002), with its focus on civilizational encounters and post-hegemonic forms of human community, has signalled a new step in his ever-evolving critical thinking.

This interview was conducted between 14 and 16 June 2009 in La Barboleusaz, Switzerland.

Life and influences

You grew up in the Anglophone sector of Montreal, a son of politically conservative parents. Yet, very early in your life you became interested in French Canadian nationalism of the 1930s and 40s – which was radically opposed to the milieu of your family background. Later in your life, expressing your admiration for Edmund Burke's organic approach to society as a link between conservatism and socialism, you argued (Cox 1996b: 24) that this form of conservatism was congenial to democratic socialism. Does your background explain the development of your thought?

Montreal was a very divided city when I grew up. I lived where English-speaking people lived and then – even as a youngster – I became aware that there was a whole different world, not very far from me. I used to take long streetcar rides down into the East end of Montreal, just to see what it was like. I would go to political meetings in the French-speaking areas of town. This was something completely different from, and which hardly existed in, the English-speaking areas – because politics was hardly discussed in public there.

It interested me that there was this other society and that they had radical ideas in different directions from those in my own milieu. There was a strong nationalist movement, part of which was channelled through the dominant provincial political party and part in more radical directions, and also fascist ideas were very current there in the 1930s. The Catholic Church was important there, not just in terms of the dominant orthodox Church Catholicism, but also because of the currents within it – the Jesuits, for example, introduced the concept of cooperative movements.

I became sympathetic to the idea of more autonomy for French Canada, although the vocabulary in those days was different from today's. When growing up, I used to read *Le Devoir*, which was the intellectual French language paper (you might compare it to *Le Monde* in France). I was more or less in the current of experimental social ideas in French Canada, which was only beginning in English Canada. In English-speaking Canada there was a movement called the Cooperative Commonwealth Federation, which later became the New Democratic Party. It did not have much impact in Montreal, but affected other parts of English-speaking Canada. I would say that these experiences of living in Quebec, with its then tight division between linguistic and ethnic groups and my small personal efforts to bridge those divisions made me more of an 'international' person in vocation.

I thought of myself as a conservative, philosophically – but not as a supporter of the Conservative Party. I read Burke's *Reflections on the Revolution in France* (1999) and from that drew the idea of society as an organic thing in which everyone had responsibility towards everyone else from their position and role in society. I thought that was the diametrical opposite of the exaggerated individualism that came to be represented much later by the likes of Margaret Thatcher as conservatism, which seemed to me nothing but a doctrinal revival of nineteenth century free market capitalism. Burke's conservatism, for me, was closer to social democracy as embodied in the radical movements growing up in Quebec in the 1940s – like the *Bloc Populaire Canadien* led by André Laurendeau, who became the editor of *Le Devoir*.

And then you started working with the International Labour Organization (ILO). How did this happen, and what made you leave the ILO and work in the academia?

Yes. It was against this background, just when I was in my graduating year, that the Principal of McGill University, Dr. Cyril James, called me into his office and asked if I would like to be interviewed for a job in the ILO, which was housed by McGill during the war. I really jumped at the offer because it was an opportunity to leave the Anglo-Canadian segment of Montreal – which was almost cut off from the rest of the world – and to go to Geneva and work in an international environment. This was a very important formative experience in developing my thinking. Not that the ILO was an especially radicalizing environment, because it was very much part of the newly established world order.

When I was recruited at the end of the war, the ILO was opening up to a wider part of the world. The mass independence movements of the 1960s had yet to come about. The decades immediately following World War II saw considerable innovation in social policy. The ILO had a central role during those post-war years. However, by the 1970s I was beginning to wonder whether that phase of encouraging social initiatives hadn't passed. Bureaucracies never die, but they perpetuate themselves by doing over and over again what they did the last time, and I had a sense that that was happening in the 1970s. So it was a combination of personal frustration and the sense that I also wanted to be free to develop intellectually that led me to think of leaving the ILO.

With the permission of the Director-General, David Morse, for a couple of years I had taken leave from the ILO to teach at the Graduate Institute of International Studies in Geneva. I began to enjoy the opportunity of thinking for myself, and I began to write a little. I started off thinking about the structure of power internally – about business, labour and the role of government. I had written a piece about leadership in international organizations based very largely on my experience of working closely with David Morse. I showed it to Harold Jacobson, a close friend and professor of political science at the University of Michigan with whom I had been working on my own critique of international organizations, and who was in Geneva at the time. He liked it and took it to Hamilton Fish Armstrong, the editor of *Foreign Affairs* in New York, who agreed that it should be published. The problem was that as a serving official with the ILO I was precluded from publishing under my own name, so from my point of view it should be anonymous. Armstrong hesitated because the policy of *Foreign Affairs* was to identify authors; however, he ultimately agreed. The precedent was George Kennan's famous article signed X (1947). My article was entitled 'The Executive Head' (1969) and was modelled on Machiavelli's *Il Principe*. So the article appeared with N. M. – for Niccolò Machiavelli – as the author.

Of course, it soon became widely suspected in ILO circles that I had written the article and all hell descended upon me from the authorities! This showed me that if I wanted to be able to express myself, I had better be someplace else.

Your work has been labelled in different ways all over the years. Mark Hoffman (1987), for example, has portrayed you as a critical International Relations theorist, whilst John Adams (1989) referred to your work as 'watery Marxism'. Meanwhile, Anthony Leysen (2008) has preferred to highlight your tolerance for diversity and eclecticism. Is it useful to try to categorize your work?

I think Susan Strange used the word 'eccentric' – she added 'in the best English sense of the word'.[1] That's probably what I am: a non-conformist. I don't belong to any school or espouse any doctrine. You can see from the people I quote that they come from different contexts; they are not the ones other people tend to use. How many International Relations (IR) scholars write about Giambattista Vico, Georges Sorel or R.G. Collingwood? These are not thinkers that authors in this field today are necessarily familiar with. Since my itinerary or socialization into the discipline has been different from that of most people in IR theory, I don't know a lot of the things that they know.

For example, take the Critical Theory of the Frankfurt School. I know about the Frankfurt School, but not much. That is, I have never read the works of scholars associated with it so thoroughly as for it to be part of my intellectual canon. Yet, people often say, 'but if you're a critical theorist you must have had some influence from the Frankfurt School'. I just never came about my work from that direction! I am perfectly agreeable to the idea that the Frankfurt School did a lot of useful things, but they were not part of my intellectual inheritance.

At the same time, you are widely regarded as one of the key neo-Gramscian scholars in IR and International Political Economy.[2] How did you come across Gramsci, and how did he influence your thought?

I discovered Gramsci after I left Geneva. The first time I remember hearing his name was around 1970 from a graduate student at the University of Toronto, when I was on a kind of sabbatical from Geneva. This young man talked about someone he called 'Gramski' whom he said 'was very interesting'. I'd never heard of him before, so I just made a note of the name in my mind. Then, while I was at Columbia, there was a professor in the Italian department who was interested in Gramsci and with his permission I sat in his undergraduate class on Italian literature.

I found Gramsci congenial to my own way of thinking because he takes an organic view of society and he does make the link between economics and ideas a central theme. One of the first things I wrote about his work was the piece published in *Millennium* on his concept of hegemony (Cox 1983). It seemed to me that Gramsci's idea of hegemony was very different from the current meaning of hegemonic power as the dominant military or economic power. His idea of hegemonic power was a process of thought, whereby people began to see a certain set of power relationships as normal. This understanding of hegemony seemed to me a far more realistic way of thinking about world politics and world power. I read and thought a lot about Gramsci at that time and people started to call me a neo-Gramscian. I wondered, 'what was the *neo* for?'

However, I do not take Gramsci's thought as a package of doctrines to be applied systematically to any problem that I come upon.

Do you consider yourself a pioneer or a 'field leader', as Hoffman has put it?

I have never thought of myself as a 'field leader'. I know that I am fairly widely read, probably more so in Britain and in Europe and other parts of the world than in the

United States, where, as Jerry Cohen (2008) suggests, I am more of an underground author. You may not find me on many of the prescribed graduate reading lists or in bookshops at universities, but you will find that I am read by graduate students.

I don't regard myself as a leader, just as I don't regard myself as founding a school or being a member of a school. I do my own work as an individual. The fact of having worked in a rather bureaucratic mode for about 25 years in an international organization like the ILO gave me a certain experience of the way things happen internationally and nationally – particularly as regards the interactions between unions and management and governments. So I am inclined to think in terms of what is the real world today and what are the opportunities for breaking into something new – but not in terms of redesigning the whole picture or bringing it about in accordance with some master plan.

Critical theory

If, as you have so famously stated, 'theory is always for someone and for some purpose' (Cox 1981: 128), what would you say is the purpose of your theory and who is it for?

That statement was an admonition to be critical – a call to get one to find out what any particular theory is for. It was also, if you like, a sceptical or critical reflection on the nature of theory, a reminder that theory is not something which exists in some absolute sphere. Whoever is developing a theory is trying to achieve some goal. Often, that goal is not explicitly stated but it should become evident with some reflection upon the work and the circumstances in which the theory was developed. That phrase was a general encouragement to be critical, to refuse to accept a theory at face value, to look at it and see where it comes from, what it was designed to achieve, the context in which it was developed.

I did not anticipate the impact that the article 'Social Forces, States and World Orders' would have. I am however pleased that it did have such impact. At the time, the article was not conceived as a breakthrough or a major contribution, but merely as a sketch of the way my own thinking was going. It was Susan Strange who suggested I publish the text. It might have been the most succinct statement of my process of thinking that I have ever published!

In that article, I argued that E.H. Carr was an example of the historical approach and that Hans Morgenthau was much more in the American (positivist) mould, which tried to reason like the physicists and the chemists. I don't think history is related to that kind of science at all. I still follow the approach laid out in my book *Production, Power and World Order* (1987): we need to look at the material conditions, ideas, institutions, production relations and world orders but not in any systematic form. I hope that my thinking is not fixed in rigid form. I hope that it is continually evolving – at the moment, perhaps more in the realm of ideas and civilizations, rather than in terms of thinking about political structures. I like to think historically and I feel that thinking in this way is more in line with continually evolving thought, rather than with thought that follows rigid parameters to be applied to all circumstances.

So my intention was not to prescribe a method to be followed, but rather a set of ideas that may lead to further ideas. Basically my approach is historical. Theories arise out of historical situations and the problems or dilemmas they create for the people who are experiencing them. The theoretician is the person who can synthesize all this and propound a way to think about it. I have sketched a number of factors that frame any situation and need to be taken into account in theorizing – like the prevailing institutions, the material conditions and the prevalent ideas and ideologies. My purpose is normative, and my aims could be summarized as the achievement of greater equity in people's material life, a greater sense of understanding and tolerance of differences in culture and ideas, as a means of moderating conflict among peoples. This is no small matter, as I see economic crisis leading to more inequality, economic inequalities embittering cultural, religious and ethnic conflict, and the whole becoming very unsettling for global and regional peace.

But do you still agree with the distinction between 'problem solving theory' and 'critical theory' (Cox 1981: 129)?

Yes, I think so. At the time, I thought that people might find it useful. Recently, someone suggested that the distinction was now pretty much *passé*. All I meant to say was that 'problem solving theory' is something useful. It is useful in circumstances where you can bring together all of the constraints bearing on a situation and find a solution within that situation. In other words, it works within the assumption of overall stability.

Critical theory, in my mind, is much more a historical mode of thinking. It recognizes that the existing situation is a transitory one and that maybe what one needs to be looking for is not just to solve the problems that are inherent within it, but to look for the openings that are likely to bring about structural change in the future. So I think that critical thinking is directed more towards historical change, whereas problem solving means thinking within the existing historical structure about how to overcome the difficulties that might arise.

In this context, what is the role of the critical theorist?

The role of critical theory is to examine current proposals and doctrines and to – I do not know whether the term 'deconstruct' is appropriate in this circumstance – to show how they have originated, what are the things that they protect and, if you are hoping for change, what possibilities exist within them. It requires thinking of alternatives. Critical theory is a mode of thought that exposes the common current doctrines as inadequate in dealing with global problems, and that tries to find other elements that could be thought of, either separately or collectively, as an alternative.

Yet it is difficult to foresee how an alternative view arises other than accidentally, that is, provoked by specific events that shock people into rethinking their circumstances. I think that is probably more likely to happen that way than for people to be convinced by sophisticated argument.

The role of the critical theorist, then, is to be aware of forces of opposition to the established order, and to bring them to the light so that others are not only aware of them but can evaluate them in terms of their own thinking – assessing whether there are compatibilities and common aims. I am talking about working from the level of society rather than from a formal institutional structure. We need some sort of feeling at the base of societies, so that people can recognize more common concerns with 'others'.

This movement will also have to be one that bridges different civilizational groups or national entities that represent civilizations. This is very difficult because at the base of society people are mostly concerned with their survival as individuals and families and cannot afford the luxury of thinking about what is happening in other parts of the world. Yet, I think more and more people are becoming accustomed to things that are global or at least regional in scope. Developing a transcivilizational way of thinking will be a long and gradual process; and whether it will be able to save the world is still an open question. But I believe that recognizing and accepting difference is a minimal requirement for long-term survival – minimal but essential.[3]

Do you think that there is the danger that we have become too socialized within existing structures for alternatives and possibilities of change to emerge?

Maybe this is putting me in the optimistic category, but I think that people's sense of where they are in the world is subject to pressures that are global in character. I do not want to use the word globalization because I think that, like democracy, it has been used in many different ways, mainly supportive of the idea of a gradual convergence towards a global free market economy, which would be dominated by the United States. By 'global pressures' I mean those problems that arise in different parts of the world, and which no longer affect just a particular local area, but everybody else.

Now, as people become more and more aware of this process, their mentality is being forced to change by the very things that happen – rather than by preaching and propagation of ideas among people. It may be that feeling the impact of these global pressures will induce people to change and will feed into the support of civil society groups that have been pushing for such changes. But we are speaking in very abstract terms as behoves intellectuals!

Let us be more specific, then. Do you think that there is any global pressure nowadays that can force people to rethink their circumstances?

I would probably put my bet on the environment issue: saving the biosphere. I think there is some evidence to suggest that people have become alive to that in most parts of the world. Even in China, a country bent on economic growth, which is consuming more and more of the oil reserves of the world and is polluting more, there is a real concern – on the part of the government at any rate – for the implications of this growth in terms of climate change and the environment. This is because China is a very vulnerable place in terms of its land surface and what it can produce. It does not have expendable land resources to be able to feed itself with its massive population growth, so it has to be concerned about the global environmental situation. In various ways, it seems to me that this concern is spreading.

However, when there is an economic crisis, these concerns retreat. We saw that in Canada when Dion's campaign for a green policy was rejected by the electorate.[4] The main chance for green parties lies in becoming a platform for the expression of ideas that are sometimes picked up by civil society movements. However, developing a sense of collective responsibility about the environment is a very gradual process, and it seems to wither whenever there arises a crisis related to something as immediate as the economy. When confronted with an obstacle in the global economy the problem of the environment is deferred.

What about the role of political programmes?

I was reading an article in *Le Monde* a couple of days ago by Edgar Morin, a French sociologist and philosopher who has broadened the field of Sociology into a way of thinking about the world as a whole.[5] This piece focused on the issue of climate change and the issue of, not just developing policies, but of working towards a fundamental change of people's sense of their relationship to nature. In other words, a kind of long-term reshaping of people's mentality in what concerns the relationship of humanity to nature.

I think he was probably right in suggesting that this will either come about through a series of shocks, or it will not come about at all. But I don't think I can see any existing programme or a set of existing institutions that could make it happen. Certainly, we need to develop and spread ideas that question who we are in relation to nature, that make us of think of ourselves as part of nature, rather than nature as something to be exploited for the benefit of mankind.

This requires a rather radical change of the way people think about themselves and the world. I do not think there is any programme that you can devise that will make that happen. But it may take place as a result of a whole series of negative circumstances that shock people into questioning the way they think about themselves now.

In your work, critical theory is connected to history. How do your critical-theoretical concerns reflect in your choice of research methods? In particular, what is the importance of the synchronic and diachronic analysis of historical development? And how does your dialectical methodology work?[6]

Braudel is very good in synchronic analysis.[7] He wrote about a particular period of world history, exploring the interrelations of different peoples and countries at one particular period. Nonetheless, he was also very sensitive to the development going on within each of those areas. Sometimes the development is synchronically interrelated because what is developing in one country will have an impact upon other people who are in contact.

One can say, therefore, that the diachronic and synchronic dimensions go together – especially in the broad landscape of regional or global history. It is not a question of selecting one over the other. Yet most of the social sciences do focus solely on the synchronic dimension, which prevents them from observing patterns of change over time. This is where the idea of critical thinking comes in: its purpose is to examine the synchronic for the elements in it that are breaking down and opening up opportunities for change. It is a question of keeping the two together rather than picking one or the other. But I do think the synchronic is more conducive to problem-solving theory, since its method takes one slice of time and ignores the potential for change.

In regard to dialectics, very simply there are antagonisms in life and world history, and these antagonisms create change. Yet I don't think there is any way that you can predict change. Change is going to happen, but you cannot predict what that change is going to be. This takes you back to what Collingwood (1994) called the 'inside' and 'outside' of history.[8] The outside is what positivism sees, what the observer of events records, what you can measure and quantify. The inside is the thought process that appraises the reality of the outside and introduces the direction of change. History will see both the inside and the outside. Whereas positivism just sees the outside and assumes that the observer is separate from what is being observed, the historian understands that the very act of observing is an act of doing that makes the observer part of the action. This too is the role of the critical theorist. You don't examine things just to see what they are; you have some intention of improving the situation, of moving it in a direction you find more beneficial for mankind.

Emancipation, progress and the post-modern critique

The defining feature of critical IR theory is said to be its emancipatory interest. While you do advocate greater social equity in the transformation of society, this has always been done within the context of a pessimistic philosophical position. In fact, you claim 'the pessimism of the intellect and the optimism of the will' (1996a: 527, 531).[9] How does your thought relate to the concept of emancipation, given that you never referred to it directly and are pessimistic about its attainment?

Emancipation, to me, means emancipation from slavery. I suppose that in general terms it is probably used to mean making things better or allowing people to express themselves more freely. But I have never found that I could use this word comfortably. This is because I have always felt that it might mean more than I meant, or it might not mean what I meant. It is one of those words that create a question mark in my mind. So I have just avoided it. However, I understand it when other people use it and I try to interpret exactly what they mean by it. I am neither for it nor against it, but I don't use it because of how people may read it if I were to use it.

I think the idea of being critical is bound with the concept of emancipation, since, after all, you are criticizing the established way of thinking. The established way of thinking is usually something that works to the benefit of an established power or social structure, so that if you are writing critically you are writing with the implication of some kind of change that can be made to that social structure. You are not accepting the world just as it is; you want to see where the existing world can open up, where there are cracks in the existing social establishment of power, and you try to envisage those cracks in such a way as to advance, I would say, social equity, meaning less inequality in material circumstances and in life opportunities.[10] This is a very vague concept, it is true, but I feel I can use it a little more easily than emancipation.

You are, however, pessimistic about the achievement of social equity…

I'm thinking of criticism as being in the interest of the improvement of conditions for the general mass of people. However, I am doing so *pessimistically* because, first of all, you have to be aware of all of the constraints that make the present order the way it is, and the resistance to change that it embodies. That is the pessimistic part, if you like – and you can call it realism as well – so as not to assume the utopian standpoint, according to which if you think 'nice thoughts' they are something that can necessarily be achieved. For this reason, I have put emphasis on the realities that are being faced in making such attempts, but also on trying to find a way through those realities in order to move things in a much more socially equitable direction.

But how does this pessimism connect with the optimism that is inherent in every theory that assumes the possibility of change?

I don't think that the two terms are necessarily the negation of each other. I think pessimism is a keen sense of obstacles and not necessarily a rejection of the possibility of change. Pessimism is an appreciation of all the difficulties inherent in making significant change.

Recently, there has been tremendous optimism over Obama's win – and yet when I see that he's appointed Hilary Clinton, that Robert Gates is still there, or that the same team from the Pentagon is still there, then I don't see much evidence of change. What they are doing and intending to do in Afghanistan and Pakistan seems to be a reinvigoration of old policies. It seems evident that there are entrenched institutions and forces. Even if Obama wanted to change them, he couldn't. Maybe there is some hope for health care in the United States, but of course there is a very powerful group of forces aligned there against it, forces that could never accept a single payer system. So you end up with a series of compromises. You promised change to the world but you aren't going to be able to give them much change.

But what you have is the creation of a sense of optimism after the years of George W. Bush, after the negative raw feeling about that regime. They have a new positive feeling but is there going to be much change? Things will probably be done with a more generous spirit, but by pessimism I mean that I do not expect too much.

What about progress? Is it too optimistic or naïve to think in those terms?

'Progress' is one of those words like 'emancipation'. Perhaps my reaction to emancipation is that it seems to have connotations with the European Enlightenment, and most of the thinkers I have followed have been critics of the Enlightenment. The whole idea of pessimism that I have described goes back to Georges Sorel, whose thought was, like Vico's, a reaction against the Enlightenment. Sorel wrote a book at the end of the nineteenth century called *The Illusions of Progress* (1969), in which he argued that the idea of progress was traceable to the Enlightenment and to the idea that mind could create the future. While Sorel identified progress with the Enlightenment, others identified it with the industrial revolution, the imperial expansion of the nineteenth century and, more recently, in the reasoning behind the neo-conservative expansionists of the George W. Bush administration. Anything that is expanding seems to engender that idea of progress.

So I steered away from the notion of progress because, to me, it can mean everything and nothing much. I prefer to think in terms of concrete forms of change than to think of a general category of progress.

You quoted Isaiah Berlin's remark that '[t]o realise the relative validity of one's convictions and yet stand for them unflinchingly is what distinguishes a civilised man from a barbarian'. You argued that while this offers no philosophical grounding for our commitments, it nevertheless avoids the ethical nihilism of postmodernism.[11] *How would you describe your relationship with the post-modern critique of Critical International Relations Theory?*

I don't think I ever really understood the post-modern criticisms of critical theory. Yet I would feel that I am immune to such criticisms because I have always called myself a conservative. I don't mean that in the American sense, where conservative means something like a radical nineteenth century liberal, *laissez-faire*, believing in the free market and in 'everybody for themselves'. Rather, I mean it more in the sense of Burke, who would say that society is an organic structure and that in a healthy society people have to be able to behave towards each other as members of a collectivity.

I remember Margaret Thatcher's statement that 'there's no such thing as society' (1987: 8). To me, that is the absolute negation of what a conservative is. Society is there and it is organic in the sense that people are bound together in some way. It develops, it grows, it changes, and it should be encouraged to change. But you should not have a plan for remaking society, as this would lead to the Soviet problem, where you have a blueprint for a society and are willing to use all sort of dastardly methods to bring it about. That, to me, is a complete negation of an organic society where people are really responsible to each other and can encourage change – but not by killing and reshaping forcibly.

So I think the 'Other' (with a capital O) that post-modernists refer to seems to mean some alien creature to whom various characteristics are ascribed, most of which are the contrary of those that you think of as your own. My whole argument has been to learn how to think empathetically, to be able to get inside the mind of these 'others' and to try to understand why they think the way they do.

Thinking about the present: globalization and pluralism

If, as you have just remarked, critical theory should seek to engage with concrete circumstances and possibilities of change, what are your most pressing concerns and objectives at the moment?

My central concern is to find a peaceful way out of the neo-conservative dream of the whole world becoming unified in the American idea of democracy and free enterprise capitalism, and the cultural hegemony that accompanies it. The Bush administration made this dream very explicit, and I do not see much change in the Obama administration – just a more effective expression of that hegemonic goal. Obama is less aggressive, and the notion that people can be brought about to adjust to your own concept of world order is more effective through ideas than through force, but I don't think the outcome differs substantially.

Against that, I am thinking more and more about the idea of pluralism in the world. This idea of a more plural world entails that one uses empathetic understanding to try to get inside the minds of other cultures and civilizations – to try to see from the inside how they view the world, and then to see what compatibilities or arrangements can be made to carry on in a peaceful way. The secret is in the extent to which people are able – or become able – to insert themselves into the minds of others. I think this is the only way in which one can hope that plurality – meaning different patterns of society and different moral codes – will work out. While different groups may be opposing or supporting different objectives, they may have some things in common. An ability to understand each other's motives and actions is conducive to becoming aligned to one another for certain goals.

At the same time, the fact of being able to think into the minds of other people changes your own way of thinking. It doesn't mean you adopt other people's values and ideas, but by understanding them for what they are there is a feedback influence on the way you think yourself.

Also, this does not mean necessarily that you will necessarily agree with others when you do understand them. The point is just to understand the connections of thought that make them think and act the way they do. To me that means *overcoming* the concept of the "Other". That is the primary goal of my critical thinking.

What consequences do you envisage from the current economic crisis in terms of the neo-liberal ideology, and what you refer to as hyper-liberalism?[12]

I would say the global financial crisis has sounded the beginning of the end of the neo-liberal ideology and of the notion of the hyper-liberal state. The very fact that the people whose interests were most identified with neo-liberalism are now the ones asking government to pour massive amounts of money into the stability and maintenance of their industry is both bizarre and inconsistent. According to their own ideology, they should let these industries collapse and develop other ways of production – and yet they are the ones who are now shouting for protection!

Neo-liberal ideology does not have much of a long-term future. I would move away from the idea that the free market is the basis of freedom and that individual independence is the goal of mankind. My sense is that if there is a goal, it is one of responsible freedom and of the ability to make individual activity compatible with the needs of the broader social groups and communities. So, going back to an organic notion of society, I think individualism is an extremist doctrine. It has value when it is a matter of allowing people to develop their thinking in whatever way they choose. However, when it comes to applying it to society, you have to be more attentive to its implications.

I think that what is likely to come out of this – just as Keynesianism emerged out of the Great Depression – is that some other concept of economic policy may be pieced together. Alternatively, economic policy may just become fragmented as different countries will see themselves as benefiting from a more heterogeneous form of economic theorizing. In terms of the effect on international institutions such as the World Bank and the International Monetary Fund, it is still very much an open question. However, if they do survive, they will survive as different kinds of institutions. This crisis represents a challenge to these institutions to reinvent themselves and to discard the doctrinal views that they have been associated with – the fixed views about what was good for the world and good for everybody. It is interesting that Jeffrey Sachs, the economist who was associated with the rather brutal application of 'shock therapy', consistent with neo-liberal doctrine, has since turned his attention to the problem of poverty and development, climate change and ecological sustainability.[13]

In one of your works you talked about the internationalization of the state.[14] *Do you think that this crisis will have an impact at the level of the state?*

People who talk about globalization were too quick to write off the state. In my opinion, the state is still the focal point – especially for people who feel deprived in society and that look for recourse and rectification of their situation. The state is the closest thing able to do something. You cannot ask the United Nations or some sort of global government to act for you, because they are too far away and too remote from effective power. Moreover, with the economic crisis, states have to act to protect their own societies and economies. Therefore, the state will continue to be an important force. The question will be 'how do you reconcile the potential conflicts among states?' Here, I do not mean just over territory, but in terms of the kind of economic policy they follow.

Does this mean that the solution is multilateralism between states?

Multilateralism has been frustrated because of the fact that the United Nations was not in a position to accomplish anything without the consent of the great powers – who could not agree. In these circumstances, the world moved towards forms of organization that were improvised, and which resulted from the fact that the United Nations was not what it was thought to be. You had the world economy being organized by the G7 – in other words, the major capitalist powers – while the Soviet bloc was excluded from being part of it. That arrangement functioned for a while, but some parts of the world that were not represented have become more important – witness, for example, the phenomenon of what they call the 'BRICs' – Brazil, Russia, India, China.

It is only in the last few years, with the G20 meeting in London, that there seems to be some general recognition that all of these countries need to be given some voice in the construction of a global economic policy, specifically because of their growing weight in the world economy and the relative weakening of America and Europe. This global economic policy is not going to be dictated by the ideology of neo-liberalism that had seemed to be the consensual form of the G7, and which the latter wanted to impose on the rest of the world. The ideology and the policies will have to be negotiable, and I think we are in that stage of movement. Now, of course it is governments that are represented, not directly people. However, I think the situation is a lot more open now than it has been before and has potentiality for new forms of multilateral engagement.

Overall, this signals a move towards a more plural world, and the recognition that all people do not have to be governed by the same social and economic structures and the same economic policies and doctrines. What constitutes change within those structures and policies is what people and governments within them want to achieve, not something that can be imposed from up high. This constitutes a movement in the direction of plurality.

And what is the role of non-governmental organizations in this process?

There has also been a greater growth of non-governmental organizations. The spread of NGOs from one country to others and the growing linkages within civil society have been a lot more important as a stimulus for change. This network of organizations is becoming more and more important as part of the multilateral picture. These are growing alongside of, but not within, the United Nations system. The UN itself tried to promote NGOs, giving them consultative status, yet I don't think that has been particularly remarkable because of the fact that consultative status didn't really lead anywhere – insofar as the United Nations was incapable of acting. There wasn't much point in trying to influence the United Nations; it was far more important to build up a set of contacts that could grow independently of those official international bodies. So I see this period as a kind of intermediate stage where NGOs are more important.

Of course, they tend to grow in countries that are expanding economically, such as China. There are people who have reached a certain level – beyond the necessary means of survival but not reaching affluence – and can express themselves collectively and form organizations to try to achieve things. I think this phenomenon is spreading around the world, and it will probably be as a result of it that the changes may come about – rather than through direct pressure on the United Nations. While the UN does give countries the obligation to meet and the possibility of discussing things together; and while it gives states the opportunity to bring forward proposals – the challenge is to try to form collective visions of the future and collective policies.

Future political challenges and directions for critical theory

Let us turn then to future challenges – political and theoretical. To begin with, do you think that alternative political visions will take the form of a backlash against globalization?

Resistance to forms of globalization has happened before, and it has been accelerated by the global financial crisis. The first signs of this resistance were clear in the Asian financial crisis of the 1990s, when Malaysia, a small state, took a stand against globalization centred on the attempt of the United States and the so-called 'Washington Consensus' to force policies on other countries. There was a surprising initiative in Japan in 1997, at the height of the crisis, to create an Asian monetary fund separate from the IMF. This was quickly squashed by the IMF and the United States, and resulted in a crisis in which the Asian countries, with the exception of China, lost control over most of their economies. In this context, the application of the 'Washington Consensus' meant in practice that the economies were effectively open to being bought out by Western capital.

As a result of this, most of the Asian countries said 'no more of that for us'. In a future crisis, as in the present time, most of the Asian countries have come out of it better than the United States and Europe because they kept and maintained their own levers of economic control. They have not become swallowed up by the West. China is a prime example: nowadays, the United States, the major predator country, is dependent upon borrowing from China.

These countries now have a better sense of self-control, and they have learned to live without the threat of globalization determining their future. Therefore, resistance comes more at the level of states – which translates into the level of people. It is hard for the peasant masses of China and India to even have a concept of globalization, let alone to organize resistance against it. But those who have experienced it and have shown some resistance against it can identify much more with political leaders who have shown how that resistance is possible.

Does this mean that a unified counter-hegemonic bloc – to use Gramsci's words – is impossible nowadays? What are the privileged oppositional forces in contemporary world politics?

I don't think that I could prescribe how to build a hegemonic bloc as a counter-society in the world today. It might be easier to do so in a specific situation, in a concrete national case.

In general, I think the class-based thinking of earlier times is no longer very pertinent. There has been a deterioration of purely class-based political parties. Class conflict was a force for change historically, but in the present it does not work so well. Changes in the nature of production are breaking down some of the more institutionalized arrangements that grew up in the era of mass production: the organization of mass unions, the concentrated power of employers, the role of the state, all of which was characteristic of a certain period. Especially since the digital revolution – which is empowering all kinds of different people in different ways – you cannot see the structure of society in quite the same rigid forms that they appeared to be in the late nineteenth, early twentieth centuries. One has to be more alive to the way in which technology has reshaped, in a certain sense, the ability of people to work together to form organizations. Even organization sounds too formal a word – one should talk about networking in order to achieve certain common goals.

One can say that today the working class is a rather strange, amorphous entity. The way economies have developed has led the working class to become so fragmented in terms of the work it does, the authority under which it works, the set of ideas that are common to its members, that the Marxist belief that there is a kind of moral entity to the working class is somewhat defunct now.[15] Contemporary movements do not usually arise out of the organized working class anymore. They come from less structured movements: people who are organizing against poverty in cities, people who are organizing on ethnic grounds and so on.

Has there been a failure of the Left in providing a source of opposition?

This particular economic crisis has turned people more to the Right, and you might say that is a failure of the Left. Being cut out of a job puts you back in the 'clinging to survival' category, where you're perhaps more likely to cling to elements of the established order that you may find available to you.[16] If you have known a situation a little better than just basic survival and are alive to persisting injustices, your mind may be more in tune with expressing collective opposition. It looks as though Europeans have moved to the Right partly because the economic crisis tells them that these parties are more likely to get the economy back on track, and there is no room for the 'luxury of experimentation'. It is hard to know why, but it does seem the Right is more generally popular and the old socialist movement is in pretty bad shape.

It is interesting to speculate why the economic crisis has not been taken advantage of by more radical movements. I think that part of the Left is bankrupt. It abandoned its basic ideology twenty years ago with Tony Blair and others. The 'Old

Left' has pretty well disappeared and those remaining on the left of the political spectrum have attempted to make movements based on personality, or on specific issues or doctrines. But I can see no example of an overall comprehensive response in society.

So I think that the strength of opposition is questionable now. One sees much more a backing away into a defensive attitude – rather than a sense of solidarity among people. I thought that perhaps an issue like the environment might produce a sense of common struggle, but that seems to be obscured by the present economic crisis. It is as though it is too luxurious to think in the long term, to plan for the future. You just think about the immediate problem of jobs and income. I do not find much in the way of a strong movement of opposition. There are lots of causes for opposition but nothing that makes it very coherent.

What about critical thinking? What do you think are the future directions for critical theorists?

My preference would be to move in the direction of a more plural concept of world order, and to facilitate the withdrawal of dominant, hegemonic power over the whole world. This would involve providing a plausible retreat for the United States from positions where it is over-extended and where it is a source of conflict. It would mean encouraging situations where peoples are able to think through their own way, and maybe make changes that they consider better in the knowledge that the world is a composite and plural entity.

One has to begin to understand that the concerns of others will thereby cease to be those of an 'Other', and become something that you can understand and relate to. Recently, at a conference in Singapore and in my book *The Political Economy of a Plural World* (2002), I have been developing my reflections in intercivilizational terms.[17] This means thinking about how people can begin to understand other civilizations – not to cease being separate civilizations but to recognise certain regions of compatibility.[18]

The normative choices would be those basic factors of sustainability or defence of the biosphere, as well as the avoidance of violent conflict amongst nations or peoples. Beyond that, I think, lies the question of different peoples being able to develop their own forms of society and organization – economic and social organization and political structures – not by having something forced upon them from the outside, but rather from their spontaneous internal development. This would entail creating forms of organization that would be good for them, but not necessarily in a uniform pattern. I would not extend the realm of compulsory norms very far, but I think that the norm of tolerance of diversity would, perhaps, be the third norm to stress after defence of the biosphere and avoidance of major conflict.

Does your focus on civilization run the risk of essentializing civilizations?

I think that Samuel Huntington (1993) provoked a useful debate about civilizations, but I think his idea of civilizations was of a series of monoliths. A civilization is an understandable whole, which has a lot of variety and conflict going on within it and which is continually in process of changing. One's own civilization and other civilizations are changing and going through this process, and each one is different. They may be identified by terms like Western, or Judeo-Christian or Confucian or Islamic or some other characteristic that is assigned to the whole – blanket terms which Huntington can apply and which most people recognize, but which do not signify a fixed entity, or monolith or a tectonic plate, which was his metaphor.

In other words, Huntington overemphasized the synchronic and under-emphasized the diachronic. A civilization is a very mobile diachronic thing. It is changing all the time. There's more change in civilizations than *among* civilizations, because most people live within civilizations and are not, all the time, thinking about other civilizations and their differences. By understanding that civilizations are changing, dialogue among them becomes possible. You are not dialoguing with monoliths that have a fixed position; you are dialoguing with people who are undergoing a process of change, which might not be similar to the change going on about you. This needs to be taken into account in order to develop some kind of compatibility about global policy.

That would be my position. It always goes back to the question how do you understand other people? How do you reduce them from a big 'Other', a capital 'Other', to a little small approachable other that is more interesting to inquire about? In this context, civil society can make changes in the way people think about things in their own countries, and can build linkages to people in other countries. This would be helpful in this process of trying to *understand* each other without *becoming* each other.[19]

A cosmopolitan solution, then?

Cosmopolitanism has to be the basis for any kind of agreement on things broader than specific interests. This brings us back to the central issue of Collingwood's 'inside' of history – the mentality which animates the material forces of institutions, economies, military organizations and so on. We need to discover and develop mentalities that are not uniform, but that understand each other and each other's difference sufficiently, so that some degree of compatibility becomes possible or at least discussable. Not everybody's cosmopolitanism is the same of course – just as not everybody adheres to the American form of democracy and free market capitalism.

At the top level, a plural world means that the major centres of political power meet each other in dialogue, hopefully to achieve some common understanding – so that the policies of one are not damaging to the others, and so as to avoid open conflict. There is always conflict, but this need not necessarily be violent. At a different level, a plural world means the development among people of the capacity to put themselves into the minds of others, in order to see why they might be inclined to act in the different ways that they do. This is a very personal level, a cosmopolitanism of gradually expanding your understanding of the difference among people.

Notes

1 Cox is here referring to Strange's back-cover endorsement of his 2002 volume (co-authored with Michael Schechter) *The Political Economy of a Plural World: Critical Reflections on Power, Morals and Civilization.*
2 On this assertion, see Germain and Kenny (1998).
3 See, in this context, Cox (2007).
4 In the Canadian general election of 2008, the leader of the Liberal Party Stéphane Dion had based his campaign on an environmental programme. The Liberal Party suffered its worst defeat in recent history.
5 See Morin (2009). This transdisciplinary perspective is presented in Morin (2002).
6 Cox's dialectical method aims at identifying the contradictions that may lead to systemic transformation; see Cox (1981: 127). See also Cox (1996c: 49–59; 2001: 121).
7 See Cox (1995: 13) for another reference to Braudel (1994: 8).
8 See also Cox (1996b: 28)
9 This is a quote from Gramsci (1971: 175), who had borrowed the maxim from Romain Rolland.
10 On this concept, see Cox (1996b: 34–5).
11 For this reference to Berlin (1969), see Cox (1996b: 22).
12 Hyper-liberalism refers to the weakening and dismantling of government-imposed regulations to protect the public from industrial and market activities. For a discussion of hyper-liberalism, see Cox (1987: 285–98; 1996a: 528).
13 'Shock therapy' refers to the immediate liberalization of a state, including privatization, withdrawal of state subsidies, regulation and welfare measures, and the releasing of price and currency control mechanisms. Sachs has since become an advisor to the United Nations Development Program and an advocate of the increase of aid to developing countries. See Sachs (2005).
14 The concept of the 'internationalization of the state' refers broadly to the subordination of domestic social pressures to the requirements of the world economy in the post-World War II environment. See Cox (1981: 144–6).
15 In this respect, see Cox's comments on the debate between André Gorz and Rudolf Bahro in Cox (1987: 3).
16 This resonates Cox's comments regarding the 1974 crisis, in which large-scale unemployment created fears and concerns for personal survival rather than collective protest. See Cox (1987: 282).
17 See Cox (2010).
18 On this point, see Cox and Schechter (2002).
19 See Cox and Schechter (2002: xx–xxi).

Bibliography

Adams, J. (1989) 'Review of Cox, Production, Power, and World Order', *Annals of the American Academy* 501 (January): 224–5.

Berlin, I. (1969) 'Two Concepts of Liberty (1958)' in *Four Essays on Liberty*, Oxford: Oxford University Press.

Braudel, F. (1994) *A History of Civilisations*, trans. R. Mayne, London: Penguin Press.

Burke, E. (1999) *Reflections on the Revolution in France*, Oxford: Oxford University Press.

Cohen, B. (2008) *International Political Economy: An Intellectual History,* Princeton: Princeton University Press.

Collingwood, R.G. (1994) *The Idea of History* (1946), revised edn, Oxford: Oxford University Press.

Cox, R.W. (1969) 'The Executive Head: An Essay on Leadership in International Organization', *International Organization* 23(2): 205–30.

_____ (1981) 'Social Forces, States and World Orders: Beyond International Relations Theory', *Millennium* 10(2): 126–55.

_____ (1983) 'Gramsci, Hegemony and International Relations', *Millennium* 12(2): 162–75.

_____ (1987) *Production, Power, and World Order: Social Forces in the Making of History*, New York: Columbia University Press.

_____ (1995) 'Civilisations: Encounters and Transformations', *Studies in Political Economy*, 47: 7–31.

_____ (1996a) 'Globalisation, Multilateralism, and Democracy', in R.W. Cox with T.J. Sinclair *Approaches to World Order*, Cambridge: Cambridge University Press.

_____ (1996b) 'Influences and Commitments', in R.W. Cox with T.J. Sinclair *Approaches to World Order*, Cambridge: Cambridge University Press.

_____ (1996c) 'Realism, positivism, and historicism', in R.W. Cox with T.J. Sinclair *Approaches to World Order*, Cambridge: Cambridge University Press.

_____ (2001) 'Civilisations and the twenty-first century: some theoretical considerations', *International Relations of the Asia-Pacific* 1(1): 105–30.

_____ (2007) 'The "International" in Evolution', *Millennium*, 35(3): 513–27.

_____ (2010) 'Historicity and International Relations: A Tribute to Wang Gungwu', in Zheng Yongnian (ed.) *China and International Relations: The Chinese View and the Contribution of Wang Gungwu*, London: Routledge.

Cox, R.W. and Jacobson, H (1974) *The Anatomy of Influence: Decision-Making in International Organization*, Yale: Yale University Press.

Cox, R.W. and Schechter, M.G. (2002) *The Political Economy of a Plural World: Critical Reflections on Power, Morals and Civilization*, New York: Routledge.

Germain, R.D. and Kenny, M. (1998) 'Engaging Gramsci: International Relations Theory and the New Gramscians', *Review of International Studies* 24(1): 3–21.

Gramsci, A. (1971) *Selections from the Prison Notebooks*, New York: International Publishers.

Huntington, S. (1993) 'The Clash of Civilisations?', *Foreign Affairs* 72(3): 22–49.

Hoffman, M. (1987) 'Critical Theory and the Inter-Paradigm Debate', *Millennium* 16(2): 231–49.

Kennan, G. F. (1947) 'The Sources of Soviet Conduct', *Foreign Affairs* 25(4): 566–82.

Leysen, A. (2008) *The Critical Theory of Robert W. Cox. Fugitive or Guru?*, New York: Macmillan/Palgrave.

Morin, E. (2002) *Pour une politique de civilisation*, Paris: Arléa, 2002.

_____ (2009) 'Le quantitatif, le qualitatif … et la politique', *Le Monde*, 13 June.

Sachs, J. (2005) *The End of Poverty*, London: Penguin.

Sorel, G. (1969) *The Illusions of Progress*, trans. J. Stanley and C. Stanley, foreword Robert A. Nisbet, Berkeley: University of California Press.

Thatcher, M. (1987) 'No Such Thing as Society', Interview with Douglas Keay, 23 September 1987, No. 10 Downing Street. *Aids, Education and the year 2000! Woman's Own*, 31 October, 8–10.

3

CITIZENSHIP, COMMUNITY AND HARM IN WORLD POLITICS

An interview with Andrew Linklater

Andrew Linklater has been a leading figure in the development of a critical theory of world politics and international ethics. His wide-ranging scholarship, including work on citizenship, cosmopolitanism and the harm principle, has been highly influential in the 'normative turn' in International Relations theory. Andrew Linklater's doctoral research came to print in 1982 as *Men and Citizens in the Theory of International Relations* (republished 1990), a work that engaged with the ethical obligations between citizens and non-citizens. After teaching at the University of Tasmania and at Monash University, he took up a professorship at Keele University before becoming the tenth Woodrow Wilson Professor at Aberystwyth University. He is a member of the Academy of Social Sciences, a Fellow of the British Academy, and a Founding Fellow of the Learned Society of Wales. Andrew Linklater's recent book *The Problem of Harm in World Politics: Theoretical Investigations* (2011), is the first of three volumes focusing on the harm principle as the starting point of a historically grounded critical-theoretical approach to world politics.

This interview was conducted between April and June 2009 at Aberystwyth University, United Kingdom.

Beyond Kant and Marx: themes and influences

When accompanying the evolution of your work, which spans more than thirty years, one is faced with the persistence of certain themes and interests that are, however, continuously pushed forward and even reformulated. What would you say are the main 'knowledge-constitutive interests' of your work, and what has changed since you began?

I think it is fair to say that the defence of ethical universalism – and support for cosmopolitanism – has been a driving interest throughout. There have been changes of approach. I began with an essentially Kantian standpoint and developed through the Habermasian discourse ethics to the current defence of a global harm principle.

Those are not fundamental changes, however, because my recent argument for a harm principle integrates the earlier standpoints. Admittedly, more work is needed to show how the different themes fit together.

The other main change is a shift in focus, from the tension between citizenship and humanity in seventeenth and eighteenth century theories of the state and international law, to the question of the expansion and contraction of the boundaries of moral and political community. In this context, my work on the English School approach to international society served as a bridge to more recent work on harm in world politics, which draws on process sociology (based on Norbert Elias's writings) to reach a higher point of synthesis in the study of international relations.[1] In a nutshell, then: there has been a shift from the problem of citizenship, to the problem of community and to the problem of harm. I explained this in the 'Introduction' (2007b) to *Critical Theory and World Politics*.

How did these shifts relate to developments in world politics in the past thirty years?

What is striking – and pleasing – from my perspective is the growing prominence of cosmopolitan ideas, both in Political Theory/International Political Theory and practice over the last few years. There has been an increase in the number of works that discuss cosmopolitanism in one form or another, and an increase in the number of people who are involved in, or broadly support, a cosmopolitan project of some kind. There has been an obvious increase in the number of people, both inside the academic world and beyond it, who recognize that rising levels of human interconnectedness require new 'post-national' institutions and ideas.[2] Part of the challenge is to create a cosmopolitan vocabulary that addresses the challenges of global interconnectedness while respecting cultural and other differences between people. The proliferation of non-governmental organizations that are concerned with humanitarian issues (such as torture, land mines, poverty, environmental issues and so forth) illustrates the small but important shift in thinking about the relationship between citizenship and humanity in the recent period.

More and more people in different parts of the world are aware of how everyday conduct affects human possibilities and arrangements elsewhere. Whether we are looking at the academic world, social movements or everyday conduct, there have been some important advances. In this regard, for all their faults, the development of International Criminal Law and the formation of the International Criminal Court are important developments. That is not to underestimate the importance of countervailing forces and ideologies, or to assume that progress in cosmopolitan theory and practice is guaranteed. It is only to suggest that cosmopolitan ideas are now far more mainstream – in academic circles and in the broader culture – than they were thirty to forty years ago when my own career began.

Your first book, Men and Citizens in the Theory of International Relations *(1982), introduced a new angle into the study of world politics. What influenced you to write this book? How did the question of 'men and citizens' become a problem for you?*

There are two answers to that question. First, in the early 1970s, and quite by accident, I came across the Carnegie Foundation Classics of International Law series. Reading Pufendorf and Vattel's writings on international law, the theme that stood out was the relationship between the law of nature, which governed all human beings in the original state of nature, and public law – or the law of the state – pertaining to relations between citizens.[3] Reading these texts led to an interest in the tension between the two moralities, and in what seemed to be a dilution of the laws of humanity once people were divided into separate states.

Second, when I was an undergraduate studying Politics and International Relations (an unusual combination at the time) at Aberdeen University in the late 1960s and early 1970s, I couldn't quite understand why Political Theory and International Relations (IR) were not more closely connected. In those years, it is important to remember, there was almost no literature on what we now call International Political Theory. However, two works on course reading lists encouraged me to think that there was something wrong about that state of affairs, something peculiar and puzzling: these were Arnold Wolfers' *Discourse and Collaboration* (1965) and Stanley Hoffmann's *The State of War* (1965). These books dealt with Rousseau and Kant on politics and ethics, in Hoffman's case, and with Weber on the ethics of conviction and responsibility, in Wolfers' case. They started me thinking about links between Political Theory and IR. Thanks to Hoffmann's book, for example, I learned about Rousseau's focus on the tension between how we treat each other within states and how we treat the members of other societies.

To go further, I was taught by Brian Midgley, a Thomist natural lawyer, who had worked on the ethical issues surrounding nuclear weapons and who was an expert in the just war tradition.[4] I received a great deal of encouragement from him about how to think about international ethics or International Political Theory. He made the inquiry seem entirely natural and legitimate at a time when there was considerable indifference – and some resistance – to that way of thinking.

Later, and as a result of reading many of Hegel and Marx's political writings (thanks to a postgraduate course at Oxford), the notion of tensions and contradictions in society started to fascinate me.

So by this odd route I ended up with the sense that there were contradictions in the way in which we manage obligations between citizens and duties to other human beings. I continue to work on that topic, but in ways that are now more influenced by sociological writings than by political theory.

The theoretical argument of Men and Citizens *was pushed forward and developed considerably in your following book,* Beyond Realism and Marxism *(1990). Could you tell us a bit more about the importance of Marx for the development of your thought?*

Men and Citizens tried to establish that there had been a degree of progress in social and political theory – and particularly in the Kantian tradition – in wrestling with the questions of sovereignty, citizenship and humanity. I was trying to show that there had been a degree of progressive thinking. Although this should not be mistaken for a linear process, nevertheless it seemed legitimate to point to advances in social and political thought. It was possible to compare, for example, ancient Greek thinking, which was centred on the polis, and international relations thinking originating from the birth of modern, secular natural law – which seemed to be struggling, more than the Greeks ever did, with some notion of the moral equality of all people, an idea that is central to cosmopolitanism. Kant's writings and his critique of the 'miserable comforters' were important influences in this regard (1970).

The reason for writing *Beyond Realism and Marxism* was that Marxism seemed to offer an alternative to the realist view that people are more or less bound to live in separate communities that compete for power and security. Marx offered a panoramic overview of how people have been drawn into larger social systems and global relations over the last few millennia. The tension between the anticipated socialist world order and the persistence of nationalism led to fascinating discussions about the boundaries of community, how they have changed over time, and how far obligations can extend beyond the nation (potentially embracing the whole species). My assumption was that comparing realism and Marxism could lead to a better conceptual framework with which to understand the problem of community in world politics.

Reading the Marxist literature also forced me to think about questions of method. When I was writing *Men and Citizens*, I was not particularly aware of Critical Theory – indeed, it did not really enter the IR discussion until Robert Cox published his renowned essays in *Millennium*.[5] In the late seventies, while teaching at the University of Tasmania, I spent a great deal of time in the company of sociologists. That led me to read works by Richard Bernstein (1976), Brian Fay (1975) and others who explained the critical alternative to positivism and hermeneutics. That also influenced the approach that was taken in *Beyond Realism and Marxism*, and the interest in immanent potentials that runs through my work on citizenship and community in the 1990s, and the current project on harm.

Can we then consider Marx as the starting point for an effective critique of realism?

I began working on *Beyond Realism and Marxism* because Marxism was an interesting way of thinking about the long-term patterns that had integrated the human species. It was also an interesting way to start thinking about the problem of community, and about the possibility of a cosmopolitan community.

Both realism and Marxism cast light on long-term developments in relations between societies; seen in conjunction, they emphasize the importance of war, geopolitics and production. However, neither approach focuses on the moral and cultural forces that shape the ideas people have about their bounded community: how exactly they are bound to it, what they believe their rights are in relation with other peoples, and what they think their duties are to the rest of the world.

Marxism did wrestle in interesting ways with the tensions between universalizing processes, such as capitalism, and clashing tendencies such as loyalty to the nation. But there was little focus on the issue of rights and duties that people believe they have as members of specific communities, and little understanding of the need to focus on what English School theorists call the society of states. That realm is as important as war, geopolitics and production for historical sociology – although little work has been done on how those phenomena influence one another and shape the development of the species as a whole.

Marx was right in arguing that over human history there has been a long-term trend towards higher levels of interconnectedness. However, he did not devote much attention to the development of ever larger 'survival units', as Norbert Elias (1978: 138) put it. Important passages in *The German Ideology* (Marx and Engels 1970) and elsewhere emphasized the importance of widening the scope of emotional identification to embrace the whole species – and the need to do that so that the species could gain control over the processes that have tied more and more people together. But the analysis suffered from presenting questions about emotional identification in class terms, a limitation that reflected Marx's views that changes in forces and relations of production are the driving force in human history.[6]

In this regard, Marx also seems to be influential by providing an understanding of human freedom centred on the capacity for self-creation. This has implications in the understanding of political community as something susceptible to transformation …

The crucial passage for me is in *The Eighteenth Brumaire*, where Marx states that 'men make their own history but not under conditions of their own choosing' (this passage refers to 'men', as thinkers did until quite recently, when they were really thinking about humanity or human beings).[7] That is a remarkable statement: it captures the point that human beings are initiators, individually and collectively, of their history, and at the same time it shows that humans do not control many of their creations. History is human product but it has been made in ways that people do not necessarily understand and do not really control.

That is manifestly Marx's view in the *Grundrisse* – and elsewhere – where he discussed how relations of personal dependence in early societies gave way to relations of personal independence under capitalism.[8] According to Marx, however, capital was what was really liberated. In modern societies, human beings became freer in some respects, but their freedoms came with subjection to impersonal forces and structures, which were clearly made by people but not necessarily in a conscious way or with a real understanding of where their actions would lead.

The issue then is how humans can use their rational powers to understand and transform social systems so that people can live under conditions that they have chosen for themselves, rather than in conditions that have been forced on them. This theme is carried forward in Eliasian or process sociology, but without the partisanship that runs through Marxism and with a more comprehensive analysis of long-term patterns of change.

The idea of an expansion of the moral community is central in your work. It would perhaps be interesting to discuss its intellectual origins a bit more. Could you explain the reasoning behind this idea, and how it draws on your Kantian and Marxist influences?

The basic reasoning is as follows: the long-term trend towards larger territorial concentrations of power has affected the scope of emotional identification.[9] People can identify with millions – even hundreds of millions of other people – in the same society. Many have a sense of solidarity with their contemporaries in other societies who have similar concerns – about the global environment, for example. More people are aware of the political implications of belonging to the human species. They are aware of how the lives of people in different societies have become more closely interwoven, and some support a politics that is concerned with the whole species. Of course, in general those identifications are weak in comparison with those that bind people to specific communities.

The idea of the expansion of moral horizons or the expansion of community is closely connected with the defence of freedom in Kant's and Marx's thought. Despite their many differences, they broadly agreed that human beings can only really take control of their history and get rid of unnecessary force and surplus constraints if they co-operate in some kind of world-wide association – whether it is the association of republican states that Kant discussed, or whatever political form Marx thought was appropriate to the condition of socialized humanity. Even for Kant, expanding moral horizons was not just about being ethically correct. It was very much about gaining more control over social processes that have become global, that are beyond the control of existing institutions. It was about eradicating, as far as possible, 'barbaric' forces, in Kant's case, or false constraints, as Marxists are inclined to argue.

The 'triple transformation' of political community that I defend – a notion that encompasses a community that is more universalistic than its predecessors, but also more sensitive to cultural differences and more committed to reducing material inequalities – draws on themes from both Kant and Marx. The vision is Kantian up to a point. The Kantian republic of sovereign states is clearly limited, but it rested on the important point that the constitution or configuration of the state matters. As Kant argued, if the domestic constitution has, at its core, the notion of human rights, then society is committed by its own discourse to the view that all people have equal entitlements to moral consideration. An action that contradicts such principles is perhaps more likely to be opposed or to cause moral unease. A hurdle is placed in the way of acting entirely on self-interested grounds. It is strengthened, as Kant argued, when states are obliged to defend their actions in global fora. That is perhaps no longer a radical thought, but most states in the history of international relations have been free from that particular obligation.

Marx never addressed such issues about the state and international politics. Here Kant has the edge, although his weakness is the absence of a consideration of class inequalities, as well as the absence of any vision of a more equal distribution of economic and social power, or a restructuring of global relations that are not accountable to the people they affect. Certainly, in recent years thinkers in the

Kantian or liberal tradition have placed questions of global justice at the centre of political theory. Marxists have provided more sophisticated analyses of global capitalist relations, but they have yet, as far I am aware, to confront the relevant ethical issues 'head on'.

The insufficiencies of both Kant and Marx in this context explain why Habermas's exercise in reconstructing historical materialism, and in developing a cosmopolitan ethical framework in the shape of a discourse theory of morality, featured prominently in works such as *The Transformation of Political Community* (1998). But Elias's writings now seem to me be to the real heir to the tradition to which Kant and Marx belonged.

The expansion of moral community and post-national citizenship

Let us explore in more detail the idea of the expansion of the moral community. You have argued that a major condition for the expansion of moral duties and commitments is the development of an estrangement, an uneasy feeling towards one's own community …

An old theme in political thought reveals what is at stake. Hegel argued that the life of the citizen in the ancient polis was unified or internally coherent. The citizen was, as he puts it somewhere in the *Philosophy of Right* (2008), entirely 'at home in the world'. Whether he was entirely correct about that is another matter, but suffice it to say that Hegel, along with Schiller, believed that the unity of the *polis* had had to be shattered in order for the species to advance to a higher level of moral and political consciousness.[10] The important thing here is not to suggest that ancient Greeks were so at one with the polis that questions about the morality of its behaviour towards outsiders did not arise. At the same time, however, there does not seem to be any evidence that Greek political thinkers (or citizens for that matter) agonized about the relationship between duties to the polis and obligations to other people – in the way that Rousseau, Kant and others have done since the Enlightenment.

I have no doubt that a sense of unease about how exactly one's community should behave towards the wider world is necessary for the development of wider solidarities. In order to move to a higher level, citizens have to go through a process of trying to establish the limits of their obligations to their community – the limits of its claims on them. A degree of agonizing over those rights and obligations is necessary to make the transition to new forms of political community, which can be more cosmopolitan than their predecessors but also more tolerant of various cultural and other differences within nation-states. This is complicated for many people who have strong attachments to the nation or state, settled views about their rights against and duties to people in other societies, and fears about new centres of power and authority.

But how does this unease come about?

Two closely related terms in sociology and social theory highlight the central issues. The first is Habermas's notion of decentration, which refers to standing back from one's own community, and understanding how its practices appear to others, and how its behaviour seems to outsiders who are affected by it.[11] The second concept is detachment, which Elias discusses in different contexts, including the relationship that people have with their community and the extent to which they can, as it were, see it from outside.[12]

Elias stressed how difficult detachment is for many people. At the same time, he has emphasized that the capacity for detachment has 'survival value' for the species and makes it possible to adapt to new circumstances such as the demands of the high levels of global interconnectedness that exist today. From that standpoint, the tension between 'involvement' in particular communities – identification with them and the sense of a personal stake in their success – and 'detachment' is likely to become more intense under those conditions.

But, as I noted earlier, various social movements have acquired a degree of detachment from their own communities; they are more alert to the problems that confront the species as a whole, including future generations who may be unfairly burdened by current structures and attitudes, and by failures to deal with issues such as climate change. Those social movements are more responsive to notions of post-national citizenship.

Let us follow that cue. Citizenship is a central concept for you, and you have argued that we are witnessing the rise of notions of citizenship that go beyond the remit of the nation-state …

The development of post-national citizenship is central for the emergence of new social and political systems that address the global problems that I mentioned. It is interesting that citizenship is a concept that is often used in that context – examples are notions of world or cosmopolitan citizenship, good international citizenship and environmental citizenship.[13]

In *The Transformation of Political Community*, I argued that there has been some movement towards creating what Habermas calls post-national citizenship and post-national communities. That means that there are new sensitivities to the various forms of suffering incurred by distant strangers, and there is the whole realm of NGO activity that is concerned with reducing transnational harm. A central claim was that the universalistic and egalitarian ideology that is central to modern political life provides cultural resources that various groups can harness to emancipatory causes that are transnational in focus.

Notions such as world citizenship are an extension of the dominant ideas about the relationship between the citizen and the state, and an attempt to equip modern peoples with the conceptual resources – which already exist within the relations that tie them together – that are necessary to deal with global challenges.

Is that the role you see post-national notions of citizenship playing in the current context?

Yes. Notions of post-national citizenship, whether encapsulated in the idea of world citizenship or good international citizenship, are important attempts to develop a vocabulary that prepares communities for the challenges of rising levels of interconnectedness. They express the view that the modern sovereign states-system is a dead end. They suggest how, over time, people can weave more inclusive notions of community into their lives.

The idea of post-national citizenship is significant because it relies on one of the great achievements of modern democratic societies: the establishment of a web of legal, political and economic rights. Over approximately the last two hundred years, there has been an overall trend towards universalizing citizenship – in other words, towards the extension of rights to more and more social strata, and to deepening the meaning of these rights so that they address the political concerns of the more vulnerable members of society.

This is no more than an overall trend – many will emphasize that social and economic rights, for example, have been weakened with the advance of market liberalism, as have civil rights since 9/11. Even so, there was, early on, an emancipatory dimension to the language of citizenship that creates the possibility of a bridge from the nation to the world, from national citizenship to good international or cosmopolitan citizenship. The idea of citizenship, notwithstanding its historical fusion with sovereignty, territoriality and nationality, provides the cultural resources that make it easier to grasp the outlines of new forms of political community that are essential to deal with global problems. Those issues have made the question of whether people can balance national and international loyalties – and overcome the old conflicts between humanity and citizenship, between 'men' and 'citizens' – a fundamental political problem and not just an interesting philosophical matter. In sum, citizenship can be a moral resource in the quest to reduce violent and non-violent harm in world politics.

States are not the problem for me and I don't regard them of necessity as 'bad' things. States have been the arenas within which there have been very substantial advances in human liberties, welfare politics, citizenship rights, and so forth. So I am not an anarchist and think the states ought to be dismantled because they are all equally bad. Rather, it is a question of what to do with the state and what other content might go into it. In *The Transformation of Political Community* I discuss the fusion of nationalism, nationality, sovereignty, territoriality and citizenship, but what I am trying to get away from is that content that renders a totalizing project in which the state is the ultimate focus of human loyalty and which has permeated mass culture. This is why notions of world citizenship are attractive to me and indeed why notions of good international citizenship are granted, because they both refer to the fact that individuals and groups, non-public groups and state structures can weave more expansive notions of community into their lives and into their ways of thinking about society and politics.

Yet, citizenship is still seen as implying an allegiance to a bounded community. Is your use of the notion of post-national citizenship an attempt to balance utopianism and realism in your analysis?[14]

In my view, it is not surprising that citizenship functions in a post-national vocabulary. True, in some sense of the word citizenship secures certain privileges for some people while depriving others of the same advantages. However, it must be noted that modern notions of citizenship have been strongly influenced by universalistic and egalitarian ideas. Visions of post-national citizenship might be regarded as an attempt to release those ideas from national constraints, thereby promoting some features of civility – a civilizing process, if you want – in world affairs. For Elias (1969 and 1982), taking the standpoint of the civilizing process entails studying how more and more people have become more and more interdependent – leading to new rules of etiquette and manners, to other civil obligations. He doesn't put it quite this way, but it is in actual fact a study of how moral life changes, how cultural transformation takes place through changed interdependencies between peoples. Constructivists take note!

Whether that is best described as balancing utopian and realist aspirations is another matter. Carr's point (2001: 12) about avoiding the naivety of utopianism and the sterility of realism was well made. But he seems at times to suggest that realism and utopianism run along entirely separate track-lines that have to be brought together. Frankfurt School theory, on the other hand, and the idea of immanent critique, suggests that it is important to understand how they develop within the same set of social relations, each influencing the other. This is also strongly suggested by process sociology. The question, then, is whether the utopian element can actually be seen as essential for the preservation of the social system or for adapting it to deal with new challenges.

What happens to separate communities like nation-states, when such understandings of citizenship are developed?

Everything hinges here on the nature of the separateness of communities, specifically whether separateness entails the right to privilege the interests of insiders over outsiders – a frame of mind that has dominated modern political life since the fusion of sovereignty, territoriality, citizenship and nationality. Separateness need not be linked with such characteristics.

In the European Union, for example, states continue to value their separateness in many ways, but without the traditional emphasis on the moral significance of distinctions between insiders and outsiders. The EU has broken with that old 'totalizing project' without surrendering the sense of national loyalties. It is an interesting experiment in combining post-national loyalties with attachments to existing national and indeed sub-state groups. As such, it provides some insights into how citizenship can find new expression 'above' and 'below' the state, and also into the nature of the obstacles to reconfiguring political communities.

The question, then, is how societies balance such loyalties with attachments to wider political associations. It is interesting that in academic circles there are now important discussions about the principles that the EU should observe in its relations with other people – and specifically discussions about the role it can play in defending human rights and democratic governance, in promoting conflict resolution and in encouraging multilateralism.[15] We seem to be witnessing a 'locking in' of cosmopolitan attachments as they are embedded in institutions and in everyday life.

And what is the role of civil society in this context?

One of the criticisms of *The Transformation of Political Community* was that there was too much focus on the state and too little consideration of civil society actors and organizations. There was a tendency in some of the social movement literature in the 1980s to argue that we should by-pass the state – the assumption being that popular movements could secure fundamental change by their own efforts. In my view, the question is rather how to transform the state so that its powers and resources are used to promote cosmopolitan as well as national purposes.

The idea of the good international citizenship is significant here. The landmines treaty is an example of how civil society groups can be successful in persuading states to support humanitarian objectives. It has been argued that there is an element of 'complementarity' between civil society and international society – a degree of interpenetration perhaps – in which states endeavour to benefit from the resources that civil society actors possess while attempting to preserve their dominance in world affairs.[16] In that process, NGOs have helped shape political agendas and, in conjunction, they have had some impact on the structure of human loyalties and on modes of identification with others.

What is important to note here is the role of civil society in the dissemination of ideas about how people in very different parts of the world have come to be interconnected, and in promoting a greater realization of the need for justice in relations between distant strangers. There have been subtle shifts in that domain in what is perhaps still a very early stage in the development of human interconnectedness. States are increasingly immersed in complex global relations with a variety of international actors that have reduced their ability to socialize people into national outlooks. People now have a variety of moral reference-points and diverse sources of information that have weakened national attachments to some degree. Again it is important not to overstate the point – only to identify trends that, even if reversible, are encouraging from a cosmopolitan perspective.

Harm and the emancipatory commitment

Your more recent work has focused on cosmopolitan harm conventions and the harm principle. One of your aims is to research how far members of particular communities have historically believed that people have an obligation to avoid harm to others. How did this project start?

The immediate interest for focusing on harm was Marx's belief that a major transformation was under way in Europe, which would eventually affect the whole world. According to Marx in *The Communist Manifesto* and elsewhere, as a result of capitalism violent harm between national populations was probably in decline – but only to be overshadowed by non-violent harm in the shape of the world-wide exploitation of vulnerable people. That comment raised the question of whether the most industrialized societies were caught up in a longer-term pacifying trend – as many liberals from the nineteenth century to the present day have argued. If so, the modern states-system may avoid the conflicts that eventually destroyed earlier states-systems. Marx's standpoint raised questions for me about how many forms of harm exist in world politics, and about how to understand them. I realized that there is no tradition of thought and no body of literature that analyses the place of harm – the development of more ingenious ways of harming other people as well as efforts to rein in that power – in the history of humanity.

Another important resource in this regard was Wight's sociology of states-systems (1979), which is a major contribution to efforts to build new connections between Historical Sociology and International Relations. I am presently in the process of trying to link Wight's project with the study of harm in world politics. This is perhaps best understood as an extension of existing Grotian themes, since various members of the English School have stated, in one form or another, that the society of states is principally concerned with restraining the capacity to harm other societies. At times, reference is made to the 'civilizing' role of the society of states, which brings to mind Elias's claim (1996: 31) in *The Germans* that the civilizing process places restraints on people within the same society so that they do not demean, injure and in other ways harm each other time and time again. Stumbling across that passage led to me to think that the study of harm in world politics is best regarded as a comparison of civilizing processes in different forms of world political organization.

What exactly does the recognition of the harm principle entail? Are we talking about negative duties of refraining from injury, or positive duties of assistance?

A few years ago I came across a discussion of Simone Weil's reflections (1952) on a basic obligation of rescue.[17] Her argument was that almost anybody encountering a complete stranger who is suffering from the effects of drought in a desert will share their canteen of water – assuming there is enough to share. There was a theological dimension to that argument which I leave to one side here, preferring instead to focus on the empirical claim that many people in many societies and in most periods of time would assist in that way. All that Weil was arguing was that most or at least many would assist – she did not go beyond that claim since she was undoubtedly aware of all sorts of reasons people can have for leaving adversaries, the members of 'culturally polluted' groups and so forth to die.

The important point is that people do not have to belong to the same community to believe they have duties of rescue of that kind – nor do they have to speak the same language. All that may matter is that they belong to the same species. Of course, many may believe that the duty is to some deity rather than to another person *per se*. But either way the question may arise for them of whether the failure to help might constitute harm.

Writers in the area of moral and legal philosophy have discussed the relevant issues in significant detail. A crucial text is Feinberg's *Harm to Others* (1984), which argues that the obligation to avoid harm extends from the more obvious proscriptions – regarding killing, assault, exploiting the vulnerable and so forth – to actually rescuing others, when there is no serious risk to the potential rescuer. Feinberg regards the failure to rescue as a potentially punishable offence and not, as some philosophers have argued, as a legitimate entitlement to withhold a benefit. It is a punishable offence, he argues, when a potential rescuer is in the position to decide whether or not a person survives and chooses to do nothing.

Thomas Pogge's book (2008) on world poverty is also important since he argues that the so-called negative obligation to avoid harm generates a positive responsibility to dismantle what he calls 'global coercive regimes' that disadvantage the global poor. Similarly, Onora O'Neil published an essay (1991) on transnational justice where she argues that all people have the right to protest against the way in which they are bound together. It is possible to anchor that claim in the 'harm principle'.

In short, then, the negative obligation not to injure others has radical implications under conditions of global interconnectedness, where people in one part of the world affect the interests of 'distant strangers' in profound ways. This can all be connected with studies of cosmopolitan democracy, transnational public spheres and so forth.[18] As a result, the 'negative' obligations that are usually associated with the harm principle do not stand alone, but come with some 'positive' obligations – exactly how far they extend is, however, a controversial matter.

Let me just add that it is important not to claim too much for the harm principle – so that it seems to cover the whole of morality – or so little that it involves simply refraining from various forms of violent and non-violent harm.

Could you elaborate on the limits to the principle of harm? It is possible to become 'pathological' in meeting its requirements – for example, fearing to leave the house in case of harming something or, alternatively, acting with brazen heroism to save others?

In Jainism, I gather, monks wear masks and strain their drinking water lest they kill insects unintentionally. Some allegedly carry small brushes to clear the path ahead them so they avoid killing unseen insects. They are also said to refrain from lighting fires or lamps in case insects are drawn towards them and destroyed. What is striking here is the high level of self-restraint – or self-limiting – compared with the dominant ideas in the West in recent centuries. This is a matter I will discuss in more detail in the second volume on harm, where the emphasis is on various efforts to place limitations on the power to harm – recognizing that the capacity to harm more and more people over greater distances in more and more destructive ways has run ahead of the capacity to curb that power. Sensitivity to harm in other cultures and in various world religions provides an interesting contrast to the dominant attitudes towards nature and towards the members of other societies in the West.

Realists will argue that states have been caught up in geopolitical relations that have made it essential to work out how to 'out-injure' actual or potential adversaries. Jainism is a luxury that states cannot afford if they intend to remain in business. Liberals have long argued that it is important to balance the duty not to harm with the right to live freely, that is, without being burdened with responsibilities or with fears about the consequences of causing harm inadvertently. The question then is where the balance lies between right to liberty and duties to avoid harming others.

Liberals themselves have disagreed about the right balance – free market liberals and welfare liberals continue to debate the limits of state power and the extent of personal freedoms. The disputes extend to notions of corporate responsibility, and to how limited or extensive those should be. These disputes have become more complicated with the rise of the so-called 'global risk society' and the realization that current generations, unless there is a change of course, may harm future generations or burden them unfairly, and thereby reduce their freedom of action.[19] Some defend the precautionary principle on the grounds that certain liberties should be withdrawn because of possible dangers and risks; others resent what they regard as an attempt to reduce liberties. They are concerned that the harm principle may lead to some of the pathological qualities that you mention in your question.

By itself, the harm principle cannot reconcile those political differences. But the notion of harm is useful for any discussion about the establishment of limits upon human action. This is particularly important given the revolutionary developments in the capacity to harm that have taken place over the last few decades. I refer here not only to revolutions in military technology, but also to the growth of unintended and often invisible harm to the environment. All those developments create pressures to think about the multiple sources of various forms of harm, and to reflect on limits to human action that have become essential for future well-being, and possibly for human survival.

What seems to underlie your concern with the harm principle is an attempt to ascertain what each member of humankind may reasonably claim from others. This was already present in your book Man and Citizens *(1982: 8) …*

Cicero (1991: Book I, 99) argued that the main obligation we have to all other humans is to refrain from harming them, adding that anyone who causes unnecessary harm is an enemy of the human race. Interestingly, that idea runs through the natural law tradition, and is evident in the writings of Pufendorf, Vattel and Kant, and specifically on their reflections on the relationship between duties to the state and obligations to the rest of humanity. Of the three, Kant (1970: 206) was alone in arguing that individuals and societies have an obligation to enter into a civil condition with anyone they might injure.

Of course, complex issues arise about the reasonable claims that people can make in their relations with each other – or about the limits on action that they need to observe if they are to live together. There is a basic distinction between not harming others and acting heroically – in a way that involves putting one's life at risk. Philosophers will continue to debate how far the harm principle extends. All I want to argue is that the 'harm principle' is now central to global efforts to establish principles of co-existence. It is central to international legal conventions that prohibit 'serious bodily and mental harm'.[20] It is at the heart of a global discourse – still at an early phase of development – about how to balance the rights and obligations that people have as members of particular sovereign states with the rights and obligations they have as members of the human race.

How does harm fit into the emancipatory project? Does your focus on the harm principle represent a retreat from emancipation to harm minimization as the goal of a critical theory of IR?

It is perhaps worth saying that those who have focused on harm have tended to offer a negative utopia – in other words, they have sometimes envisaged a future in which people are no longer subject to various forms of violent and non-violent harm. Here we appear to be a long way from the socialist utopia, which was defended in Marx's and in later Marxist writings. It is probably fair to say that those who have focused on reducing harm regard the loftier goals that Marx advocated as naively utopian.

There is probably something of the same negative outlook in Elias's writings, despite some parallels with Marx's belief that social science can enable people to take more control over processes that appear to stand over them. For Elias, the pacification of social and political relations appears to have been a core ideal, but that would represent the contraction of the Marxist emancipatory project.

It is important to stress, however, that Elias would have rejected that way of formulating the central issue. One of his laments about Sociology was that analysis often lags behind diagnosis and prognosis. The 'reality-congruent knowledge' that could in time enable people to have more control over social process could only be produced through the rigorous 'detachment' from political positions. Some of the issues are set out in a lecture on Adorno, which emphasizes the latter's failure to break with Marxist visions.[21] Elias (2007: 13) did have a clear normative position, which is evident in his hopes for a world in which people who violate human rights are regarded as either 'criminal or insane'. Indeed, at one point he suggests (Elias 1998a: 145) that the purpose of social inquiry is to understand the forms of restraint that are perhaps more or less necessary for any society to function, and those that have no other purpose than protecting dominant interests.

I do not see my research on harm as a retreat from the emancipatory project of critical theory. At its core is the question of how people can live without the burden of violent and non-violent harm including exploitation, humiliation and so forth. Elias's work, for example, has obvious parallels with Horkheimer's conception of critical theory.[22] Whether Horkheimer and Adorno had any influence on Elias – and vice versa – is not entirely clear although the Institute of Social Research and the Department of Sociology shared the same building at the University of Frankfurt. In some recent writings, I have tried to suggest that critical theory and process sociology can be brought more closely together (Linklater 2007a: 135–50). That is partly driven by an interest in certain parallels in their ethical orientation. It also reflects my belief that the efforts that Frankfurt School theorists have made to build on, or transcend, historical materialism fall short of the explanation of long-term processes of change that can be found in process sociology.

What kind of notion of emancipation would you suggest?

The question is whether or not there is a rolling back of the grander aspirations that one finds, for example, in Marx's writings. What is suggested here is a utopia of limited aspirations, one that is the direct product of what Charles Taylor calls the Enlightenment 'affirmation of ordinary life'.[23] It is a vision of 'ordinary virtues' that has appealed to many thinkers – from Montaigne and Montesquieu, Horkheimer and Adorno, Shklar and Rorty, and Primo Levi to mention just a few. It rests on a humanistic ethic but, as noted earlier, one that supports not only negative but also positive obligations. The correct balance between them – as well as between personal or collective rights and duties – is still in the process of being worked out, as we can see from many of the forms of cooperation and conflict that dominate world politics.

Critical theory in world politics: challenges and future

In an answer to a previous question, you talked about the expansion of the moral community as a matter of moving 'to a higher level'. This resonates with a passage in your book Men and Citizens *(1982: 160), in which you talk about the possibility of placing 'different social formations upon a scale of ascending types in accordance with the extent to which each approximates the conditions of realised human freedom'. For many critics, this means subscribing to the modern narrative of progress and Western superiority …*

The idea of the scale of forms was designed to highlight two things: on the one hand, the different levels of emancipation from the constraints of particular, or particularistic, social groups; on the other, different positions in relation to a cosmopolitan ethic that stressed the moral equality of people. The idea of a scale of forms, which I borrowed from Collingwood,[24] was a useful heuristic device at the time of writing *Men and Citizens*. I have not used it since, in part because it smacks of nineteenth century ideas about a natural hierarchy of peoples, or about natural distinctions between the 'civilized' and the less 'advanced'.

Nevertheless, I would still argue that it is possible – to use an unfashionable claim – to analyse forms of collective learning. The reference here is to Elias's comment (1998b: 228–9) that modern humans are still at the beginning of what may be a long collective learning process in which people within their respective groups and in their relations with others find ways of living together more harmoniously. It is certainly possible, as Kant argued, to ask what different societies contributed to ideas of world citizenship. The implication here is that different peoples might indeed be located on a scale of forms, some having contributed more than others to political ideas and institutions that can promote a more cosmopolitan world order.

Problems set in if it is assumed that some contributed more than others because of some natural qualities and endowments. Elias maintains that the idea of collective social learning is worth defending, but it should not be accompanied by the assumption that earlier peoples faced a choice between 'their values or ours', and made the wrong choice through some defect in their reasoning or some deficiency. Any discussion of collective learning has to be conscious of that point.

The idea of a scale of forms was not constructed with that thought in mind. It had the heuristic purpose of emphasizing important changes in the relationship between conceptions of the state, citizenship and humanity that marked movement towards more cosmopolitan forms of reasoning.

How does this notion of collective learning relate to your earlier points on harm?

In this context, the idea of collective learning refers to advances in understanding how humans can co-exist without the forms of violent and non-violent harm that have dominated much of their history thus far. It refers to identifying the most accessible forms of solidarity between strangers who belong to different ways of life and have competing conceptions of how they should live. Amidst the differences there are certain shared vulnerabilities and common aversions to pain and suffering that can provide the basis for advances in learning how to live together more amicably.

Your cautious approach suggests that, when thinking about the expansion of moral commitments or civilizing processes, we need to temper optimism with an awareness of the dangers of modernity …

There is indeed a 'dark side of modernity' – visible, for example, in extraordinary state powers as expressed in total warfare, genocide and so forth. It is only in more recent times that I have discovered the language that seems to capture those different dynamics rather well. I am thinking of the Elias's argument, when he emphasizes in *The Germans* and elsewhere that civilizing processes and de-civilizing processes always develop in tandem.[25] The question is which has the upper hand at any particular moment.

This strikes me as a particularly effective way of trying to capture those tensions within modern societies – that there are latent potentialities for more cosmopolitan communities in the way in which modern societies are constructed but, at the same time, they come up against various forms of power, domination and resistance. As Elias puts it, the pressures to become sensitive to the needs and interests of people over greater distances have increased, but most people remain firmly wedded to a particular state, and to the belief that the interests of co-nationals or fellow-citizens come first. So there is still a major imbalance in the way we think about obligations to our own societies and to other peoples.

It is also crucial to add that those emancipatory ideals can sometimes serve the 'dark side' – as the post-structuralist critique of 'Enlightenment thinking' has shown. Various social movements – Marxist most obviously – harnessed the language of liberty and fraternity to commit terrible acts against other human beings. This is also part of the internal tensions within modern societies. All those points could be described as raising questions about the 'material' context in which, for example, the tensions between citizenship and humanity arise and are played out. That is to say, they are designed to focus on how those tensions arose in conjunction with particular patterns of state-formation, economic development, demands to become better attuned to other people over greater distances and so forth.

How would you respond to the post-modern injunction to be sensitive to diversity, difference and plurality?

The standard view is that Critical Theory (capital 'C' and 'T') is embedded in the Enlightenment project of creating universal arrangements, whereas post-modernism/post-structuralism, which is sensitive to threats to difference, takes issue with Enlightenment Reason. Foucault (1984a: 32–50) famously claimed that there is no need to be either for or against the Enlightenment, which was in any case a complex mixture of ideas rather than one movement or way of thinking.

More fundamentally with respect to your question, post-modernism itself defends a universal claim which is a claim for difference, or for a sensitivity to forms of social organization, modes of discourse and so forth that marginalize and exclude other groups. Indeed, arguments about sensitivity to difference raise a universal claim. In Foucault's essay on Enlightenment (1984a), in his comments on the Vietnamese boat people (1984b), or in Derrida's work on Marx and in his comments on the European Union (Habermas and Derrida 2003), there are unmistakeable universalist claims that resonate with Frankfurt School Critical Theory.

How artificial is the distinction then?

Giddens made the point that post-modernism is a 'radicalization of modernity' (1991: 20, 51, 156), which might be taken to involve a greater questioning of the forms of exclusion that are central to modern ways of life. It is possible to take this further by bringing into the discussion Elias's distinction (1996: 25) between 'the established' and 'the outsiders', as well as his remarks about the changing balance of power between members of those strata in recent years – between men and women, adults and children, the former imperial powers and the former colonies, and so forth.[26]

In this context, the post-modern defence of difference can be seen as an expression of a long-term trend towards redefining the relationship between established and outsider groups. To that extent, post-modernism continues the so-called Enlightenment project or the project of emancipation – although many of its adherents would probably recoil at this description. At that level, then,

Critical Theory and post-modernism are not at odds, despite some efforts to drive a wedge between the two.

This idea that Critical Theory is not at odds with the post-modern concern with difference was, in fact, already present in your postscript to Men and Citizens *(1990: 209), in which you argued that Foucault's work can be 'harnessed to the task of developing a critical theory of international relations' …*

It seemed to me that was striking about Foucault's thought – and largely missing from Frankfurt School writings that I knew about – was the analysis of how the development of the modern subject was dependent on notions of irrationality, madness and criminality – in short, on negative representations of others. As far as I know, Foucault had little to say about International Relations, but as Said (1979) and others have argued, the approach can be applied to distinctions between the 'civilized' and the 'uncivilized' world. Foucault did speak out against distinctions of that kind and at least in one interview, when discussing the Vietnamese boat people, he defended the notion of being a citizen of the world who is opposed to efforts to place sovereignty above the interests of particular people.

There was at the same time an emphasis on the dangers of ethical universalism or cosmopolitanism – a stress on how such standpoints can become the basis for violence against those who are different, and who are seen as being parochial. As a result of reading Foucault and various post-structuralist writings, my work of community and citizenship in the 1990s was, I would like to think, more sensitive to the question of difference. That does not mean giving up the commitment to ethical universalism or cosmopolitanism. My approach to the universalization of citizenship rights argues that these can develop alongside the devolution of power to local communities and alongside the greater public recognition of cultural differences. Those can be seen as different sides of the same coin.

The question, then, is how to reformulate the defence of universalism so that respect for the different is a central ethical ideal. That was one of the central aims of *The Transformation of Political Community*.

Which, in your view, are the future tasks of critical theory?

Going back to Kant and Marx, I believe there are three parts to it. First, the normative dimension, which is concerned with ethical ideas and their philosophical justification. Secondly, the sociological dimension, which analyses how people are simultaneously bound together in specific communities and divided from other peoples, how more and more people have become more and more interconnected over time, and how the tensions between loyalties to particular communities and pressures to develop 'post-national' practices and loyalties are played out. The sociological dimension is where I think there is still an enormous amount to be done; however, the issues are slowly moving to the centre of the discipline. Finally, there is the praxeological dimension, which enquires into the moral and cultural resources that can be harnessed to the project of enabling people to live together amicably, with the minimum of violent and non-violent harm and with an increased capacity to cooperate in dealing with global problems that are in danger of spiralling out of control.

This is what I call the tripartite structure of critical theory. It comes down to us from Kant and Marx and, in my view, has not been surpassed.

A final question: what political role can the critical theorist have in the world today?

For some, the central question is whether academics should be overtly aligned with particular political objectives and ideal states of affairs. The dominant strand of thinking in IR has long been suspicious of value claims and committed to striving for objectivity, even though complete value-neutrality is impossible.

The so-called 'post-positivist' movement, however, argued that all forms of knowledge have political implications: they support or contest, however unintentionally, particular distributions of power and wealth, particular images of how societies should be organized, and how they can best conduct their external affairs. Cox's argument (1981: 128) that 'theory is always *for* someone and *for* some purpose' is the most influential statement of the relationship between theory and practice.

Of course, others claimed that theory is too remote from questions of policy – which led Booth (1997) and Smith (1997) to argue that critical forms of scholarship are addressed in part to the more progressive elements of global civil society. For example, I stand by the Habermasian argument that the commitment to dialogue between equals is central to cosmopolitanism and to the idea of justice between all peoples. For me, that is not just theoretically interesting but has significance for practical matters that arise in relations within and between societies, and indeed in our everyday lives. But I understand the criticism that this ethic seems remote from many practical concerns. Jean Bethke Elshtain (1999) criticized *The Transformation of Political Community* because it said little about violence; Norman Geras (1999) argued that all humans have certain basic needs and interests, and that there is an easier way to cosmopolitanism than through support for discourse ethics. Their criticisms have influenced my recent work on harm in world politics.

It is important to leave to one side International Political Theory and International Ethics, which are explicitly concerned with the case for and against particular value-judgements. As for more empirical inquiries, scholars face a choice: whether or not to embrace any specific normative standpoint. Those who chose not to should perhaps consider ways in which their approach may contribute to the perpetuation of social arrangements which some find unjust – even if the main task is explanation or understanding. Those who do align themselves with ethical standpoints need to engage with competing perspectives and confront what may be unpalatable facts. For critical theorists, the aim is not to side with contemporary political movements necessarily, but rather to take the long-term view by thinking about alternative forms of world political organization and the prospects for realizing them.

Notes

1 In *The Civilizing Process* (2000), Norbert Elias developed an approach to long-term processes of change in Western European societies that focused on the interplay between state-building and war, urbanization and capitalist economic development, and changing attitudes to the body and violence. The approach was not limited to explaining developments within the societies concerned but analysed developments in their external relations as part of a study of the transformation of human society as a whole. For further discussion, see Linklater (2011) and Linklater and Mennell (2010).
2 See Linklater (2009).
3 See Pufendorf (1927) and Vattel (1916).
4 See Midgley (1975).
5 Linklater is here referring to Cox (1981; 1983).
6 In this respect, see Linklater (2010).
7 The passage from *The Eighteenth Brumaire* goes: 'Men make their own history, but they do not make it just as they please; they do not make it under circumstances chosen by themselves, but under circumstances directly encountered, given and transmitted from the past'. See Marx (1950: 225).
8 For an edited version of the *Grundrisse*, see McLellan (1973).
9 See the discussion in Swaan (1995) and Mennell (1994).
10 See Plant (1973).
11 On decentration, see the discussion in Linklater (1998: chapter 3).
12 On detachment, see Elias (2007).
13 See Linklater (2002; 2007a).
14 See, in this respect, Linklater (2007b).
15 See Linklater (2005).
16 See Clark (2007) and Linklater (2007a).
17 See the discussion in Linklater (2007c).
18 See Held (1995), Fraser (2007) and Linklater (2007d).
19 See Beck (1984).
20 See Linklater (2001).
21 See Elias (2009).
22 See Linklater (2007d). For parallels, see Horkheimer (1993: 32).
23 Linklater is here referring to the third part of Taylor (1989).
24 See, in particular 'III. The Scale of Forms' in Collingwood (2005: 56–60).
25 See the discussion in Fletcher (1997) and Elias (1996).
26 See Elias and Scotson (2008) and Elias (1996: 25).

Bibliography

Beck, U. (1984) *Risk Society*, London: Sage.
Bernstein, R. (1976) *The Restructuring of Social and Political Theory*, Philadelphia: University of Pennsylvania Press.
Booth, K. (1997) 'Discussion: Reply to Wallace', *Review of International Studies,* 23(3): 371–77.
Carr, E.H. (2001) *The Twenty Year Crisis: 1919–1939*, New York: Palgrave.
Cicero (1991) *On Duty – De Officiis*, eds. M.T. Griffin, E.M. Atkins, Cambridge: Cambridge University Press.
Clark, I. (2007) *Legitimacy and World Society*, Oxford: Oxford University Press.
Collingwood, R.G. (2005) *An Essay on Philosophical Method*, Oxford: Oxford University Press.
Cox, R.W. (1981) 'Social Forces, States and World Orders: Beyond International Relations Theory', *Millennium* 10(2): 126–55.
____ (1983) 'Gramsci, Hegemony and International Relations', *Millennium* 12(2): 162–75.

Elias, N. (1969) *The Civilizing Process: The History of Manners*, vol. I, Oxford: Blackwell.

____ (1978) *What is Sociology?*, New York: Columbia University Press.

____ (1982) *The Civilizing Process: State Formation and Civilization*, vol. II, Oxford: Blackwell.

____ (1996) *The Germans: Power Struggles and the Development of Habitus in the Nineteenth and Twentieth Centuries*, Cambridge: Polity Press.

____ (1998a) 'An Interview in Amsterdam', in J. Goudsblom and S. Mennell (eds) *The Norbert Elias Reader*, Oxford: Basil Blackwell.

____ (1998b) 'Technization and Civilization', in J. Goudsblom and S. Mennell (eds) *The Norbert Elias Reader*, Oxford: Basil Blackwell.

____ (2000) *The Civilizing Process: Sociogenetic and Psychogenetic Investigations*, Oxford: Blackwell.

____ (2007) *Involvement and Detachment*, Dublin: University College Dublin Press.

____ (2009) 'Address on Adorno: Respect and Critique', in N. Elias, *Essays III: On Sociology and the Humanities*, Dublin: University College Dublin Press.

Elias, N. and Scotson, J. (2008) *The Established and the Outsiders*, Dublin: University College Dublin Press.

Elshtain, J.B. (1999) 'Really Existing Communities', *Review of International Studies* 25(1): 141–46.

Fay, B. (1975) *Social Theory and Political Practice*, London: Allen and Unwin.

Feinberg, J. (1984) *Harm to Others: The Moral Limits of the Criminal Law*, Oxford: Oxford University Press.

Fletcher, J. (1997) *Violence and Civilisation: An Introduction to the Work of Norbert Elias*, Cambridge: Polity Press.

Foucault, M. (1984a) 'What is Enlightenment?', in P. Rabinow (ed.) *The Foucault Reader*, London: Penguin.

Foucault, M. (1984b) 'Face aux governments, les droits de l'Homme', *Libération*, 30 June-1 July. Reprinted as 'Confronting Governments: Human Rights' in *Power: Essential Works of Foucault 1954–1984* (2002), vol. 3, ed. J.D. Faubion, London: Penguin.

Fraser, N. (2007) 'Transnationalizing the Public Sphere: On the Legitimacy and Efficacy of Public Opinion in a Post-Westphalian World', *Theory, Culture and Society* 24(4): 7–30.

Geras, N. (1999) 'The View from Everywhere', *Review of International Studies* 25(1): 157–63.

Giddens, A. (1991) *The Consequences of Modernity*, Stanford: Stanford University Press.

Habermas, J. and Derrida, J. (2003) 'February 15, or What Binds Europe Together: A Plea for a Common Foreign Policy, Beginning in the Core of Europe', *Constellations* 10(3): 291–7.

Hegel, G.H.W. (2008) *Philosophy of Right*, trans. S.W. Dyde, New York: Cosimo.

Held, D. (1995) *Democracy and World Order: From the Modern State to Cosmopolitan Governance*, Cambridge: Polity.

Hoffmann, S. (1965) *The State of War: Essays on the Theory and Practice of International Politics*, New York: Frederick A. Praeger.

Horkheimer, M. (1993) 'Materialism and Morality', in M. Horkheimer, *Between Philosophy and Social Science: Selected Early Writings*, Cambridge: MIT Press.

Kant, I. (1970) 'Perpetual Peace: A Philosophical Essay', in M. G. Forsyth, M. Keens-Soper, and P. Savigear (eds.) *The Theory of International Relations: Selected Texts from Gentili to Treitschke*, London: Allen and Unwin.

Linklater, A. (1982) *Men and Citizens in the Theory of International Relations*, London: Macmillan.

____ (1990) *Beyond Realism and Marxism: Critical Theory and International Relations*, London: Macmillan.

____ (1998) *The Transformation of Political Community: Ethical Foundations of the Post-Westphalian Era*. Cambridge: Polity Press.

____ (2001) 'Citizenship, Humanity and Cosmopolitan Harm Conventions', *International Political Science Review* 22(3): 261–77.

____ (2002) 'Cosmopolitan Political Communities in International Relations', *International Relations* 16(1): 135–50.

____ (2005) 'A European Civilizing Process?' in C.J. Hill, and M. Smith (eds) *The International Relations of the European Union*, Oxford: Oxford University Press.

____ (2007a) 'What is a good international citizen', in A. Linklater, *Critical Theory and World Politics: Citizenship, Sovereignty and Humanity*, Abingdon: Routledge.

____ (2007b) 'Introduction', in A. Linklater, *Critical Theory and World Politics: Citizenship, Sovereignty and Humanity*, Abingdon: Routledge.

____ (2007c) 'Towards a Sociology of Global Morals with an "emancipatory intent"', in *Critical Theory and World Politics: Citizenship, Sovereignty and Humanity*, Abingdon: Routledge.

____ (2007d) 'Public Spheres and Civilizing Processes', *Theory, Culture and Society* 24(4): 31–7.

____ (2009) 'Human Interconnectedness', *International Relations* 23(3): 481–97.

____ (2010) 'Global Civilizing Processes and the Ambiguities of Interconnectedness', *European Journal of International Relations* 16(2): 155–78.

____ (2011) *The Problem of Harm in World Politics: Theoretical Investigations*, Cambridge: Cambridge University Press.

Linklater, A. and Mennell, S. (2010) 'Retrospective: Norbert Elias, The Civilizing Process: Sociogenetic and Psychogenetic Investigations', *History and Theory* 49(3): 384–411.

Marx, K. (1950) 'The Eighteenth Brumaire of Louis Bonaparte', in *Karl Marx and Frederick Engels: Selected Works in Two Volumes*, vol. I, Moscow: Foreign Languages Press.

Marx, K. and Engels, F. (1970) *The German Ideology*, ed. C.J. Arthur, New York: International Publishers.

McLellan, D. (1973) *Marx's Grundrisse*, Herts: Paladin.

Mennell, S. (1994) 'The Formation of We-Images: A Process Theory', in C. Calhoun (ed.) *Social Theory and the Politics of Identity*, Oxford: Blackwell.

Midgley, E.B.F. (1975) *The Natural Law Tradition and the Theory of International Relations*, London: Elek.

O'Neil, O. (1991) 'Transnational Justice', in D. Held (ed.) *Political Theory Today*, Cambridge: Polity Press.

Plant, R. (1973) *Hegel*, London: Allen and Unwin.

Pogge, T. (2008) *World Poverty and Human Rights*, 2nd edn, Cambridge: Polity Press.

Pufendorf, S.V. (1927) *The Two Books on the Duty of Man and Citizen According to Natural Law*, trans. F.G. Moore, New York: Oxford University Press.

Said, E. (1979) *Orientalism*, New York: Vintage.

Smith, S. (1997) 'Power and Truth: A Reply to William Wallace', *Review of International Studies* 23(4): 507–16.

Swaan, A.D. (1995) 'Widening Circles of Identification: Emotional Concerns in Sociogenetic Perspective', *Theory, Culture and Society* 12(2): 25–39.

Taylor, C. (1989) *Sources of the Self: The Making of Modern Identity*, Cambridge: Cambridge University Press.

Vattel, E.D. (1916) *The Law of Nations or Principles of Natural Law Applied to the Conduct and to the Affairs of Nations and of Sovereigns*, intro by A. de Lapradelle, trans. C.G. Fenwick, Washington, D.C.: Carnegie Institute.

Weil, S. (1952) *The Need for Roots: Prelude to a Declaration of Duties Towards Mankind*, London: Routledge and Kegan Paul.

Wight, M. (1979) *Systems of States*, Leicester: University of Leicester Press.

Wolfers, A. (1965) *Discourse and Collaboration: Essays in International Politics*, London: Johns Hopkins University Press.

4

CHALLENGING THE IDEAS THAT MADE US

An interview with Ken Booth

Ken Booth spent most of his career at Aberystwyth University, where he is currently Senior Research Associate at the Department of International Politics and Editor of the journal *International Relations*. Besides having contributed to the consolidation of Critical International Relations Theory, he was one of the pioneers of Critical Security Studies with his articles 'Security and Emancipation' (1991a) and 'Security in Anarchy: Utopian Realism in Theory and Practice' (1991b). His emphasis on the application of critical theory to the study of security issues is explicit in his more recent book *Theory of World Security* (2007). Ken Booth is also Fellow of the British Academy, an Academician of the Academy of Social Sciences, and in 2004 was recipient of the International Studies Association Susan Strange Award.

This interview was conducted between December 2009 and April 2010 at Aberystwyth University, United Kingdom.

Beyond realism: the origins of a critical approach to security

How do you think that your upbringing as a white male British citizen in the twentieth century affected your thinking?

I think I was very lucky. I don't say this in a nationalistic sense – one of the curses of our age – but having been brought up in the UK at this period of history was like drawing one of life's winning lottery tickets. The world is a terribly inhospitable place for so many.

I was fortunate in my upbringing (once the village where I was born was no longer under the flight-path of Hitler's bombers). For all its problems, postwar Britain had a lot to offer to families like mine. This experience, I believe, has helped me appreciate the significance of basic security. As a result, I am irritated by those who want to 'celebrate' insecurity: they just don't understand. As a child needing urgent hospital treatment, I benefitted right at the start of the National Health Service. Two of my uncles had wanted to go to a famous grammar school in the next town, and had the ability to do so, but my grandparents in the 1930s could not afford it for one of them, and then for only a short time for the other. By the time I got the opportunity to go, education was free. And this later included university. I was also lucky in escaping conscription (I suppose!) by 18 months: better still, I wasn't born 18 years or so before a World War, which was the fate for boys of my parent's and grandparent's generations. I therefore appreciate my luck in the roll of the cosmic dice – for one's life is so shaped by that simple fact. I hope this makes me somewhat sensitive to the lack of fortune of so many other people – individuals and groups who through no fault of theirs live diminished lives as a result of abject poverty, political tyranny, incompetent governments, or any of the oppressions that give individuals little or no scope to explore living beyond mere survival.

There are two other circumstances that are significant, and I mention them to show that I take seriously the Critical Theory claim that all observers of the social and political world are historically-situated. First, there is my experience as a 'war baby'. For a boy brought up in the 1940s, playing soldiers was unavoidable, and as a pupil in a very traditional British grammar school in the 1950s, I enjoyed official afternoons off to go to the local cinema to watch the latest great war movie. This, I am sure, meant that I was primed for realism when I became a student of International Politics. But the second set of circumstances pulled in a different direction. I was born and brought up in a fiercely Labour Party-dominated area of the West Yorkshire coalfields. Both my grandfathers were coal miners, we lived in a poor pit village where the 'well-off' were as alien as foreigners, and where strikers had been shot within living memory. This bit of personal history meant I was primed to recognize the solidarities of the Left – class and common humanity.

How and why did you become a student of International Politics?

Accident played a big part in this. To the extent I had a career plan it was to become a civil engineer – the idea of building bridges appealed to me. But more than that I wanted to be a sports journalist. Why neither of these happened is a complicated story – involving ill-health, failed and deferred university applications, teachers' advice, and chance. Somewhat to my surprise – because it had originally been my least preferred choice – I arrived at the University College of Wales, Aberystwyth, in 1961 to study physical geography. I had discovered that there was the opportunity in the first year to study something called 'International Politics' – a subject that had in a sense been invented in Aberystwyth, but which I had not heard of until I read the University's undergraduate prospectus. This was a definite attraction, as History had been a great interest in school, and I assumed that 'Inter Pol' was simply up-to-date History. Within weeks of beginning the course, I was hooked, though I was overwhelmed by all we needed to understand, and intimidated by some authoritative lecturers. I was particularly fascinated by interwar history, diplomacy,

Comparative Politics and Strategic Studies. Who could not have been at that time? The victory of 1918, merely a prelude to another World War within a generation, was only yesterday for the parents of my cohort of students. And who could not have been fascinated by the superpower confrontation at the time of the Cuban missile crisis, which occurred shortly before we began a course on nuclear strategy? Eventually, I had the chance to do research in International Politics, and this led me to appreciate the challenges and promise of an academic life. When I started teaching, I was lucky to get a job in Strategic Studies, which at the end of the 1960s was the most vibrant sub-field in the discipline.

In your book Theory of World Security *(2007: 40–87) you discussed in detail your theoretical influences, including your interest in critical theorizing as developed by Marx, Gramsci, and the Frankfurt School. However, you never explained how you first got involved with critical theory. Was it an accident or the result of a conscious theoretical pursuit?*

It is a messy story, not the result of a 'conscious theoretical pursuit'. It involves many twists and turns, involving specific choices, hopes, ignorance, and plenty of accidents. That said, and with some hindsight, it is possible to make a story that is somewhat coherent. It falls into two stages: first, working out my dissatisfactions with the political realism that I learned as a student; and second, searching for something to take its place (which led eventually to the concept of emancipation).

You mentioned that your early experience had 'primed' you for realism: how then did those dissatisfactions creep in?

Within a few years of starting lecturing, I became somewhat uncomfortable – I put it no stronger than that at the time – with some of the analyses and prescriptions of realism. In time this solidified into a stronger view that realism's analyses were too narrow and static, while its prescriptions replicated a potentially catastrophic Cold War confrontation. A significant break came when I came across the idea of ethnocentrism, and I attempted – starting in the early 1970s – to insert the concept into the Strategic Studies literature. I began to emphasize culture as an explanation for strategic behaviour, and not merely some universal strategic logic. (Putting it like that – in 2010 – makes it seem so obvious, but I can assure you that at the time it did not seem so, to me at least.)

I came to see the institution of war (my driving intellectual interest), and even the world of states, as a cultural phenomenon – and not 'natural' or a historical necessity. An important driver in this context was my interest in Soviet history, and in what came to be called 'strategic culture'. These interests led me to think that the game of nations could be played according to different logics than the one being put forward by (overwhelmingly) US professors of International Relations (IR). However, the book that emerged, *Strategy and Ethnocentrism* (1979), proved to be much more cautious in questioning the norms of Strategic Studies than the position I was then taking up as a citizen.

Shortly after the publication of this book, I became involved with the anti-nuclear campaigning of the 'second' Cold War. As this confrontation threatened to boil over, thinking about the danger of nuclear war became all-consuming for many of us. I got involved with the academic wing of anti-nuclear advocacy, which became known as the 'Alternative Defence' or 'Alternative Security' approach. Meanwhile, various contacts with people in Eastern Europe and beyond brought home the sheer barbarity of threatening nuclear war.

Could you tell us a bit more about these 'Alternative' approaches, and how they influenced you?

Those who gravitated in this 'Alternative' direction did not think the Cold War was a simple confrontation between a peaceful 'Free World' and an aggressive Communist East. We thought that much of what the Soviet Union did (which seemed to Western governments to be threatening and potentially expansionist) could be interpreted as defensive and reactive in intent, if not appearance. In other words, the dynamics of the 'security dilemma' were at work. For the Alternative school, the way out of the dilemma was to move towards non-provocative defence.[1] This approach was much derided both by academic defence experts and NATO governments. They were wrong. Signalling defensive intent by strategic reform became an important dimension of Gorbachev's 'new thinking', and played a critical role in his contribution to ending the Cold War.

Alternative defence involved a rich interplay of ideas about weapons and doctrines. Denuclearization was seen as central to dampening chronic fears, while movement towards an associated non-provocative posture in conventional forces sought to create 'defensive deterrence'. The basic idea was to raise the entry-price of any aggression while ruling out as far as possible those strategies and weapons that would appear to the other side as offensive. By changing the balance between threat and reassurance, it was hoped to loosen what Robert Jervis called the 'spiral' of security dilemma dynamics.[2] A changed set of ideas about strategy would create a changed military posture, which would then reshape the whole security landscape. In the course of time it was hoped that predictable peace based on politics would emerge, consigning to the rubbish heap a potentially catastrophic order based on nuclear fear. As these ideas developed, politics came to have a bigger role in thinking about the Cold War confrontation, with the spread of democracy and human rights being seen as central to security in Europe. Some people now chose to use the term Alternative *Security* to describe this broader approach, rather than the narrower conception of Alternative *Defence*. Eventually, some hitherto sceptical Western governments came to change their labelling, no longer seeing defence and security as synonymous.

You mentioned earlier that the story of your intellectual development was messy. So far it has sounded very coherent! Were there other things going on?

Real life was going on, and some of the accidents fed importantly into my academic work, and helped to channel my steady disenchantment with realism. I wrote about this at length in a piece sub-titled 'Reflections of a Fallen Realist' (1997) in the mid-1990s, and identified contacts with three people at the end of the 1970s/early 1980s whose own interests encouraged my reappraisal of various academic positions. One (a peace activist) forced me to engage more with relevant anti-war groups outside the seminar room; another (an Amnesty International supporter) made me think more seriously about human rights (and rethink 'the state'); and the third (my wife) discovered feminism and encouraged me, via gender, to rethink 'human nature'. Each of these influences, in different ways, impacted on how I thought about the various levels in Waltz's 1959 book, *Man, the State and War* – which I regard as one of the few truly indispensable books in our discipline.

And what about IR theory?

I spent the turn of the 1970s/1980s in Canada, and it is interesting – looking back – to reflect that most of the stimuli for my thinking about international politics during this time came more from events (Cold War challenges) and sources external to 'the discipline', than from the discipline itself. The 'Great Debate' of the time – sparked by Waltz's 1979 book, *Theory of International Politics* – passed me by. I confess to being very late in reading the book and catching up with the controversy it caused.

In the 1980s neorealism did not distract me; rather, two other approaches fed into my Alternative Defence agenda. First came the World Order approach associated with Richard Falk (Booth 2007: 59–64). Later – and thanks to Nick Wheeler – I became interested in international society thinking (the work of Kissinger 1957, 1973 and Bull 1977) about 'legitimate international orders'. This fitted very well with what I thought Gorbachev was attempting to achieve with his notion of a 'Common European Home' (Booth 1990a).

What appealed to you about the World Order approach?

What particularly appealed, in comparison with the standard realist posture at the time, was that it was *explicitly* normative, had a concept of social change, was future-oriented, and assumed multi-causality (seeing war as part of a 'system' for example). Falk, together with Samuel Kim, produced an excellent textbook which in 1980 I bought at a massive discount (another accident) and then used for many years on a course entitled 'War, Politics, and Strategy'. In this book, *The War System: an Interdisciplinary Approach*, there was an essay by Falk (1980), dating from the 1970s, titled 'Anarchism and World Order'. It is a very short piece but it was eye-opening. I was drawn to the way in which Falk's idealism was never remote from discussions of power and authority. In this particular piece he made a persuasive case for global reform looking towards a bifurcation of power, away from centralizing all decision making and loyalty at the level of the 'nation-state' and instead splitting it: 'upwards' in order to promote sensible global functionalism in the interests of common humanity, and 'downwards' in order to decentralize power in the interests of smaller communities. Such views were not common at that point.

And when did you become interested in critical theory?

By the second half of the 1980s, I was dissatisfied with the explanations and prescriptions of mainstream realism – a self-fulfilling 'theory' which helped perpetuate the eyeball-to-eyeball Superpower confrontation. At the same time, I was witnessing (and celebrating) Gorbachev's 'new thinking' and the way it was transforming international reality in front of all our eyes. I was ready for a theory that would help me put the bits together. Onto my desk dropped the copy of *Millennium* containing Mark Hoffmann's seminal article 'Critical Theory and the Inter-Paradigm Debate' (1987). It pointed towards the avenues of thought I needed. As a result of this inspiration, I started bringing critical theory ideas into my teaching at undergraduate level immediately.

Shortly afterwards, I started working on what later became the article 'Security and Emancipation' (1991a). Whilst playing around with the notion of emancipation, I was also trying to rethink Carr's realism. For my professorial Inaugural Lecture, Nick Wheeler had encouraged me to try and take on Carr's challenge to bring together utopia and realism – something Carr thought impossible. The result was the article entitled 'Security in Anarchy: Utopian Realism in Theory and Practice' (1991b).

These early explorations with critical theory, emancipation and utopianism struck a chord with a number of excellent students, and in particular they helped persuade Richard Wyn Jones to do a PhD trying to put together critical theory, security, and Strategic Studies. I became his supervisor, and this experience was of crucial significance, and meant that my thinking moved more consistently in the direction of the Frankfurt School. As a result of the need to keep in touch with Richard's thesis, I read Gramsci and Robert Cox's seminal article (1981) on problem-solving and critical theory for the first time.

And how much did critical theory influence the subsequent trajectory of your work?

As I mentioned, critical theory had no direct influence on my thinking until 1987, by which time I was in my twentieth year as a teacher. After that point, it had an increasing role, and helped me put all the disparate parts together. In other words, it played no explicit role in my early efforts to hold up a mirror to the problems of realism, but it was crucial in the search for what was to replace it. And what was to replace it – the second stage I mentioned at the beginning of this interview – was the ideal of emancipation. The picture of these two stages involves a complete reversal of the usual picture of critical theory, which normally emphasizes its strength in critique and its weakness in political prescription. For me, critical theory was irrelevant in my original disenchantment with realism (though it later helped tidy up what I thought was wrong), but it was essential in my rethinking of how we might act.

I tried to make clear in *Theory of World Security* (2007) that I am not a purist in theoretical terms. I have tried to combine various approaches in my 'critical theory of security' – even if the combination does not please purists. I adopted Arendt's predatory 'pearl-fishing' approach to ideas, and attempted to organize them in a framework based upon Philip Allott's broad conception of theory.[3] So, my 'theory' of world security (the scare quotes are for those – social science ultras – who would not regard what I offer to be *theory*) is influenced by critical theory, but it is also dependent on other approaches and understandings of international life, including historical sociology, Kantian social idealism, feminism and so on.

You have described the Frankfurt School as 'an inspiration to critique rather than a particularly coherent system of thought' (Booth 2007: 44). How exactly were you inspired by the Frankfurt School?

The Frankfurt School represents for me a necessary but not sufficient anchorage for thinking about International Politics. It could not be 'sufficient' because it represents a way of thinking rather than being a comprehensive system of thought (a *theory*) of International Politics as such. For students of International Politics, Frankfurt leaves many blanks: there is no 'Frankfurt School International Relations theory'.

What was inspiring was the congenial combination of theoretical commitment and political orientation. To be specific, the key ideas of Frankfurtian-style thinking that appealed so much at the time were the recognition of the historical nature of knowledge in the social world (rejecting hubris about 'objectivity'); the importance of reflexivity (including being critical of critical theory); the relative merits of holistic as against reductionist thinking; the inseparability of politics and ethics; the practicality of understanding theory as constitutive; the pragmatic idealism of immanent critique; and the anchoring of theorizing in a notion of emancipation.

What about Marx? Given that the project of the Frankfurt School was a reconsideration of the Marxist legacy, why do you think that we still need to engage with Marx (Booth 2007: 49)?

No Marx: no Frankfurt School – and so much else.

If you do not engage to some degree with Marx, you are shutting off trying to understand the history of the past century and a half. Marx helps us think about structural interpretations of society, about the material basis of life and thought, about big historical change, about class, about imperialism, about globalization, about progress, about the role of philosophers – and on and on. He was a better analyst than practitioner or predictor, but was without doubt one of the world's great thinkers. His ideas – right or wrong – remain at the centre of the agenda of the social sciences. Marx had relatively little to say about International Politics, of course, or the place of ethics. When I had started to become familiar with Kant – through teaching a course on IR theory – the convergence of ethics and the international became clearer; Marx did not provide a helpful recipe book here.

This dissatisfaction with the Marxist framework led some people to turn to Gramsci. How exactly did his notions of common sense and hegemony influence you?

As I said, I had not read any Gramsci until I became Richard's PhD supervisor in 1989. What I particularly liked in Gramsci was the cultural dimension he brought to Marx. I saw links between his notion of common sense and where my thinking had been going about ethnocentrism: human society developed (through the workings of power) a particular common sense about what should be done. Gramsci's idea of hegemony helped me understand better the constitutive role that ideas can have in replicating structures that serve the powerful. Cox's distinction between 'critical' and 'problem-solving' theory was also helpful (I sometimes call this 'outsider' versus 'insider' theorizing, to avoid the frequent criticism that 'critical' thinkers see themselves as removed from solving problems).

You have mentioned Kant a couple of times already. What part did he play in the development of your ideas?

In a nutshell, Kant became important for me by helping me think about the limitations of the traditional distinction in IR between the search for survival 'outside' and the search for the good life 'inside', while giving due attention to the dynamics of the international level. I was drawn to an approach that said that the search for the good life should be universal (a categorical imperative) and that it could not be achieved within one's own state boundaries without the universal project being completed.[4]

It is worth adding that I doubt whether I would have read as much Kant, and about Kant, had I not been advised by Howard Williams, who became a colleague when the Politics Department in which he worked was merged with the International Politics Department in which I worked – another accident.

'Security as emancipation'

You have talked about 'playing around' with the notion of emancipation in the beginning of the 1990s.[5] Can you tell us how you came across the concept?

As you can tell from what I have already said, there was a lot of stuff swirling around in my head in the late 1980s. I was trying to find a way to make sense of it all – to level with the powerful (and enduring) dynamics of international politics while at the same time engaging with all the things going on in world politics in that historic moment – human rights abuses, the realization of globalization, the end of the Cold War, and so on. I knew what I was going away from in a theoretical sense – mainstream realism – but it was not yet clear where I was heading. The answer proved to be emancipation. Emancipation became an organizing principle, a way of trying to put it all together.

I have to confess, however, that I cannot remember exactly when or how I thought: 'Let me put "security" and "emancipation" in the same sentence.' But here are some pointers. First, on a beautifully sunny Spring morning in 1977 – it must have been around 7.00am or earlier – I found myself alone at the Lincoln Memorial in Washington DC. I looked up at old Abe, read the words on the walls, thought about slavery and emancipation, and then had a walk by the river where the cherry blossom had just come out. Cheesy, perhaps, but this was a moving experience, and I suspect it might have planted the word 'emancipation' irrevocably in my head. Second, anybody who knows the literature I have been mentioning – Kant, Marx, Frankfurt School, etc. – will be aware that emancipation is a value running through all of them. Finally, I am sure that the first time *in print* I put 'emancipation' and 'security' together was in a booklet produced by Saferworld, a then new NGO based in Bristol. I wrote a short introductory piece entitled 'A New Security Concept for Europe' (1990b), in which I discussed the 'traditional' concept of security and the pressures for a new one. I proposed, and outlined, a security strategy of emancipation.

Among the key sources I mentioned in that piece was Andrew Linklater's *Beyond Realism and Marxism: Critical Theory and International Relations* (1990), which I must have read at the very moment it came out. He categorized the 'primary concerns' of the three traditions in IR (represented by Hobbes, Grotius and Kant) in terms of power, order and emancipation (Linklater 1990: 8). As it happens, there was a decidedly Kantian slant in the Saferworld article, for I argued that a good place for starting to think about the framework for emancipation was the Atlantic Charter and its Four Freedoms (of speech, of worship, from fear, from want). Later that year I elaborated these preliminary thoughts in the Plenary Address at the December 1990 British International Studies Association conference. I had been asked to do this by Barry Buzan, who was then the Association's Chair. Barry had been a key figure in encouraging the profession to think theoretically about security; here he proved to be an important (if unlikely) catalyst for the development of the idea of security and emancipation!

In the article that came out of that Address, the influences of Peace Research are stronger than Frankfurt. Aren't there important overlaps between the notion of security as emancipation and Galtung's ideas for example?

I agree. As I suggested earlier, some aspects of Peace Research (broadly understood) have been very important, and as you have just suggested, Galtung's work was very interesting for me, in particular because of its stress on structures. I incorporated some of Galtung's ideas into my teaching in the 1980s, together with other giants of Peace Research, notably Kenneth Boulding and Anatol Rapoport. In 1976 I had stood on a mountainside in mid-Wales and received a personal mini-lecture from Rapoport about shifting paradigms in human thought and behaviour, just before visiting Harlech Castle. Ten years later I saw him and Boulding do a marvellous double act in London. I was already familiar with Boulding's notion of 'stable peace' – peace based on the politics of cooperation rather than on mutual fear. All these Peace Research influences, together with Galtung's 'structural violence' and 'positive peace', undoubtedly helped to prepare the ground for security and emancipation.[6] It is a great pity their work is ignored (for the most part not even known) by so many students of IR these days.

As much as I admired such work, I was uncomfortable with some aspects of Peace Research (or do I mean some peace researchers?). There was too often a certain naivety with respect to power, a knee-jerk anti-military attitude, and a congenital anti-Americanism. I thought 'security' to be a more useful concept than peace: not only are the meanings of 'peace' so varied, but crucially in the international realm it is possible to have peace without security – one only needs to surrender. To surrender to power is to invite insecurity, and to renege on the prospect of emancipation.

You have worked with the concept of emancipation for over twenty years, and the concept is still prominent in your book Theory of World Security. *Did emancipation play the same role in your thought in this period? How has it developed?*

From the time the idea started firming up in 1990, the challenge has been to work out its implications, in theory and practice, and also to make it more palatable. An important part of both these tasks has involved saying to critics: 'this is not what I mean'. In particular, I am constantly having to defend myself against those who seem to think that 'emancipation' is a dreamy notion removed from power, against mindless critics of the Enlightenment, and against those who assume that my starting point is that 'we' (in the West) are emancipated and that it is my aim is to get the rest of the world to catch up with us.

'Power' is central to my concerns, and that is why I call my approach *emancipatory realism*,[7] and why I tend to concentrate in my research on the international level of world politics (where so much power is concentrated). I use the term 'realism' to indicate a continual concern with power in a generic rather than IR schoolism sense; power in all its forms needs attention. We need to uncover it, to see how it works, who benefits and so on. At the international level military power is traditionally central, but other dimensions are also causal.

I do not see the values of the Enlightenment as 'essentially' European, nor do I believe that 'we' are emancipated and 'they' need catch up. As it happens, at this moment in Western countries there is much moving away from what I consider to be the road to emancipation. This is apparent, for example, in slippages in ideas of social justice (growing inequality and more mean-spirited welfare schemes), in economic unfairness (nationalizing the losses of banks while privatizing profits), and in reneging on duties beyond borders (from the sorry state of the UN to the tough face shown to asylum-seekers). There is emancipatory work to be done everywhere.

Why do you think that emancipation is such a controversial concept? Why are so many people suspicious towards it?

Is it *such* a controversial concept? And are *so* many people suspicious of it? In my view it is a widely understood concept, and what some people are 'suspicious' of is not emancipation as such, but particular claims made on its behalf – what I have called 'false' as opposed to 'true' emancipation (Booth 2007: 113). There are critics, of course, and they belong to three main groups – all of whom I am happy to welcome as opponents.

First: conservatives. They do not like the idea of emancipation because in their minds it is exclusively identified with 'failed gods' like Marx, 'disastrous political experiments' like the USSR, and discredited 'left-wing' projects in the West smacking of 'socialism'.

Second: 'doctrinal realists' in IR. This group operates on the assumption that the task of IR specialists is to contemplate the theory and practice of survival – not engage in the Kantian inside/outside holism I mentioned earlier. For these realists, talk about emancipation smacks of idealism and utopianism – two labels that are not seen as good career moves for those wanting to be taken seriously in the corridors of power.

Third: post-structuralist/postcolonial thinkers. For this group the idea of emancipation – quite erroneously – is seen to be synonymous with Eurocentrism, and particularly with the ideas and values (and especially the 'metanarratives') of the European Enlightenment of the eighteenth century. To advocate emancipation is therefore considered as a form of cultural imperialism.

But is there not a danger that emancipation will fall in the trap of being a metanarrative?

Every idea ever invented has the potential to be a 'trap': think of love, of family, of community. That said, metanarratives need not be a 'trap' in the sense that critics claim. There are more or less emancipatory metanarratives, and at this point in the twenty-first century I believe that emancipatory grand theories must be part of the solution to the problems of a world that is not working for countless millions of people. Leaving aside post-structuralist reactions against Western 'canons', 'dead white men', 'binaries' and 'metanarratives' – all of which criticisms need to be turned back into post-structuralist thinking, incidentally – my main pragmatic point is that on a shrinking planet, threatened by global problems, grand theorizing in the interest of the human collective and the natural world on which we all depend is a historic necessity.

But instead of drawing attention to the voice of the critics of emancipation, I would turn your earlier question round, and ask: why are there are so many people in so many places who are *keen* on exploring the idea of emancipation in contemporary conditions? When I began thinking about emancipation in the context of security, it was a novel idea; now it is not. It has resonance, and especially beyond Western Europe and North America. I have received positive comments about this idea in many different places, especially parts of the developing world. Emancipation makes sense to most audiences, even if they do not quite know how to fit it into how they have been taught to think about IR. It makes sense as an organizing device to many people who know – look around! – that human society needs a different organizing principle about how to live globally.

Earlier you implied that the idea of emancipation came with much political and historical baggage: how do you explain it to those not familiar with the term?

At the beginning, I played with different definitions – not a way to engage audiences. I believe I made a leap forward in explaining the term when I came across the title of a book written by the Chartist William Lovett (1876), which contains the words 'Bread, Knowledge and Freedom'. For many I talk to, using these three words as the basis for discussing emancipation has made it seem more understandable, more concrete, and both more local as well as universal. Right across the world, folk tales and histories recognize iconic struggles against oppression: struggles for material necessities ('bread'), struggles for truth in the face of dogmatic authority ('knowledge'), and struggles to escape from political and economic tyranny ('freedom').

You claim that security as emancipation is about opening up space in people's lives, about removing constraints on free choice so that life can naturally unfold. Can you explain what you mean by this state in which people will be able to decide freely about their lives?

I do not accept the idea of life 'naturally' unfolding. What humans do (and should do) is highly 'unnatural'. If life were simply natural, it would involve remaining trapped in our animal 'natures'. The development of our minds has enabled us to create new social and political worlds. This is what I mean by equating emancipation with the creation of the possibilities to explore what it might mean to be human. Such exploration is a highly 'unnatural' exploration of the freedom which our biological make-up allows.

'Removing constraints' is not synonymous with 'no constraints'. I assume there will always be constraints; I cannot imagine life otherwise, and would not want it so. I do not want a society where I am free to carry a gun, or where companies are free to exploit workers. Emancipation is about constructing a world of humane constraints that promise reasoned freedom (consistent with everybody else's). This is the tradition that conceives freedom in terms of the ability of individuals to live their lives within a structure of rules (including laws). But what I am concerned with in the first instance in removing those brutal, demeaning, and determining constraints on peoples' lives such as poverty, racism, patriarchy, war and so on. The starting point for thinking about security/emancipation must be insecurity. Insecurity is synonymous with living a determined life. Such a life is one of daily necessity not choice.

Does the idea of 'security as emancipation' assume that true emancipation claims are ultimately compatible and harmonious?

Emancipation is a journey, and I cannot imagine what might *ultimately* be possible. But as humans are not born wiser than their parents, I expect there will always be work to do. In the event of a stage in human history being reached in which universal emancipation could be announced – with bread, knowledge and freedom everywhere, with the setting free of the dove of world peace, and with the raising of the flag of humanity above the parliament of humankind – then critical theorists would need to turn their theoretical commitment and political orientation inwards, to discover what oppressions might exist in this new stage in the journey. Critique is a way of life.

As the journey proceeds, I believe there is much potential for the compatibility of values across cultures, and harmony between groups. For that to happen, humanity needs to free itself from what Allott (1998: 323) termed the 'deformed ideas of what it is' – ideas such as 'human nature', 'the human condition' and so on. We are still very much engaged in the Enlightenment's struggle against regressive ideas.

On this journey, if you are faced with a particular situation in which two emancipation claims are contradictory, what do you do?

This is a question of practical politics, and politics is an art not a science. In specific situations one has to learn as much as possible about what is going on, examine the words and behaviour of those involved, and make a decision as to which party seems the more likely to advance the emancipatory package of 'bread, knowledge and freedom'. The political arena is messy, and wrong choices can be expected. In the heat of the kitchen, the recipe books of political theory are guaranteed not to work out as well as they promise in the seminar room. This is as true for theories about emancipation as it is for other principles.

In Theory of World Security *(2007: 110–16), you talk about resistance as an intrinsic part of emancipation. Could you elaborate on the relationship between the two concepts?*

Resistance is part of the operational logic of emancipation, in the sense that emancipation is concerned with forms of oppression. To be emancipatory, acts and strategies of resistance must be driven by an explicit ethic – an 'idea of the ideal'.

Resistance to 'the ideas that made us'[8] is for all of us. It does not have to be grandiose in scale or heroic in form. We can only do what we can do, given our circumstances. This might be anything from writing letters to the press, voting for the most progressive party on offer, talking to friends and family about asylum-seekers, and being kinder to Nature. The choice of one's PhD topic is not a neutral act. Together we can do something to help bring about cultural changes about how to live globally – changes that, when enough people think the same, can help improve the daily realities for real people in real places.

Might resistance also be violent? If so, what guidelines do you offer?

Theory of World Security (2007: 253–6 and 428–41) has a section on ends and means, and the theme is about using means that are compatible with the ends that you are trying to achieve. If you want to live in a lawful world, then you should try not behave illegally. If you want to live in a non-violent world, this means that violence must be avoided if possible.

So your position is not a pacifist one?

No. I would like it to be, but I cannot go that far in this complex world. I do not believe that good will necessarily triumph, so some things – literally – have to be fought for. But I think the cases are getting fewer and fewer where the use of force by one state against another is justified.

I was tempted in the 1990s by the idea of humanitarian intervention. However, I quickly came to think that such interventions were likely to cause more problems than they would solve. Unlike most of the people I mixed with, I was against NATO (the United States essentially) acting as judge, jury, and executioner in the Kosovo conflict. It remains to be seen whether I was wrong: the Kosovo imbroglio, in which NATO legitimized one set of ethnic cleansing over another, has not yet run its course. Sometimes one has to accept that one cannot solve every problem – and certainly not by sending in troops. Sometimes, one has to let people work it out between themselves, however bloody. (There are limits to this general posture of non-intervention, however, and trying to prevent or stop genocide is one of them – but even in this case it would have to be a pragmatic not a principled decision. One has to accept that one's military response would be radically different if the perpetrator were the government of a Great Power as opposed to that of a weak and failing state.)

If such a position looks like passivity and complacency, I offer two practical reactions to distant humanitarian crises that do not involve sending in the troops. One strategy is simply to strengthen one's commitment as a citizen to improving one's own polity – trying to make it the force of a good example. This shapes my view of the EU. Some time ago I read an article saying that 'Europe needs to get its act together or it can't become a world power like China and the US'. Well, I don't want the EU to become a traditional Great Power. I want the EU to be the force of a good example to the world. I want – unfashionably – 'Europe' to be a normative power, a civilian power. With that in mind, the disillusion with the EU within Europe today is one of the most distressing features of the current scene. If Europeans, through regressive nationalism, economic protectionism, and complacency let things drift to collapse it would be a political failure of truly historic significance.

Second, there are alternatives to sending in the troops both for governments (who can try and strengthen relevant multilateral organizations and their non-military instruments) and for individuals. In face of a crisis, individuals might choose to give money to development or relief agencies, or become members of human rights organizations – or just decide to become better citizens more generally, in the interest of creating a more civilized society. There is plenty of humanitarian work to be done – work equivalent to being a citizen of the world – instead of assuming we know best and think we can solve complex problems by projecting military power.

I am aware that these will look like 'weak' responses to egregious human rights abuses, but I am also aware that 'strong' responses are rarely the answer. Look at the disaster of the Iraq war.

Engaging with the critics, engaging with realism

In Theory of World Security *(2007: 41) you wrote that 'not all critical theories are equally useful when thinking about security'. This implies that you have tried reading some of the post-structuralist work, for example, but perhaps do not intend to any more. What exactly is your position?*

I do not think that sentence can be read to mean that I do not intend ever to read any post-structuralist writing that purports to be about security or international politics. However, I probably have read enough post-structuralist work for the moment; I know I have a long list of reading which is of far higher priority. I do not need to be persuaded that it is about time I re-read *War and Peace* after 40 years, but I do need persuading that I should read the next interpretation of Foucault, Derrida, Agamben and so on in an IR journal. I will need persuading that such work will tell me something of real usefulness in relation to the things I primarily want to know about – which, in brief, is how *the dynamics of international politics* shape the distribution of security, prosperity, and ideas across the world.

I think the great thinkers in the realist tradition have more to say about these things than the poststructural canon. For a long time I have been especially interested in some of the great realist thinkers of the mid-twentieth century (notably Carr, Morgenthau, and Herz). Their prescriptions for a world of what they considered to be obsolete institutions and revolutionary technology transcended what was and is taken to be the orthodox realist tool box. While he does not attract the 'utopian realist' label I have sometimes given to such earlier realist thinkers, Waltz's work is crucial to critical theorists because his focus on structure and on the enduring 'texture' of the international constantly reminds those of us who want to envisage alternative worlds of how great the obstacles are.[9]

You say that there has been an 'unproductive stand-off' (Booth 2007: 54) between, on the one hand, the legacy of Marx and the Frankfurt School and, on the other, those drawn to poststructuralism and continental philosophy. This implies that there has been some sort of debate – but where is it?

I do not think there has been a debate: there has been a dialogue of the deaf. I think it is probably too late for such a debate to happen: those drawn to poststructuralism seem keen to remove themselves from the concerns of the IR agenda, and some are drifting into other fields, while those drawn to the legacy of Marx and the Frankfurt School seem more concerned to engage directly with the disciplinary power of realism than with self-marginalizing poststructuralism.

Is your diagnosis therefore that these two strands of critical thinking are incompatible and increasingly so?

It depends what you mean by 'incompatible'. There are areas of shared interest: for example in the history of words, in the way ideas about society evolve, and in the variety of ways power works. But there are areas where there appears to be an unbridgeable gulf. These include substantive issues, such as universalism/ particularism and emancipation/relativism, and matters of style, notably what often appears to be the deliberate obscurantism of post-structuralist writing.

Don't get me wrong. I believe in principle in pluralism, because it helps to keep us all honest. When I was Head of Department I appointed various people with views different to my own. But that does not mean we have to agree or find lowest common denominators to try to construct bridges.

You have emphasized the importance of the International Politics agenda, and equated that – more or less – with that of traditional realism. Let us talk about realism then. To begin with, does it still make sense to talk about a realist orthodoxy in the field, or are we just building a 'straw man'?

There is indeed a risk of creating a straw man of realism, and I may have played a part in this by my own criticisms over the past twenty years. In my defence, I have always tried to keep a distinction between the great thinkers of realism and their mainstream followers. Waltz, to give one example, is much more complicated – and his work is much richer – than the straw man created by many critics, notably in Richard Ashley's (1984) well-known attack on what he considered the 'poverty of neorealism'. Some mainstream realists have contributed by their bar-room tough-mindedness to the stereotyping of the whole tradition.

All students of International Politics must engage conscientiously with realism: it is a constitutive theory, one of the ideas that made us. For critical theorists in particular, realism is a crucial issue because it helps replicate the international status quo, which is one of the problems critical theorists in this field want to address.

The realist agenda – states, distribution of power, relative gains and all those things that have become fixtures in the way world politics has evolved through history – is very important. This is the strength of Waltz's theory: he does explain 'a few big and important things', to use one of his well-known expressions. Anarchy is causal; states do want to survive; and capabilities matter. By such reminders, realist theory can provide a reality check against naive progressivism. But there is another side: 'anarchy', 'states' and 'international politics' are only ideas and as such – to paraphrase Wendt – are what humans make of them. With difficulty, we can rethink a different reality.

Do you envisage a more fruitful discussion with realists than with post-structuralists?

I think so, because at least we share some sort of commitment to what might be called the International Politics project. I think critical theorists in IR (a small group) do try to level with the international, so I have not given up hope of a more fruitful discussion with realists. It is worth recalling in this respect Waltz's rather ignored endorsement of Cox's well-known distinction between 'problem-solving' and 'critical theory'. Waltz expressed no fundamental problem with this categorization, calling it a 'nice distinction'. He made clear, however, that it was not his own preferred approach to International Politics. Critical theorists, he said, 'would transcend the world as it is; meanwhile we have to live in it' (Waltz 2008: 50). There is plenty of scope for positive discussion there, focusing on the meaning of 'the world as it is' and whether trying 'to live in it' under contemporary conditions with traditional ideas is a recipe for disaster – and so we must 'transcend' it.

Talking of transcending the world 'as it is', it is interesting that many (indeed most) mainstream realists are unaware of the radical vision of some of their key figures. I referred earlier to the way in which some of the great thinkers of realism – in the face of the historic threats of mid-twentieth century – sought to develop strategies that were quite contrary to the statist and militarized tool-box of mainstream realism. I refer here to Carr's view that the nation-state was dead, and his embracing of the idea of expanding community, economic planning, and functional coordination. And to Morgenthau, who shared the view that the nation-state was obsolete, and developed ideas about world community as the basis for world government, nuclear disarmament as the basis for security, and functional cooperation as the basis for community building. And also to John H. Herz, who saw the territorial state as obsolete under the nuclear threat, and who looked for universalist solutions to the new global threats of the time – going beyond International Relations to 'survival research'.[10]

Would you say then that the role of a critical theory in this regard would be not to replace realism but rather to unlock the potential of realism?

No: the 'potential' of realism (in disciplinary IR terms) has been unlocked already, and as both theory and practice it has had an enormous influence.

Realism in that sense needs locking up, not the opposite. But above all it needs understanding.

I need to clarify the juxtaposition of critical theory and realism in your question. They are not opposites; they are not even comparable when it comes to International Politics. Realism is a distinct theory of IR. For example, it tells us what the key referents are (states), explains their motives (to enhance security and prosperity), and recommends a menu of strategies (such as balance of power). Critical theory is not a worked-out theory of IR in the same way. Instead, as represented by the Frankfurt School, it offers a critical approach to understanding society, and hopefully changing it. Over the past 80 years critical theory has been characterized by a heterogeneity of theories concerned with social critique and transformation. It has not delivered a 'theory of International Politics'. It has produced a set of ideas, which some contemporary thinkers, notably Andrew Linklater, have attempted to develop into a coherent normative, sociological and praxeological framework for International Politics.

IR, as I mentioned earlier, has been a minor theme of critical theory, but I join with those who think that some Frankfurt School ideas help us to engage in a sophisticated way with the biggest questions of the discipline of Politics (What is real? What can we know? How might we act?) in the biggest arena of politics. Because of this, I do hope that critical theory will 'replace' realism as the primary thought-way for accessing the international. But because realism is so implicated in the international, it will remain part of the problematique for the foreseeable future.

Theory and practice: beyond the 'Great Reckoning'

How do you go about applying your theoretical framework when faced with a particular issue? What are the necessary steps and the things to avoid?

The main point to stress here is that critical theory is not primarily a recipe book to deal with immediate issues. The first task of a critical theorist is to try and stand outside the contemporary situation as far as possible and hold up a mirror – to try to show people what the world is like and what it will continue to be like if behaviour remains dominated by the traditional ideas that made us. This was very much the view of the early members of the Frankfurt School. A second task – and the Frankfurt School was less successful in this respect – is to contemplate ways in which emancipation might be furthered. Clearly, the critical theorist's timescale is not that of the typical decision maker, policy analyst, journalist, or academic-with-one-foot-inside-the-corridors-of-power.

I stand by that as the general orientation, but it would be an odd critical theorist not to be interested in the present, and how best to get from an oppressive *here* to a better *there*. To the extent one gets involved in a particular issue – and that will depend on multiple contextual considerations (your power, your location, your history and so on) – it is a matter of directing the three big questions I mentioned earlier at the micro-level. *What is real?* Which referent group is to be secured?

What is the oppression? In the famous words of Marshal Foch from the Great War: *De quoi s'agit-il?* (What is it all about?) *What can we know?* It is a primary responsibility of critical theorists to try to discover reliable information about the situation, remembering always that governments are not truth machines and that information often comes in nationalized packages. *How might we act?* When contemplating a particular critical issue the first step is not particularly a 'critical' one – it is about not doing extra harm. One carries out this task alongside conducting immanent critique, the idea that all situations have within them the possibilities for something better. Immanent critique involves identifying the unfulfilled potential in all situations in order to nudge emancipation forward.

Could you give us examples of particular political issues that interest you, where you have to try and engage all these dilemmas and provide coherent policy-relevant thinking that deals with the present, immediate, and long-term future?

I will give you two. First, nuclear abolition. Working in a timetabled way towards ridding the world of nuclear weapons is a way both of recognizing common humanity as a meaningful political referent, while working practically to reduce the immense danger of nuclear proliferation and extending community across historic boundaries. Nearly all politicians talk loosely about abolition, but consign it to some point beyond their lifetimes. When they do this, I do not believe they are really serious. I include Obama in this. You need to have a plausible timetable, one which to some degree you control. You can only have some control if you are willing, on occasion, to be a unilateralist.

The second example is European integration. As mentioned earlier, I desperately want the EU to succeed as a positive civilian power in world affairs, and am depressed about the apathy and casual (and not so casual) nationalism around these days. The European project may, if we are not careful, become victim of its own success. There is much in need of improvement in Europe: there is a democratic deficit, the EU is run like a capitalist club, and the Euro-elite is often remote from those they are supposed to represent. But 'Europe' is a process, and different ideas can make a different reality. Europe is the best model around pointing the world of states to the potential of supranational governance above the 'nation-state' level – and the desirability of subsidiarity below that level.

In the past ten years or so you have been warning about a 'world-historical crisis', and more recently you have been calling it 'The Great Reckoning' (Booth 2007: 395–426). How serious is the danger you outline?

I think it is very serious. The Great Reckoning is my phrase to describe history's way of catching up with human society's traditional ways of thinking and behaving across the planet. As we approach the middle of this century human society will come increasingly and dangerously face-to-face with global 'business as usual', and the potential outcome is a concatenation of dangerous crises – 'climate chaos', food shortages, energy conflict, water deprivation, economic distress, poverty, social unrest, security dilemmas, nuclear proliferation, population pressures, 'clashes of ignorance' between ethnic and other identity groups. As these threaten to converge, the age of nationalism and statism of the past few centuries will be tested to the limit, and perhaps beyond. There is a parallel with the Thirty Years' War, and the way it tested the age of religion to the limit. And beyond.

But this image of a world in turmoil in the 2030s/2040s is an extrapolation, not a prediction. It is my attempt to hold up the mirror to the consequences of human society's traditional ways of behaving globally (ways shaped by the ideas that made us). The political challenge for human society over the next couple of decades is to develop collective ways of decision making (above and below the 'nation-state') to head off the worst consequences of 'business as usual'.

What do you think is the most important challenge facing a critical approach to security and politics?

The big question of our time is this: how at this point in world history, can human society organize locally and globally, with more justice and harmony, to overcome the consequences of the fact that on an ever-smaller planet there are ever-more of us who need to eat every few hours, who have an instinct to survive and to reproduce, who need jobs, and who have active and massively evolved minds which are collectively stuck in regressive ideas about how the world works? I think the perspectives critical theory gives in terms of understanding reality, accessing knowledge and developing emancipatory praxis offer the best anchorage for tackling this big question.

In this context, our duty as critical theorists is to change the collective consciousness of society, to challenge the ideas that made us. These ideas, on a global scale, have constructed a world that is not working for so many of our fellow human beings, and much of the natural world on which we depend. Patriarchy, nationalism, gender, race, statism and nationalism, proselytizing religions, consumer democracy – these are the ideas that made us into the ethically diminished species we have become, whereby some people are willing to behave with extreme cruelty in the name of the race or the nation, or manliness or capital.

In the face of these ideas, for whom and for what purpose is your theory?

For whom? Common humanity. And for what purpose? Emancipation.

How is humanity 'common'?

The common sense has it that humanity is naturally 'nation sized'. The famous argument of the Stoic philosopher Diogenes is that to become cosmopolitan is to become a sort of exile. In contrast, I want to argue that to become cosmopolitan should be regarded as going home. The ideas that made us through history (with their associated institutions and power plays) have kept humans apart. Patriarchy, statism, nationalism, racism and so on exile us from each other. We should not only behave as if we have 'equality' in a formal sense, but should start from the understanding (as Darwin taught us) that we are the same.

But how confident are you that academics like yourself can have political impact?

The closer one gets to political power in our field the less one becomes an academic in the true sense, because one has to move onto the agenda of those in power. Various experiences in the 1970s led me to think there is limited value in spending much time with politicians and policy makers, because they only want to use academics as a bureaucratic resource. They are only interested in one's work if one has something to say about their agenda. Occasionally, it is possible to have a useful interchange between governments and academics, but our skills are not best employed to serve the interests of particular governments and their agencies or 'nations'.

However, one should not define 'political impact' narrowly, in terms of the agenda of the political elite. If impact is defined more broadly, then I think academics can have an important influence – though that impact is likely to be broad, diffuse, probably long term, and certainly beyond the horizons of the so-called 'metrics' beloved by the managers of higher education (especially in the United Kingdom). We should always be very modest about what we can achieve as academics, especially in the short run (except for teaching as well as we can). This is always perhaps particularly the case for the critical theorist working in the inhospitable field of IR. As 'outsider' theorists, our role is to hold up a mirror to present realities, and to provide alternative ways of thinking and behaving. As such, we must appreciate the privilege of being among the relatively small number of people on Earth with the time and opportunity to think about world politics in this way. Our aim must be to make some contribution, however little, to changing human consciousness about living globally – for common humanity and towards emancipation.

Notes

1 On the state of the debate, right at the end of the Cold War, see Booth and Baylis (1989).
2 On the 'spiral model', see Jervis (1976: 58–113). See also Booth and Wheeler (2008: 45–50).
3 See Allott (2001: 14–38; 2002).
4 See, in this respect, Booth and Williams (1996).
5 The most influential statement of 'security as emancipation' is provided in Booth (1991a). Here, he defined emancipation as 'the freeing of people (as individuals and groups) from those physical and human constraints which stop them carrying out what they would freely choose to do' (1991a: 319). This concept became central to his security theory. For a more recent formulation, see Booth (2007: 110–12).
6 See Galtung (1971: 81–117), Boulding (1978), and Rapoport (1974).
7 On emancipatory realism, see Booth (2007: 249–76).
8 This formulation, which denotes the structural networks shaping how human society lives globally, can also be found in Booth (2000; 2007: 21–7).

9 Booth (2010) has recently edited a collection of essays on Waltz's theorizing.
10 On Carr, see Booth (1991b). On Morgenthau, see Booth (2005). On Herz, see Booth (2008).

Bibliography

Allott, P. (1998) 'The future of the human past', in K. Booth (ed.) *Statecraft and Security: The Cold War and Beyond*, Cambridge: Cambridge University Press.

_____ (2001) *Eunomia: New Order for a New World*, Oxford: Oxford University Press.

_____ (2002) *The Health of Nations*, Cambridge: Cambridge University Press.

Ashley, R. (1984) 'The Poverty of Neorealism', *International Organization* 38(2): 225–86.

Booth, K. (1979) *Strategy and Ethnocentrism*, London: Croom Helm.

_____ (1990a) 'Steps Towards Stable Peace in Europe: A Theory and Practice of Coexistence', *International Affairs* 66(1), 17–45.

_____ (1990b) 'A New Security Concept for Europe', in P. Eavis (ed.) *European Security: The New Agenda*, Bristol: Saferworld.

_____ (1991a) 'Security and Emancipation', *Review of International Studies* 17(4): 313–26.

_____ (1991b) 'Security in Anarchy: Utopian Realism in Theory and Practice', *International Affairs* 67(3): 527–45.

_____ (1997) 'Security and Self: Reflections of a Fallen Realist', in K. Krause and M. Williams (eds.) *Critical Security Studies: Concepts and Cases*, London: UCL Press.

_____ (2000) 'Where are we now? Between helplessness and hope', paper presented at the Millennium Lecture Series, University of Wales, Aberystwyth.

_____ (2005), 'Morgenthau's Realisms and Transatlantic Truths', in C. Hacke, G. Kindermann and K. Schellhorn (eds.) *The Heritage, Challenge, and Future of Realism*, Gottingen: Bonn University Press.

_____ (2007) *Theory of World Security*, Cambridge: Cambridge University Press.

_____ (2008), 'Navigating the "Absolute Novum": John H. Herz's Political Realism and Political Idealism', *International Relations* 22(4): 510–26.

_____ (ed.) (2010) *Realism and World Politics*, London: Routledge.

Booth, K. and Baylis, J. (1989) *Britain, NATO and Nuclear Weapons: Alternative Defence versus Alliance Reform*, Houndmills: Macmillan.

Booth, K. and Wheeler, N. (2008) *The Security Dilemma: Fear, Cooperation and Trust in World Politics*, New York: Palgrave Macmillan.

Booth, K. and Williams, H. (1996) 'Kant: Theorist Beyond Limits', in I. Clark and I. Neumann (eds.) *Classical Theories of International Relations*, London: MacMillan Press.

Boulding, K. (1978) *Stable Peace*, Austin: University of Texas Press.

Bull, H. (1977) *The Anarchical Society: A Study of World Order in World Politics*, London: Macmillan.

Cox, R.W. (1981) 'Social Forces, States and World Orders: Beyond International Relations Theory', *Millennium* 10(2): 126–55.

Falk, R. (1980) 'Anarchism and World Order' in R. Falk and S. Kim (eds) *The War System: An Interdisciplinary Approach*, Boulder: Westview Press.

Galtung, J. (1971) 'A Structural Theory of Imperialism', *Journal of Peace Research* 8: 81–117.

Hoffman, M. (1987) 'Critical Theory and the Inter-Paradigm Debate', *Millennium* 16(2): 231–50.

Jervis, R. (1976) *Perception and Misperception in International Politics*, Princeton: Princeton University Press.

Kissinger, H. (1957) *Nuclear Weapons and Foreign Policy*, New York: Harper.

____ (1973) *A World Restored: the Politics of Conservatism in a Revolutionary Era*, London: Victor Gollanz.

Linklater, A. (1990) *Beyond Realism and Marxism: Critical Theory and International Relations*, London: Macmillan.

Lovett, W. (1876) *The Life and Struggles of William Lovett, in his Pursuit of Bread Knowledge, and Freedom; With Some Short Account of the Different Associations He Belonged to, and of the Opinions He Entertained*, London: Trübner & Co.

Rapoport, A. (1974) *Conflict in a Man-Made Environment*, Harmondsworth: Penguin Books.

Waltz, K. (1959) *Man, the State and War: A Theoretical Analysis*, New York: Columbia University Press,

____ (1979) *Theory of International Politics*, London: McGraw-Hill.

____ (2008) 'Reflections on Theory of International Politics: A Response to My Critics, 1986', in K. Waltz, *Realism and International Politics*, New York: Routledge.

5

THE TEST OF PRACTICE

An interview with Richard Wyn Jones

Richard Wyn Jones has been an unavoidable reference in Critical Security Studies since the publication of *Security, Strategy, and Critical Theory*, in which he introduced Gramsci and the Frankfurt School to the study of security issues. In a chapter titled 'On Emancipation: Necessity, Capacity and Concrete Utopias' (2005), he further contributed to the theoretical development of the critical security field by arguing that a commitment to 'emancipation' can be seen as a common feature of different strands of critical thought. Following from his experience as an activist in the Welsh language movement, in recent years Wyn Jones has published extensively on Welsh Politics and has been a regular media commentator on developments in Wales. After 18 years as a member of staff at the Department of International Politics at Aberystwyth University, he is now the Director of the Wales Governance Centre and Professor of Welsh Politics at Cardiff University.

This interview was conducted online between March and May 2010.

Activism and theory

Your academic studies were conducted in Aberystwyth. That's also where you started your career as an academic. Why did you choose to attend that university?

To answer this requires a biographical digression. I first got interested in political thought and analysis through my involvement from the age of around 15 in the Welsh language movement, and in particular Cymdeithas yr Iaith Gymraeg (the Welsh Language Society).[1] By coincidence, the activists that I joined were a group of people (a generation older than myself) who had all been influenced by the post-'68 upsurge of radical thought. Unusually, I suppose, they represented a real cross-section of leftist currents who managed to eschew the typical left tendency towards factionalism and sectarianism, both because of the innate good sense of the people concerned as well as the very real sense of crisis surrounding the fate of our communities and culture. The early 1980s were not a happy time.

What was particularly important – indeed formative – for me was that our meetings would involve detailed analysis of the socio-economic context of whatever particular problems we were focusing on. I suppose this was a first introduction to the theory-practice dialectic. It was also, as you can imagine, something of a crash course in what I now understand to be the assumptions of historical materialism.

This led me very rapidly to start reading for myself; particularly the various debates around the then very influential *Marxism Today*[2] and, even more importantly, the work of the Welsh historian Gwyn Alf Williams. Williams (1960; 1975) was one of the very first people to write about Gramsci in English. Although once in the Communist Party, by the early 1980s he had joined Plaid Cymru and was almost certainly the leading ideologue of the national movement in Wales. His influence played an important role in ensuring that that movement – or at least the part with which I was engaged – became heavily Gramscian in orientation.

Anyway, the end result of all of this was a determination to study politics and international politics. And for a young Welsh activist, there was only really one place to study, namely Aberystwyth – the epicentre of language activism since the early 1960s.

What was the particular appeal of Gramsci in that milieu?

In general terms I suppose it was the fact that he took culture seriously, offering a way out of the stale and often philistine economism that characterized so much leftist thinking, very much including the Labourist tradition so dominant in Wales. For those of us concerned with the survival of a marginalized and threatened culture, this was in itself an important source of external validation. More specifically, the whole constellation of concepts developed by Gramsci (hegemony, common sense, historic bloc, civil society, organic and traditional intellectuals, and so on) seemed helpful in understanding the world around us. Their usefulness was demonstrated and underlined in Gwyn Alf Williams's magnum opus *When Was Wales?* (1985). But they also underpinned the ideas of Plaid Cymru's 'National Left' and the journal *Radical Wales* (Wyn Jones 2007: 181–260).

An added dimension was Gramsci's Sardinian roots – something scarcely noticed in conventional accounts but brought out and stressed by Williams (1984). This certainly added to the allure. As, of course, did the whole story of Gramsci's Calvary in Mussolini's prisons. I certainly recall being very moved reading Fiori's biography (1973) (translated, by the way, by Tom Nairn – another huge influence on the national left in Wales through his *The Break-up of Britain* (1977)).

You stress Gramscianism rather than Marx or Marxism more generally. Is this because the latter were not a direct influence on you, either then or subsequently?

Even if they were from and of the Left, I must stress that the activist group I was fortunate enough to encounter were not the cadres of any political party, nor did they have any particular academic or specialist knowledge of political thought of what we now seem to call 'theory'. They were rather animated by a practical interest in trying to understand and do something about the socio-economic and politico-cultural crises around us. So in terms of 'theory' it was all pretty eclectic and, to be sure, a little haphazard. And so was my education in all of this. I would pick up snippets from them; some of the basic conceptual vocabulary of Marxist thinking. But then, because I found it stimulating, I would go off and read whatever material I could lay my hands on. And because Gramsci was important for both the Euro-communist controversy then raging across the western European Left as well as the particular constellation in Wales, his ideas came to the fore very quickly. Thereafter Marxism as a broader corpus of ideas came into focus through Gramsci and the controversies of the mid-1980s. In retrospect it was all very unsystematic. But this was also a function of the ultimately practical nature of the engagement.

Moreover, while there are obvious downsides and limitations to this as a way of developing academic knowledge – and I remain acutely aware of the yawning gaps in my own – it is not without its positive sides either. It was a way of avoiding even a hint of sectarian navel gazing and in-fighting. In contrast to the members of the British/Unionist Trotskyite sects I met in university, we did not spend our time arguing about what really happened at Kronstadt!

In addition, the practical focus on the British state meant that one was quickly drawn to some really sophisticated and challenging material that would not have come into focus if the main aim had been to develop a systematic understanding of Marxian social theory for its own sake. This included not only the debates about the nature of Thatcherism and the Labour Party conducted in and around *Marxism Today*, but also even more fundamental debates about the nature of state development in the United Kingdom. In the latter case, through reading Tom Nairn's *The Break-up of Britain* (1977), I received my first introduction to the ideas that Nairn had developed in conjunction with Perry Anderson – the so-called Nairn–Anderson thesis – on the implications of English developmental priority for the contemporary UK. (This is something I have returned to again and again in my more recent work.) I also tackled things like Michael Hechter's *Internal Colonialism* (1999); a book unlikely to appear in any introductory course!

Still, I don't think this is sufficient answer to your question as to where Marx fitted in. Hindsight is, of course, dangerously seductive territory, but looking back I do wonder if engagement with the Marxist classics was made less attractive by the great nation chauvinism of Marx and Engels. Apart from their romantic attachment to the Irish struggle, they were not particular sympathetic to small nations and in particular their languages and cultures.

Even more fundamentally, having now read Allan Megill's superb book (2002) on Marx which demonstrates – with exemplary scholarly care and sympathy – the deep limitations of Marx as a political thinker, I also wonder if the practical focus would have made Marx and classical Marxism less attractive even if the conjunction had not favoured an engagement with Gramsci. What we required was above else some kind of political strategy. Whatever his own limitations as a political thinker, we were more likely to get that from Gramsci than Marx.

Theorizing in academia

Did being part of the Department of International Politics at Aberystwyth have any special influence on your intellectual development?

You must understand that the 'Interpol' of 1984, which is when I arrived, was very, very different from the department it had evolved into by the mid 1990s. Far from being the intellectual powerhouse it was to become, it was then hidebound and – at the senior managerial level, at least – pretty much moribund. Indeed I found the place very alienating. Culturally the student body was dominated by English public school boys, with all that that entails. Intellectually it all seemed very complacent. As I recount in *Critical Theory and World Politics* (2001: 1), the tone was set in the opening remarks in the very first lecture that was given by the then Head of Department. He told us that there were two types of theory, normative and positive. The former was the preserve of theologians and philosophers, 'moralizers': by contrast we were to concern ourselves with the latter, and view the world as it really is. And so on … Pretty grim stuff.

In retrospect, however, I now recognize that what were actually taught had precious little to do with realism let alone positivism. Instead it was a deeply unreflective worldview buttressed by regular appeals to 'common sense'. Indeed, from a Gramscian perspective, the choice of language was almost too good to be true because this was truly a case of 'folklore' rather than philosophy: the ruling ideology of the age reproduced in a 'fragmentary, incoherent and inconsequential' form.[3]

Lest I appear wholly negative, let me also stress that there were three things that made the Aberystwyth of this period a stimulating environment, for me at least. First I was still politically engaged, which of course meant that I was engaging with authors and ideas that took me in very different directions from those approved of by the self-appointed guardians of common sense!

The second was the fortuitous discovery of Robert Cox's work whilst spending a few hours reading in the University library. For me, at least, his Gramsci article from 1983 was even more important than the seminal 'Social Forces' article (1981). Not only was it the first thing of his that I read, leading me to his other work, but it was also the first thing that I read that allowed me to conceive the possibility of combining my non-academic with my academic interest in politics. Two decades later I still vividly recall my excitement reading it for the first time.

The third saving grace was the presence of Ken Booth in the Department.

In the acknowledgements to Security, Strategy and Critical Theory *(1999: xii) you credit Ken Booth's influence on your work. Can you tell us how that relationship developed?*

I first came into regular contact with Ken Booth around 1986/1987 when I took an undergraduate level course with him on Soviet foreign policy. Even before then, I was aware that Ken was not only coming from a different intellectual direction from the remainder of the staff, but was a somewhat marginalized figure among them. Among my student contemporaries in the department he had a reputation as a supporter of the peace movement – which was certainly not a sentiment that would endear him to most of them!

But the real formative impact came when I decided to stay on in Aberystwyth to study for a Masters degree. Somewhat bizarrely, in retrospect, I was allowed to design my own Masters programme around a core course on 'Strategic Studies' (in the shadow of the second Cold War I had long decided that this was far too important to be left to proponents of MAD and assorted Nuclear Use Theorists). This led to me taking Ken's justly celebrated undergraduate course on 'War, Politics and Strategy', which I had actually missed out when I was an undergraduate.

So in parallel with reading for the ultra-orthodox Strategic Studies course, Ken's course was encouraging me to read all kinds of innovative stuff: all that Non-Offensive Defence material; some of the things coming out of Peace Studies; Carol Cohn (1987a; 1987b); John Mueller (1988) on the essential irrelevance of nuclear weapons; the literature on humanity's alleged disposition towards violence, which Ken has always been so interested in; and so on. It was also around that time that I first read that little gem of a book of his, *Strategy and Ethnocentrism* (1979).

How would you characterize Ken Booth's influence on your ideas?

Initially, at least, it was Ken's attitude that had most influence on me, rather than any of his specific ideas – recall that his pivotal 1991 articles were still in the future.[4] He was unusually wide-ranging in his own reading and encouraged that in his students. So when I tried – however incoherently – to start combining my interest in security and Coxian 'critical theory' he was very encouraging in pushing me to continue in that direction, even if neither of us had any idea at all where (if anywhere) it might lead. In fact, he was instrumental in ensuring that I was awarded a studentship to pursue this wild hunch at PhD level.

The other thing that I took from Ken was a concern with trying to write well, by which I simply mean writing clearly and, where possible, pithily. Partly this was an (inadequate) attempt at emulation. In my view Ken is *the* great literary stylist of contemporary International Relations and it his high time he be recognized as such. Nobody writes better. And if you are writing for him, as well as reading his work, there is a natural desire to avoid embarrassment on that score! But it is also, to his great credit, something he has always sought to actively encourage amongst his students.

Later on, 'Security and Emancipation' became a central point of reference for me. In particular, I was fascinated by – and perhaps, in retrospect, beguiled by – his aphorism that security and emancipation are 'two sides of the same coin' (Booth

1991a: 319). That said, and returning to your question, I would still maintain that Ken's most formative influence on me was attitudinal rather than ideational.

So where did the Frankfurt School influence come from? What in particular did you find interesting or useful there?

Given where I ended up in *Security, Strategy and Critical Theory*, you may be surprised to hear that I had no knowledge at all about the Frankfurt School when I embarked on the PhD project that was to lead to that book. As I have said, when I started out (in 1989) the idea was to combine my interest in Coxian critical theory with my interest in security. Luckily for me, this was still a period in which postgraduate study in most UK universities was non-commercialized and pretty small scale (so, for example, I think I may have been the only PhD student in my year in International Politics at Aberystwyth) which meant that you could embark on doctoral study without a clear idea of the endpoint – or even if there was a viable endpoint at all. That allowed someone like me a great deal of freedom.

My problem was that once I started digging into Cox's distinction (1981) between critical theory and problem-solving theory there was not much there beyond an attitude and intuition. A helpful attitude and important intuition to be sure, but there was not enough there to build the kind of argument and critique that I felt was necessary. What did seem more promising, though, was work of the Frankfurt School that I had (once again) stumbled across in the library. Obviously this was just before the huge explosion of (English language) interest in their work that one can date to around the mid-1990s. Fortunately for me, however, one of the first things I found was David Held's excellent *Introduction to Critical Theory* (1980). This led very rapidly to Horkheimer's 'Traditional and Critical Theory' (1972: 188–243) essay, after which I was hooked.

What was it that appealed to you in those readings?

What pulled me in initially, I suppose, were the ways in which Horkheimer's distinction between critical theory and traditional theory chimed with Cox's critical theory/problem-solving theory distinction, while also being much more developed and, to me at least, more persuasive. But the further I dug the more intrigued I became by the way Horkheimer and his colleagues had come to criticize traditional Marxian understanding of emancipation as the domination of nature, as well as their (changing) conception of the role of emancipatory thought. Even if they could not always provide answers that were persuasive, they were clearly asking the right questions. I also thoroughly approved of their complete disregard for disciplinary boundaries. To get hung up on disciplines and disciplinary boundaries is, to my mind, a confusion of means and ends. The Frankfurt School are a great example in that regard.

The other thing that chimed was the way that the Frankfurt School opened up a window onto the issue of technology – at least after I had read Andrew Feenberg's

Critical Theory of Technology (1991). I always thought that it was vital that what we now know as Critical Security Studies (CSS) should be able to do more than add things to the traditional agenda – broadening to non-military issues; extending to other referent objects beyond the state, and in particular to individuals; deepening to understand the underlying assumptions about politics and the nature of conflict.[5] Rather, it should also be able to offer new insights and perspectives on the subject-matter central to that traditional agenda. It was also clear to me, at least after reading Raymond Williams (1980) on nuclear deterrence, that it was a critique of the technological determinism of so much post-war Strategic Studies that offered the route towards doing that. But it was through reading the Frankfurt School that I found a way of at least beginning to take that insight further.

Following on from this, your own understanding of Critical Theory has clearly been influenced by Horkheimer and Adorno quite as much, if not more, than by Habermas – and this despite the latter's contemporary prominence. This seems to be true of CSS more broadly. Why has this been the case?

While there is very much to admire about Habermas the exemplary public intellectual, I must confess that I have never found his work particularly conducive. In broad-brush terms, I am not convinced by the sociology – or social ontology – of *Theory of Communicative Action* (1985; 1987). Politically, I think he concedes too much as a result of it; to the market, to be sure. His apparent inability to view the category of 'nation' through anything other than the lens of German history is another problem. While the latter might be understandable given his own biography and the particular intellectual context he inhabits, it nevertheless seriously limits his relevance as an analyst and, indeed, an advocate.

As a result I have tended to follow those who have viewed Habermas as providing answers to a series of questions posed by the founding fathers of the Frankfurt School (and, indeed, the western Marxist tradition more generally). These are questions that were not only answered in different ways at different times by the founding generation – compare and contrast Horkheimer's 'Traditional and Critical Theory' (1972) and Horkheimer and Adorno's *Dialectic of Enlightenment* (1972) – but have also been answered in different ways at different times by Habermas himself. Moreover, my own hunch is if we survey the contemporary scene, we might find that someone like Axel Honneth (1993; 1996) or, on a different tack, Moishe Postone (1993), might well be providing more persuasive answers than the great man himself.

I would add as a codicil here that I suspect that part of the issue here is stylistic. Despite his universalist aspirations I get the feeling that Habermas' apparent determination to try to head off all counter-arguments and tie up each and every loose end not only makes for pretty turgid reading, but also serves to limit his work to a particular time and place. By contrast, the shorter forms favoured by the Horkheimer circle – aphoristic, suggestive, open – seem to me to allow for possibilities beyond those that their authors could possibly have envisaged. I find that a really attractive and exciting characteristic.

Your recent work has focused on your native Wales and political developments there, rather than in CSS or critical International Relations more generally. Could you explain why? And what, if any, relationship is there between this work and your previous contributions?

You are right, of course, and the explanation is very simple. At almost exactly the same time as I completed *Security, Strategy and Critical Theory*, affirmative votes in two referenda, first in Scotland and then in Wales, led to the establishment of devolved parliaments and governments for both countries. You will have understood enough about my background by now to realize why this was such an important development for me personally. I had already been publishing occasional things about Wales even before devolution, but once it was clear that a major institutional transformation was imminent I was very strongly of the view that it was vital that this be accompanied by serious academic engagement with the whole process. It was also clear that due to my very privileged position in the (by then flourishing) Aberystwyth International Politics department, I was probably uniquely well placed to do something about this. So I did. While I continued to teach CSS on the Masters course as well as supervise doctoral students working in the area until 2005/2006, most of my intellectual energy after about 2000 was taken up with developing the study of Welsh Politics, both intellectually and institutionally.

The relationship between my work on CSS and my subsequent work is more complicated. At one level there is no connection at all, in the sense that I seem to inhabit two wholly discrete professional worlds. I don't think that anyone who has read my CSS material has actually read my Wales/devolution output; or vice versa!

At a deeper, level, I do think that there is a lot of common ground. For one thing, some of the influences and concepts are the same. Gramsci and his conceptual vocabulary has remained a constant point of reference. And while the Frankfurt School has been less visible, my work on Wales has drawn heavily on New Left thinkers like Perry Anderson and Tom Nairn.

But of course, one's thinking does not remain static. Working closely with colleagues like Roger Scully, I have become much more interested in political institutions and much more knowledgeable about, and appreciative of, Political Science. Moreover, through initial contact with political sociologist Anthony Heath, I came to appreciate how useful quantitative analysis can be; and also, again through Heath, I became aware that some of the most sophisticated quantitative scholars do not make a fetish of that approach but are rather open to all kinds of other approaches and ideas. That was an important realization, especially given all that positivism versus post-positivism 'willy waving' around the turn of century.

I could try to dress all of this up by referring to the fact that the Frankfurt School were open in practice, if not always in theory, to quantitative work, and claiming that I have been consistent all along. But that would be disingenuous! More honest is to say that there has been a lot of continuity between both personae, for want of a better word. But there has also been some change. And that is as it should be.

To what extent did your Welshness and your engagement in Welsh politics impact upon your work on CSS and critical International Relations?

Oh, hugely! In particular, I suspect, with regards to my attitude towards the state and statism.

To belong to a stateless nation, especially if – like me – you have no emotional attachment to the official identity of the state you inhabit, leads to a particular kind of detachment from state structures: disenchantment may be a better way of putting it. This certainly makes the 'extending' move in CSS away from an exclusive focus on the state towards other referent objects seem both obvious and obviously progressive. Indeed, if you'll forgive the cod psychology, I have often wondered if it might be one of the sources of difference between the kind of approach to security associated with Aberystwyth and that associated with Copenhagen. To be sure, both Wæver and Buzan have attempted to shrug off the skin of state-centrism that undoubtedly clothed early versions of the securitization thesis. But on my own (I hope sympathetic) reading, I think that more than a hint of it remains. Could this perhaps be because those things that appear self-evident or obvious in Copenhagen or London are less so on the west Wales coast? Speaking for myself – and I would guess for Ken too – the most vocal, persistent and in some ways successful securitizing moves to which I have born witness in my own life have focused on nuclear weapons (through the peace movement) and the Welsh language (through the language movement). Despite the modifications, securitization theory seems to me to struggle with the complexities of political life in the Marches and at the margins.

The arguments about practice in *Security, Strategy and Critical Theory* are also, to be sure, heavily influenced by a particular experience of Welshness. Indeed, in retrospect, the nigh on exclusive focus on social movements as a practical locus for emancipation-oriented intellectual activity evokes a Wales of the 1980s and early 1990s. Indeed, I think this is one of the real limitations of the book. While I would completely endorse and stand by the 'extending' argument, I am very conscious of the limitation of the discussions of practice found in that book. To that extent it is far too Welsh!

What, then, are those limitations when viewed from your present perspective?

Even on its own terms what I had to say about practice failed to take sufficient account of the huge challenges for emancipatory politics that arise from the collapse of any kind of credible, let alone desirable, party-vehicle – Gramsci's 'Modern Prince' – that might co-ordinate and even arbitrate between different progressive agendas. Nor does it face up to the huge problems that arise from the collapse of any kind of credible alternative political-economic strategy. Of course, these are the problems of the Left in general, and so I might be permitted to temper my self-criticism to some extent in this regard! I am very far from being alone in having buried my head in those particular sands.

I am, however, far more culpable for my lack of interest in political institutions: how they work; how they interact, etc. While I was at pains to distinguish between statism as an ideology and the state as a nexus of institutions, and while I would want to maintain that distinction, nonetheless in practice I was not interested enough in states. Instead I concentrated exclusively on what might be termed anti-state politics. This in turn allowed me to avoid asking some very pertinent theoretical questions about the relationship between critical and problem-solving theory, for example, such as those explored by Alexander Wendt in his wonderful essay 'What is International Relations for?' (2001). It also meant that the discussion of possible strategies for emancipatory practice was very one-dimensional. I regret that.

This seems to be an example of your subsequent work on Welsh politics leading you to rethink your previous work on CSS. Is that right? If so, are there other examples?

I am sure that is right. Engaging with the politics of state institutions, of political parties, and so on, has certainly helped to highlight the aporias and mistakes of previous work. But there have been other influences as well. While ploughing the Welsh politics furrow I have also been reading some of the academic literature on security, talking to friends and colleagues who have been involved in the contemporary debate, following real world events and so on. All of these things interact in unnoticed ways and have almost certainly had a cumulative effect, so it is quite difficult to identify what has been doing the work and how.

Let's unpack that a little. Can you give some indication of what you have been reading on security that you have been impressed by?

In terms of capitalized Critical Security Studies, and in addition to Ken's prodigious endeavours, I have been particularly struck by the way Columba Peoples (2009) has taken some of the ideas on technology and pushed them much further than I was capable of doing. In addition, I think Eli Stamnes' interventions (2004) around peacekeeping were not only theoretically innovative – in particular her use of Honneth – but were instrumental in advancing a much-needed critical orientation in that field.

In terms of other alternative approaches to Security Studies, I have been encouraged by the synthesizing ambitions of the c.a.s.e. collective (2006). While I suspect that my own synthesis would look different to theirs, I wholeheartedly applaud their attempt to search for common ground rather than accentuate differences.

But beyond these, and somewhat to my own surprise, I would have to point to two very different interventions around realism. First, reading Mike Williams' magnificent book on *The Realist Tradition* (2005) forced me to confront a much more nuanced and persuasive version of that tradition than I had encountered before. In terms of political interventions I hugely admire what John Mearsheimer and Stephen Walt have been doing with regards the United States' policy stance towards Israel and the Middle East (2008). They have shown exemplary intellectual courage. Indeed one could argue that Mearsheimer has become the most significant critical intellectual working in contemporary International Relations; something that should give pause to self-proclaimed radicals. It is certainly all a very long way from what passed for realism when I first encountered it.

That is the positive side. But it would be remiss of me not to point out that I have been less impressed by the intellectual reaction to the so-called 'war on terror'. Perhaps I have just been looking in the wrong places, but while superb critical-historical and contemporary-empirical accounts of the various conflicts abound, I must confess that I have been less persuaded by the conceptual-theoretical response so far. For example, while one can understand and sympathize with the intentions underpinning the Critical Terrorism Studies move, the concern must be that one ends up reinforcing the terms of conventional discourse, and in particular the fetishization (in a classic Marxist sense) inherent in the focus on 'terror'.

Your remarks suggest that we have made a straw man out of realism …

I think that one would have to admit that there was some over-simplification. There were always more strands to realism – more nuances – than allowed for in the various attempts to reduce realism to an essence for the sake of critique. All reification is a forgetting, as Horkheimer and Adorno (1972: 230) put it. That said, I would suggest that the real problem was that far too many realists caricatured themselves – certainly the ones I came across during my education. In particular, too many tried to adapt their credo to the demands of scientific-objectivism, thus losing much of what was truly interesting and even unique in that tradition. In fact, I would go so far as to suggest that the critique of realism from less orthodox directions has been instrumental in encouraging realists to re-engage with the richness of their own tradition in a more thorough and creative way.

Theory and practice

In your work on security you have laid great stress on practice and the theory/practice nexus. In particular, you emphasize the imperative of 'speaking truth to power'. That seems to imply that power does not know 'truth' and, secondly, that one can speak in ways that might be heard. Can you expand a bit on the idea of 'speaking truth to power'?

This is, of course, hugely complicated territory, and one that I have had cause to reflect on a great deal since writing *Security, Strategy and Critical Theory*. The theory/practice nexus raises all kinds of questions, from the most fundamental epistemological issues to narrower but still important questions about the operation of the various domains through which intellectuals might try to communicate their ideas. Even if I had the intellectual firepower to do so, I am afraid that there is no way I can even begin to do justice to all of this here.

But as a starting point, and limiting our discussion only to the academy, we must begin by acknowledging that few if any academics consciously view themselves as setting out to speak untruths for the sake of power. I have certainly never met anyone who might fall into that category. And yet so many of us fail to subject received opinion to sufficient critical scrutiny; so many of us temper our views of findings for fear of offending the various powerbrokers that govern the structures surrounding *homo academicus*; so many of us orientate our research agendas towards those issues that count in the eyes of fund holders or other gatekeepers, rather than persevering with issues or questions that we ourselves view as central or important. This suggests to me that there is an imperative on all of us to be ruthlessly self-reflexive about where we – as projects or individuals – fit into those structures of power that we inescapably inhabit. It is only on that basis that we can hope to negotiate our way through them whilst maintaining some kind of integrity. This, by the way, is not to expect colleagues to adhere to some impossible standards of purity. There are complex multi-level games to be played: gaining kudos or (in Bordieusian terms) earning various forms of capital in one direction can and does allow one to make important contributions or interventions in others. So one can and should be strategic about these things. But above all this requires honest self-reflection.

In relation to this, another thing that we need to recognize is that there are different possibilities inherent in different fields of academic practice – Security Studies compared to Welsh Politics, for example. Different societies and political systems also offer different possibilities. The latter point has been brought home to me quite sharply in recent years as I have spent quite a lot of time in Oslo. The dynamics of security politics – and the nature of the theory-practice nexus – are clearly very different in small, social democratic, if resolutely Atlanticist Norway, as compared to the post-imperial United Kingdom. Patterns of media production and consumption are also different. As an example, I fear that whether they be critical or not, the possibilities for any security analyst gaining a wider public hearing in the UK are heavily circumscribed by the sheer parochialism of the London-based media. All of which again underlines the need to be self-reflexive about the structures we inhere within.

Your point about speaking in ways that might be heard is a very interesting one. I have been very fortunate to be able to use different media to communicate ideas. In addition to conventional academic writing, I have published a stream of commentary-type pieces and also been able to do quite a lot of stuff on television and radio; all of this in two different languages. Obviously, these opportunities allow one to come into contact with people who would never dream of picking up an overpriced academic book. But, again, in doing this kind of thing one comes face to face with various compromises and trade-offs that inevitably come into play and need to be negotiated or sometimes rejected. That said, and without wishing to minimize the downsides or difficulties, there are clearly different ways to be heard. And as the examples of Juan Cole and Stephen Walt demonstrate, it may well be that the so called 'new media' offer possibilities for doing so that are less laden with the compromises that inevitably come into play when one engages in the production process for TV programmes, for example.

Finally, though, even if we do manage to find an audience willing to listen, we need to recognize that, as even the most basic reception theory reminds us, there can ultimately be no authorial control over what is actually heard. But that is just the nature of the beast, I suppose! It should not deter us.

You mentioned audience. If all theory is for someone and for some purpose, could you narrow down the audience you envisaged for your work on security? How does it differ from the audience for your subsequent work?

That is actually a difficult question for me to answer in the context of the work on security because, for the biographical reasons already outlined, by the time the *Security, Strategy and Critical Theory* book was published I was already working on other things. This meant that the book was very largely left to its own fate. Because of this, even if it had been capable of securing a wider audience – which I very much doubt – any impact was confined to the specialized academic audience: other academics and graduate students. Since then, some of those ideas have been taken up by some of those readers who have added their own inflections or pulled them in different directions. Slightly bowdlerized versions have turned up in various textbooks. And so on. All very conventional…

The more recent work is different. In this case, in addition to seeking an academic audience, I have made a conscious effort to communicate with other, wider audiences. The plural is important here. There are different audiences that one is trying to communicate with, through different media, saying different things – or at least saying things with a different inflection. But with the partial exception of contributions to the mass media that can reach the populace at large, or direct contact with members of the governing class, my own feeling is that most so-called public intellectuals are actually engaged with communicating with various actors active in civil society. This is certainly the location that matters most as far as I am concerned and it is the space that I have found most receptive and conducive, even in the Welsh context of a relatively weak civil society.

But as ever there are trade-offs and compromises to be negotiated. One that I am particularly conscious of is the choices one has to make regarding involvement in party politics. Within the political context I have inhabited over the past decade and more – that of devolved Wales with its new and initially fragile institutions – my own decision has been not to associate with a particular political party as this would have made communication with other actors (and parties) difficult or even impossible. So I have deliberately kept a distance and even on occasion bit my tongue. But given the vital importance of effective political parties for democratic life, I do regret not being able to make a contribution in that direction. But one has to make choices and I suppose that one might hope for an indirect influence by way of the 'force of the better argument'?!

What of purpose, then? Accepting that no author can ever control the use that is made of their work, what purpose or purposes have you been attempting to serve?

With the work on security the aim was very much to try to propound, or at least clarify, an alternative to what I termed Traditional Security Studies. I have always been more interested in reconstruction than deconstruction and, in that sense, critique was not enough. The only alternative that I had been exposed to was Peace Studies. I had been fortunate enough to attend the pilot semester of the European Peace University at Stadschlaining that was effectively a master class in Peace Studies in which all the leading figures in the field (Galtung and the rest) did a 'turn'. Although I found it very interesting and, of course, sympathized very much with the intent, I was rather underwhelmed by the conceptual side of what was presented to us. So I thought it would be helpful to try to pull together and perhaps clarify the various 'moves' in the more critical literature on security, while also trying to locate it all in a wider framework of social theory. The hope was that, in conjunction with the work that other people were doing at the time, this kind of work would prove helpful to those people engaged with the vitally important issues involved, both in the academy and ultimately beyond.

With regards the subsequent work on Wales, as I have already indicated the purpose was to try to bolster the devolution process. My view was that the new institutions would have a better chance of success if they were being held up to critical academic scrutiny. Allied to this was a hope that it would be possible to demonstrate to other academics that by taking Wales seriously, some really interesting and significant intellectual questions that would otherwise be ignored could come into focus – thereby hopefully encouraging them into the field.

To what extent has there been a dialogue between Critical Security Studies and Peace Studies?

I must be honest and admit that apart from that brief, if very intensive, exposure at the end of the Cold War, Peace Studies is not a field that I have engaged with to any significant extent since then. So I have no idea whether or not CSS has had any impact there. Nor am I aware of any direct dialogue, although Ken Booth would have been the interlocutor if there had been any: he was both interested in Peace Studies and was very much respected by people working in that field.

I do recall a conversation several years ago with Ken in which we tried to work out how capitalized Critical Security Studies differed from Peace Studies. We even scribbled down some notes on a piece of paper. But I have no idea what happened to that subsequently. I guess there were more important priorities.

Has your work with different media and audiences affected your views on the role of intellectuals and the possibility of change?

My views on this have certainly evolved. You will already have gathered that I am more sanguine about the potential to influence those working within the system as well as anti-systemic forces – at least in some places and circumstances.

In terms of the academy, and having gone off to plough the Welsh politics furrow, I am also much more conscious of the importance of what might be termed 'infrastructure' – journals, conferences, audiences – in rendering critique and reconstruction possible. Intellectual life in the academy is so path-dependent. If there is a debate you can plug into, that makes it so much easier to get your voice heard. The development of CSS was greatly facilitated by the fact that it coincided with the burst of interest in conceptual issues that accompanied the end of the Cold War. To that extent I should perhaps be more sympathetic with Critical Terrorism Studies than I was in a previous answer. But at any rate, all this may well be just another way of saying that I am now much more aware of the nature of the games that *homo academicus* is forced to play.

Emancipation

From the beginning of your academic career, you have placed great stress on the concept of emancipation. How do you explain its centrality?

To me there are two reasons why we should be concerned about the question of emancipation. It is a matter of ethical responsibility and, in the case of anyone who views themselves as producing work that is in any way critical, it is also a matter of internal coherence.

Of course, Marx's injunction in his 'Theses on Feuerbach' (1998) looms large here, but it is not just for inheritors of the Marxian tradition that understanding the world is viewed as a prelude to changing it. One need only read Mike Williams (2005: 82–127 and 2007) or Bill Scheuerman (2009) on Morgenthau, or Mick Cox (1999 and 2010) or Ken Booth (1991b) on Carr to realize that the founding fathers were deeply concerned with what we might term human betterment. Ira Katznelson's superb *Desolation and Enlightenment* (2003) makes the same point about post-Second World War Political Science as a whole. Now of course, some of these people would probably have baulked at the use of the term 'emancipation' to describe what they were up to, but if I can set that aside for a moment, it seems to me that we should acknowledge and celebrate this ethical commitment.

What arises from this, though, is a requirement for serious engagement with the question of what a better world might look like and our bases for claiming that a particular state of affairs is to be preferred to another – which for me is what the question of emancipation is all about. Moreover, for my part at least, this is not simply a matter of following the correct procedures. Pace Habermas, and as Axel Honneth among others have pointed out, there are limits to proceduralism. There are also unavoidable questions about the nature of human potential.

Of course it should go without saying that it would be unreasonable to require a person writing a fairly traditional article on, say, Slovenian foreign policy in the late 1990s to elaborate on unfulfilled human potential! What I am claiming, though, is that these issues are ultimately related, even if in an inevitably mediated form. Moreover, for those who conceive of themselves as writing in a critical vein (from whatever tradition), there is a more direct imperative to engage with these types of questions. As I tried to demonstrate in my contribution (2005) to Ken Booth's edited collection on CSS, in this case it is a matter of internal coherence and, indeed, critical edge. If we are to take the normative projects embodied in these works seriously, then they cannot simply endlessly defer or leave implicit the question of the nature of the alternatives they espouse. Which means engaging with what I have just termed the matter of emancipation: albeit, perhaps, emancipation with a small 'e'; that is, a notion of emancipation which, in Laclau's terms (1996: 18), has been shorn of 'religious and modern secularised eschatologies'.

That said, while I would insist on the centrality of emancipation, I would want to distinguish between taking emancipation seriously and defining security in terms of emancipation. While I still think the former is imperative, I am now much more dubious about the later, even if it was a pivotal argument in Ken's 'Security and Emancipation' piece as well as in my own subsequent work. We have been rightly critiqued on that score, and I think Ken moved away from his 'two sides of the same coin' image even before those criticisms were levelled. But while that initial impulse to equate security and emancipation may have been too crude, the concern with emancipation can and should remain absolutely central.

But you haven't offered a definition of emancipation yourself …

No, you are right. What I was trying to do was to demonstrate that the Frankfurt School tradition offers some useful and interesting ways of thinking through these issues, hopefully encouraging further exploration from some of those who have not come across this literature before. What I also wanted to do was to underline (as so many have done previously) that to discuss emancipation does not entail developing some kind of blueprint for the perfect society. While I would very much want to retain the concept of utopia for political thought, and consider its absence from the contemporary scene as a classic case of throwing out the baby with the bathwater, one can be utopian in ways other than those associated with Thomas More.

If you were going to force me to adopt, if not a definition of emancipation then at least a conceptual framework for thinking about the questions involved, I would probably choose the schema offered by Honneth in this *The Struggle for Recognition* (1996). Very crudely put, he argues for the existence of three realms – the personal, the civic and the world of work – in which there exists a pre-theoretic desire for recognition, and then explores the three different logics at work within them, namely love, rights and solidarity. While I have my doubts about his characterization of the economic realm in particular, I would nonetheless want to argue that, in broad terms, this is a really useful way of thinking about the issues involved.

You have argued (2005) that a concern with emancipation could prove to be a common ground on which different critical approaches could meet. Have those hopes been realized?

No, absolutely not! There is obviously a marked reluctance among the various varieties of post-structuralism and constructivism to engage – even though some of those who originated these approaches were not so reticent.

Why the reluctance?

To be honest I really struggle to understand this. If we are to accept that the great gains brought about under the banner of emancipation – of slaves, women, the immiserated working class – were so sullied by the undeniable silences and hypocrisies of those movements; if we are going to claim that the heinous crimes associated with Liberal Imperialism and Marxist socialism were such as to render null and void any attempt to redeem the language and concepts associated with them – then, if we are to be consistent, I guess we would have to abandon all of those concepts that have given normative direction to the politics of modernity. Goodbye liberty, equality, fraternity and so much more. But that does not seem to be the case. For some reason emancipation manages to elicit a particular ire. There also seems to be a particular determination not to engage with what those of us who focus on emancipation actually say, but just to assume that were are some kind of latter day Maoists intent on forcing a particular conception of the good life on all. As I say, I really struggle to understand why this is the case.

More generally, you have tried to stress the fundamental commonalities and overlaps between critical theorists and post-modernists. Why do you think that positions are growing more entrenched on both sides?

I am not entirely sure I agree with your analysis. Things like the c.a.s.e. initiative seem to me to suggest that some, at least, are seeking to build bridges. I find it particularly encouraging that those involved were predominantly younger scholars. So perhaps there is hope. But if – depressingly – you are right, then I would suggest that the best place to look for an explanation of this entrenchment is not in the texts of the various protagonists themselves. Frankly – and as I have tried to argue elsewhere (2001) – I just do not accept that the differences are that great or fundamental, especially when one looks at the substance of what is being said rather than the forms of argumentation. I would suggest, rather, that we need to look at Bourdieu's dissection of the life of *homo academicus* (1984) and bear in mind the various forms of capital that are generated by having distinctive schools and accentuating the differences between them. The point about the 'what really happened at Krondstadt' type of argument is that, while it might have been utterly irrelevant to the politics of the mid 1980s, it was nonetheless very useful in maintaining the internal cohesion of the groupuscules involved and the status of their respective ideologues. I am sorry if this appears overly cynical, but that is the only way I can make sense of it. And by the way, I do not spare myself from the implications of what I am saying here.

Critical Security Studies

Ken Booth and yourself are regarded as the co-founders of the Welsh School approach to Critical Security Studies. Are there any fundamental differences between you in terms of the way that you conceive of this approach?

First I have to say that I am highly amused by the fact that the term 'Welsh School' seems to have caught on, especially given that I think it was first used by Ken Booth as a kind of in-joke aimed at gently tweaking the tails of some of our Aberystwyth colleagues who were forever extolling the virtues of the 'English School'. It should certainly not be taken too seriously. I recognize, of course, that scholars can and do find such labels helpful. But while Ken and I were clearly trying to mark out a distinctive intellectual position, there was never any attempt to establish a 'Welsh School' with the kind of infrastructure that one might associate with that term. No journal or research centre, for example. In fact, we only ever wrote one thing together, and in that case there was a third author involved (Pinar Bilgin) and it was only a very brief piece anyway (1998). So while I think there was a huge amount of common ground between us, this was far more the result of serendipity and mutual influence than any deliberate attempt on our parts to work out an agreed 'party line'. You must also remember that there were also other people around in Aberystwyth who brought another perspective to bear on Critical Security Studies, most obviously Mike Williams.

Given this method of working, and given also that we both have different intellectual histories and interests, it would be surprising if there were not also significant differences between Ken and myself. They are pretty obvious politically, I suppose: with regards the category of nation, for example, or on the European Union. Broadly speaking, I think that there are more progressive possibilities inhering in the former that Ken tends to admit to, while I am much less sanguine than he is about actually-existing integration. More generally, I suspect that the huge synoptic approach he has adopted in *Theory of World Security* (2007), in particular, means that he has had to work out his views on more questions than I have. Even if I am a fairly opinionated character, in 'social survey' terms there are simply more issues about which I would be forced to tick the 'Don't Know' box! We also have a different attitude to other work such as that of the Copenhagen School, for example. But all that said, I am sure that the similarities are more apparent and far more important than any differences.

What of the future? Where do you hope CSS goes from here?

Given that I have spent recent years doing other things, I am not sure that I have any moral authority in terms of suggesting where those with the intent of developing

CSS might go from here. It really is up to the cadre of young academics and postgraduate students who are interested in the approach. And given they will have imbibed a different intellectual atmosphere compared to the 'old guard', as well as inhabited a different historical context, they will have their own views about what is important and worthwhile. But from my slightly detached perspective, I would hope that there is more work on the conceptual side of things. I think that there is a lot of unfinished business there. In particular, I genuinely do think that a meaningful synthesis of the various critical strands is possible. I would also urge much more serious critical engagement with the military dimensions of security – with those issues that fall under the rubric of Strategic Studies. Finally, I would hope to see some of the people coming into the field making a concerted effort to communicate their ideas beyond the academy. Perhaps it is too much to hope that CSS scholars might have the same impact on public debate as, say, Mearsheimer and Walt, but it surely must be possible to establish a CSS version of the latter's 'Foreign Policy' blog, for example.[6] I am very well aware that this will not be easy, but at the end of the day, there has to be an attempt to impact upon practice; that remains the ultimate test of the usefulness of the critical approach

Notes

1 The Welsh Language Society was established in 1962 as pressure group attempting to secure equal legal status for the Welsh Language as well as a future for Welsh speaking communities. The Society is best known in Wales for its use of non-violent direct action. Several hundred of its members have spent time in prison as a result of their activities.
2 The political magazine *Marxism Today* was published between 1971 and 1998.
3 See, in this respect, Hoare and Smith (1971: 419).
4 Wyn Jones is referring to Booth (1991a; 1991b).
5 See Wyn Jones (1999: 93–124).
6 Available online at <http://walt.foreignpolicy.com> (accessed 23 May 2011).

Bibliography

Bilgin, P., Booth, K. and Wyn Jones, R. (1998) 'Security Studies: The Next Stage?', *Nação e Defesa* 84(2): 131–57.
Booth, K. (1979) *Strategy and Ethnocentrism*, New York: Holmes and Meier.
——— (1991a) 'Security and Emancipation', *Review of International Studies* 17(4): 313–26.
——— (1991b) 'Security in Anarchy: Utopian Realism in Theory and Practice', *International Affairs* 63(3): 527–45.
——— (2007) *Theory of World Security*, Cambridge: Cambridge University Press.
Bourdieu, P. (1984) *Homo Academicus*, Stanford: Stanford University Press.
c.a.s.e. collective (2006) 'Critical Approaches to Security in Europe: A Networked Manifesto', *Security Dialogue* 37(4): 443–87.
Cohn, C. (1987a) 'Sex and Death in the Rational World of Defense Intellectuals', *Signs: Journal of Women in Culture and Society* 12(4): 687–718.
——— (1987b) 'Slick'ems, Glick'ems, Christmas Trees, and Cookie Cutters: Nuclear Language and How We Learned to Pat the Bomb', *Bulletin of the Atomic Scientists*, 43: 17–24.
Cox, M. (1999) 'Will the Real E.H. Carr Please Stand Up?', *International Affairs* 75(3): 643–53.

___ (2010) 'E.H. Carr and the Crisis of Twentieth-Century Liberalism: Reflections and Lessons', *Millennium* 38(3): 1–11.

Cox, R.W. (1981) 'Social Forces, States and World Orders: Beyond International Relations Theory', *Millennium* 10(2): 126–55.

___ (1983) 'Gramsci, Hegemony and International Relations', *Millennium* 12(2): 162–75.

Feenberg, A. (1991) *Critical Theory of Technology*, Oxford: Oxford University Press.

Fiori, G. (1973) *Antonio Gramsci: Life of a Revolutionary,* trans. Tom Nairn, New York: Schoken.

Habermas, J. (1985) *The Theory of Communicative Action: Reason and Rationalization of Society,* trans. Thomas McCarthy, vol. 1, Boston: Beacon Press.

___ (1987) *The Theory of Communicative Action: Lifeworld and System – A Critique of Functionalist Reason*, trans. Thomas McCarthy, vol. 2, Boston: Beacon Press.

Hechter, M. (1999) *Internal Colonialism: The Celtic Fringe in British National Development*, New Brunswick: Transaction Publishers.

Held, D. (1980) *Introduction to Critical Theory: Horkheimer to Habermas*, Berkeley: University of California Press.

Hoare, Q and Smith, G.S. (eds/trans) (1971) *Selections from the Prison Notebooks*, London: Lawrence and Wishhart.

Honneth, A. (1993) *The Critique of Power: Reflective Stages in a Critical Social Theory*, Cambridge: MIT Press.

___ (1996) *The Struggle for Recognition: The Moral Grammar of Social Conflicts*, London: Polity Press.

Horkheimer, M. (1972) 'Traditional and Critical Theory' (1937) in *Critical Theory: Selected Essays*, New York: Herder and Herder.

Horkheimer, M. and Adorno, T. (1972) *The Dialectic of Enlightenment*, trans. John Cumming, New York: Herder and Herder.

Katznelson, I. (2003) *Desolation and Enlightenment: Political Knowledge After Total War, Totalitarianism and Holocaust*, Columbia: Columbia University Press.

Laclau, E. (1996) *Emancipation(s)*, London: Verso.

Marx, K. and Engels, F (1998) *The German Ideology: Including Theses on Feuerbach and an Introduction to the Critique of Political Economy*, New York: Prometheus Books.

Mearsheimer, J. and Walt, S. (2008) *The Israel Lobby and US Foreign Policy*, London: Penguin Books.

Megill, A. (2002) *Karl Marx: The Burden of Reason (Why Marx rejected politics and the market)*, Oxford: Rowman and Littlefield.

Mueller, J. (1988) 'The Essential Irrelevance of Nuclear Weapons: Stability in the Postwar World', *International Security* 13(2): 55–79.

Nairn, T. (1977) *The Break-up of Britain: Crisis and New Nationalism*, London: New Left Books.

Peoples, C. (2009) *Justifying Ballistic Missile Defence: Technology, Security, and Culture*, Cambridge: Cambridge University Press.

Postone, M. (1993) *Time, Labour and Social Domination: A Reinterpretation of Marx's Critical Theory*, Cambridge: Cambridge University Press.

Scheuerman, W.E. (2009) *Morgenthau*, Cambridge: Polity Press.

Stamnes, E. (2004) 'Critical Security Studies and the United Nations Preventive Deployment in Macedonia', *International Peacekeeping* 11(1): 161–81.

Wendt, A. (2001) 'What is International Relations for? Notes Toward a Post-Critical View', in R. Wyn Jones (ed.) *Critical Theory and World Politics*, Boulder: Lynne Rienner.

Williams, G.A. (1960) 'The Concept of "Egemonia" in the Work of Antonio Gramsci: Some Notes of Interpretation', *Journal of the History of Ideas* 21(4): 586–99.

_____ (1975) *Proletarian Order: Antonio Gramsci, Factory Councils and the Origins of Italian Communism, 1911–1921*, London: Pluto Press.

_____ (1984) 'Marcsydd o Sardiniwr ac argyfwng Cymru', *Efrydiau Athronyddol* 47: 16–27.

_____ (1985) *When Was Wales? A History of the Welsh*, London: Penguin Books.

Williams, M.C. (2005) *The Realist Tradition and the Limits of International Relations*, Cambridge: Cambridge University Press.

_____ (ed.) (2007), *Realism Reconsidered: The Legacy of Hans Morgenthau in International Relations*, Oxford: Oxford University Press.

Williams, R. (1980) 'The Politics of Nuclear Disarmament', *New Left Review* 1(124): 25–42.

Wyn Jones, R. (1999) *Security, Strategy, and Critical Theory*, London: Lynne Rienner.

_____ (2001) 'Introduction: Locating Critical International Relations Theory', in R. Wyn Jones (ed.) *Critical Theory and World Politics*, Boulder: Lynne Rienner.

_____ (2005) 'On Emancipation: Necessity, Capacity, and Concrete Utopias', in K. Booth (ed.) *Critical Security Studies and World Politics*, London: Lynne Rienner.

_____ (2007) *Rhoi Cymru'n Gyntaf: Syniadaeth Plaid Cymru, Cyf. 1*. Cardiff: University of Wales Press.

PART II
Rethinking the Origins

6

THE 'SECULAR' SUBJECT OF CRITICAL INTERNATIONAL RELATIONS THEORY

Mustapha Kamal Pasha

Introduction

In its originary promise, Critical International Relations Theory (CIRT) is emancipatory. This is not a romantic ideal, but the theory's defining theoretical and practical manifesto. The deepening structures of rationalization have powerful resources to diminish agentic coherence and moral capacity. Ideology effectively draws a wedge between appearance and essence. Structures of representation can disguise the sources of injustice and inequality. An administered society erases the political subject. The atomistic quest for self-fulfilment can displace the desire for moral community. Technique dislodges human interests. However, these challenges do not spell ultimate closure or doom, a sentiment widely entertained by the original protagonists of Critical Theory (CT) during the dark times of fascism and genocidal war. For CIRT scholars, particularly those discussed in this retrospective volume, human energies for moral advance cannot be eradicated, nor can emancipation be abandoned in the face of old or new challenges; emancipation is a *sine qua non* for renewal and transformation. It is also CIRT's *raison d'être*.

The centrality of *emancipation* to CIRT springs from the theory's durable location within post-Enlightenment thinking flanking its progressivist leanings. It is also guided by a refusal to accept the *status quo* as a natural state as in 'traditional' (Horkheimer 1972) or 'problem-solving' (Cox 1981) theory. 'Humans need emancipatory politics as a guide for judgement and action' Booth affirms. 'Without belief in ideals, traditional power elites and their oppressive common sense will perpetuate human wrongs, and humanity will never be what it might become' (Booth 2005: 181). The indissoluble theory/praxis link in CIRT is another source of its emancipatory ambition. Recognition of structures of inequality and the violence and injustice they perpetuate in the world is not an exclusive preserve of CIRT. It is, however, the aspiration for transformation that sets it apart from the *status quo* preserving edicts of either structural realism or the reformist vision of liberalism. Normative commitment for human flourishing engages both CIRT and liberalism with the potential within the latter to appear as yet another form of idealism (Jahn 1998). CIRT, however, repudiates the image of harmony of interests either in the domestic or the international arena. Social orders are marked by hegemony, violence and injustice. Within the structured spaces of international society, there are also sites of resistance. These sites form the basis of emancipation. CIRT offers the intellectual resources to identify sites of resistance, empower them with theoretical prowess and guide political practice.

Secured by reflexivity and critique, the self-aware subject of CIRT is capable of both recognizing and overcoming the strictures of instrumental reason. The subject not only possesses the agency to escape the rationalized cage of capitalist modernity, but also the vision to construct alternative worlds. On a similar assurance, CIRT repudiates the pessimism of realism (both classical and structural) and its conception of an unchanging world order. Unlike the terrified subject of realism, one perpetually unable to escape the paradox of liberty/security, the self-conscious subject of CIRT is not cowed down by anarchy – an imaginary tale invented to authenticate the need for authority (cf. Walker 1997). Freedom, not security, steers the subject's journey. CIRT equally rebuffs narrow variants of liberal imaginings that confine selfhood to mere self-seeking. The self-conscious subject is a self-reflexive agent capable of moral action. Reflexivity, not avarice, structures the life-world of the subject of CIRT. This is not the subject driven by the instinct of self-preservation, but moral obligation. It can resist the seductions of the cultural industry (Adorno and Horkheimer 1979) that are procured by the liberal promise of market freedom. Similarly, the subject of CIRT can mount resistance to cultural homogenization generated by neoliberal globalization. In sum, emancipation lies at the centre of subjectivity visualized by CIRT.

As other commentators in this volume suggest, CIRT has come in various colours and shades (Devetak 1995), leaning on the Frankfurt School in one instance (Linklater 2001), revisionist readings of Gramsci in another (Cox 1981), or dependent upon open engagements with French poststructuralism and deconstruction (Ashley and Walker 1990) in yet another attire. CIRT, as Wyn Jones notes, is 'best understood as a constellation of different approaches, all seeking to illuminate the question of emancipation in world politics' (2001: 9). Divergences, however, nullify any attempt to formalize a unified conception of CIRT. In a nutshell, CIRT refers to 'a cluster of themes inspired by an emancipatory intent' (Bronner 1994: 3, cited in Wyn Jones 2001: 7). 'Marxian-inspired Critical Theory', as Linklater notes, 'should be distinguished from post-modern critical theory which displays considerable scepticism towards the emancipatory project associated with Marxism' (Linklater 1996: 279). Linklater's 1996 description still provides a valuable summary of 'the achievements of CIRT': refutation of positivism and its imaginary tale of the neutral observer; rejection of the 'immutability thesis' in which the durability of existing structures ends up rationalizing inequalities of power and wealth; post-Marxist recognition of the varieties of forms of social exclusion; and appreciation of 'post-sovereign forms of political life'. Above all, CIRT is about the *international*, not the domestic sphere of CT. This brief commentary addresses only that variant of CIRT in which 'a universally emancipatory ethics' (Jahn 1998: 614) provides the principal thread in the narrative.

Emancipatory promise

Emancipation in CIRT, understood either as transcendence from an existing social order, commitment to equity and justice, or recognition of the need for transformation, ultimately depends upon the post-Enlightenment promise of progress and the civilizing process (Linklater 2005). Anticipation of a better world is a necessary complement to critique in which the world order is found to be grossly unjust and unfree. As with the Enlightenment *philosophes*, the practitioners of CIRT hold on to the limitless capacity of Reason to facilitate better futures. Once liberated from its instrumental fetters, Reason can reflexively usher in a world of equal communicability, recognition or freedom. Is this promise attainable? CIRT does not proffer easy answers to this important question. The goal of emancipation can only be achieved through struggle, theoretical and political, both inextricably linked.

Any assessment of a theoretical enterprise based on a linear accounting of time has its predictability: excavation of shortcomings and fault lines with compulsory references to ellipses and silences against the image of an unfulfilled promise. In this vein, many critics have examined the strengths and pitfalls of CIRT, both previously (Rengger 1988; Lapid 1989; Price and Reus-Smit 1998) and in this volume. To the ledger of pitfalls one can also add the suspicion about teleological desires that continue to inspire CIRT's essential commitments. The world will become a better place – eventually. This belief, once abandoned during the bleak period of the earlier phase of the Frankfurt School, but reinstated and reworked subsequently as in Habermas (1985; 1987), Honneth (2009) and others (Neufeld 1995; Hoffman 1987; Linklater 1996), is unshakable. It rests perilously on the fault lines of a critique of instrumental reason and the world that has been conjured up in its long shadow, and redemptive promise. Alternatively, there is also the ever-present risk for the theory's normalization within commoditized structures – a process effectively and tirelessly interrogated by the Frankfurt School. Despite CIRT's abiding reflexivity and pronounced aims of transforming the world, it has followed a trajectory not dissimilar from other 'dissident' thinking: celebrating marginality without suffering the travails of banishment. Perhaps this is inevitable within any academy that enjoys an isomorphic relation to the wider capitalist exchange economy. CIRT, however, has avoided irrelevance by continuous self-examination and cross-fertilization with cognate perspectives. In the final analysis, there is the enormous hazard of sheer exhaustion for a theory so deeply wedded to the claims of Western modernity (Inayatullah and Blaney 2004) in the midst of global and globalizing cultural currents and new awareness (cf. Hobson in this volume, Chapter 8). Without globalizing its optic, especially expanding its cultural field, CIRT can only anaemically nourish an understanding of multiplicities and difference (cf. Pensky 2005). The task in this brief commentary is not to rehearse these issues, but to shift, quite modestly, the focus onto a different terrain: to ambivalences within CIRT over the assumed 'secular' agent of emancipation – the object of emancipation and its main subject. To the extent that the universal claims of emancipation in CIRT are inextricably tied to the individual subject, the nature of this subject is worth interrogation.

Who is the subject of emancipation? Recognizing reflexivity and historicity (Jahn 1998) as indispensable elements to the critical enterprise, CIRT embraces remarkable ambivalence towards the production of a more transparent figure. This historically contingent subject has both universal and particular attributes. As aspiration, the subject of CIRT is an artefact of critical reason. It requires no cultural address. The subject of CIRT is bound neither by locality nor identitarian features. Sheltered by claims to universality, its desire to escape the faceless structures of capitalist modernity requires no location. Neither its belief nor cultural content is relevant to the desires for liberation. Yet, the subject of CIRT is neither neutral nor culturally vacuous. Upon closer scrutiny, this subject reveals the imprint of particular historical settlements. This post-Enlightenment subject bears the signature of particular civilizational aspirations and cultural specificity. Although it appears to defy the confining horizon of Westphalian imagining of political community, this subject thinks *in and through* a particular language, grammar and syntax. Behind supposed neutrality underwritten by appeals to universal ethics, the post-Westphalian subject of CIRT carries with it the political desires of a distinctive variant of transcendence now realizable within an immanentist field of reason. The subject of CIRT is *not* a secular subject drawn from the imposing horizons of Westphalia. Rather, it is a subject in search of a vernacular expression of transcendence ensconced within the immanentist matrix of modernity.

In Ken Booth's poignant definition of emancipation, human self-creation is an essential ingredient of both CIRT's field of vision as well as its practice:

> Emancipation is the theory and practice of inventing humanity, with a view to freeing people, as individuals and collectivities, from contingent and structural oppressions. It is a discourse of human self-creation and the politics of trying to bring it about. Security and community are guiding principles, and at this stage of history the growth of a universal human rights culture is central to emancipatory politics. The concept of emancipation shapes strategies and tactics of resistance, offers a theory of progress for society, and gives politics of hope for common humanity.
>
> *(2005: 181)*

Booth's formulation presents a useful template to probe the limits and potential of CIRT. A recognition of limits, to be certain, is not an obvious claim for decentring the West-centricity of CT (Steinman 2005) on which the CIRT enterprise rests. Universal values, as Booth (2005) proposes, can originate in alternate sites. Geography is a poor guide to fix the absence or presence of a cosmopolitan impulse. From a more expansive cultural perspective, CIRT clearly has the potential to speak *the* language of universality and to speak *in* the language of universality. Paradoxically, though, it is *because* CIRT assumes that this potential has already been realized within its theoretical spaces that CIRT encounters some real difficulties. Even by shedding all residues of Eurocentrism, CIRT cannot escape a more basic constraint, namely, its location within a particular cosmology relayed in its conception of emancipation.

In the first instance, CIRT privileges an anthropomorphic conception of emancipation in which freedom is not only indivisible from the liberal subject, but the liberal subject is the pivot of the cosmological design. This prejudice, however, is not entirely without its advantages. Recognition of the individual's worth against statolatry (as in realism) is to be celebrated in any project of establishing a more just political community. Only extreme variants of relativism preferred by tyrants can expel the individual from any ethical design. However, the individual envisioned in CIRT emerges within a particular historical context of the maturing of modernity with a distinct cultural address. The idea of emancipation cannot escape the historical and cultural neighbourhood in which the (liberal) subject has grown, only to confront soulless incarceration within instrumental reason. Once this subject becomes the universal referent, it is no longer in a position, nor willing to recognize, other subjectivities arising in other locales with different ontological commitments and political desires, pursuing alternative emancipatory aims. The presumption of universality subsumes particularity rather than emerging through recognition of difference.

Recognition and redistributive justice (Fraser 1989) present two important instantiations of emancipation. However, they appear meaningful only within *a* particular cosmology. Notions of the ubiquity of instrumental reason and the triumph of technology (drawn from the Frankfurt School) present a potent characterization of social life under the dictatorship of capitalist modernity. This characterization presupposes an inescapable immanentist horizon leaving no spaces for other transcendental cosmologies to structure human existence. This picture is not designed to advance claims of civilizational divergence in which some societies elect to swim in the unpatrolled waters of immanence while others choose to cling on to the fixed pole of transcendence. This observation merely suggests the possibility of diverse negotiations and resolutions *within* modernity. Political desires can assume multiple forms. The translation of these desires into a monotonic form silences both their richness and distinctiveness. Hence, the language of universality can only be a point of arrival, not a point of departure. Significantly, is the subject of CIRT equipped to engage in dialogue outside the parameters set by critique of reason?

To the point, the subject of CIRT is not straightforwardly a-religious, a child of the Enlightenment, but a schizoid figure abandoning a pre-conventional terrain of moral reasoning while simultaneously carrying the baggage of Christian morality. In this figure, redemptive aspirations collide with the post-Enlightenment self-image of CIRT. This ambivalence, to contextualize, lies at the centre of not only CIRT, but Western IR in general. The principal markers of ambivalence are manifest in the subject's (liberal) attachments to a progressive narrative of history, as well the recognition of the difficulty of overcoming the rationalizing force of history directed towards alienation. The subject of CIRT shares the eschatological legend of the Fall with acceptance of the possibility of redemption, albeit a secular redemption obtained through Reason and individualization. The Protestant underpinnings of this redemptive strain are not entirely opaque. Whether CIRT is sufficiently magnanimous to permit alternative pathways towards emancipation remains an open question. A related issue is CIRT's receptivity towards other languages and worldviews embedded in those languages.

The assumed secular subject of CIRT emerges amidst the haze and fog of religious settlements carrying the remains and surplus of transcendent dreams. Yet, CIRT apparently rejects its filial ties to Judaeo-Christian imaginings. CIRT adopts the 'secular' individual as its flag-bearer in pursuit of freedom, but this process is contested and ambiguous. The 'secular' individual may have left God and transcendence behind in search of an earthly kingdom of self-making and self-realization (Taylor 2007), but teleology guarantees a return to origins. The secular clothing of critical reason merely hides theological worries and yearnings.

Secularity is a contested arena of religious negotiation with no uniform resolution serving as its *telos* (Asad 1993). The conventional story of IR's origins that also serve as a hereditary table for CIRT overly simplifies the entangled history of religion and modern subjectivity. Received dualisms (religious/secular; sacred/profane; scientific/mythical) misguide the mutually constitutive nature of religion and modern subjectivity, but especially the enduring presence of theological longings in modern projects of building community and the world. Confronting difference, thus, CIRT retorts not so differently than traditional theory, perhaps with greater empathy and attention, but also revealing its inseparability from particular theological sediments. The pre-conventional religious other appears as a residue of immaturity or an inassimilable subject who must leave behind its particularity to forge a universal ethical community. Yet, it is quite problematic to sever the bonds that bind the idea of emancipation to theological enactments. Even in its supposed absence, religion makes its presence felt. As Mendieta elegantly puts it: 'today religion lives on because its promise and complaint, its yearning and sigh, have remained unfulfilled and unheard' (2005: 8). In CT, CIRT's progenitor, 'religion also becomes the site for the negotiation of critique, remembrance, and emancipatory projections' (ibid.).

Secular redemption and singularity

Despite its apparent liberation from religion in its attempts to forge a more just and equitable world, CIRT cannot easily dispel its alignment with secular redemption. In its pristine purity, the idea of emancipation is a 'secular' reconstruction of redemption. This may not be as awkward for CIRT's accepted transcendence from pre-modern modes of capture as it seems. Rather, it underscores the inextricable ties that infuse modern aspirations. The real problem, however, is one of singularity:

the implicit suggestion that the road to emancipation can only traverse the mountains and valleys of Western Reason. That journey has familiar signposts erected by the Enlightenment thinkers. The possibility of other pathways leading to different places outside the spatio-temporal horizon of Western modernity is scarcely entertained despite the invitation of dialogue. It is one thing to recognize the inherent unjustness of the existing social and political world, but an entirely different affair to limit the field of emancipation. A major consequence of this constriction is hierarchization (Walker 1999). The terms of incorporating others into a universal moral community can never be neutral. However, the possibility of agonistic contestation producing a more egalitarian dialogue is vitiated by an overly formalized set of criteria to allow subalternity to acquire speech. The issue is not one of representing 'religious' others into a 'secular' discourse (Shani 2007), but a recognition of the theological underpinnings of the story of secular redemption that bar 'other' religious voices to be heard. Secularity masks *intra*-religious divergence.

The ambivalences within CIRT concerning secularity permeate the whole gamut of Western International Relations. It is to the credit of CIRT thinkers to unmask the reified character of IR. Unlike CT (Siebert 1976/1977), however, with its explicit deployment of religion to liberate reason from 'the rigid grip of a reifying and mystifying idolatry of technology and the market' (Mendieta 2005: 2), CIRT has elected to disguise its theological intent. This has prevented CIRT to fully comprehend the role religion continues to play, not only as a sigh of the meek, but as a 'site for the negotiation of critique, remembrance, and emancipatory projections' (ibid.). Contra Mendieta, it is not important to extract an 'emancipatory' message from religion, but to recognize how so often the desire for justice, equality or dignity is articulated in the language of religion. This language congeals the memories of fractured identities, the disruptions perpetuated in life-worlds in the name of progress, but also aspirations of deliverance from tyranny and destitution. In sum, CIRT allows little space for political desires expressed in forms that escape the emancipatory logic of Western Reason.

In its neo-Gramscian variant, CIRT betrays a 'soft' Orientalism in its charac-terization of alterity. Similar to 'the paradox inherent with the neo-Gramscian enterprise of theorizing global capitalism, simultaneously as a reified totality in the core and a non-reified particularity in the Third World' (Pasha 2005: 549), emancipatory CIRT approaches non-Western alterity as a subject that sits precariously on the margins of international society. What is to guarantee its representation and full participation? A key precondition is the ability to embrace post-Enlightenment norms of civility and sociability (Linklater 1998).

Conclusion

Against the background of positivist hegemony and the realist/liberal entente, the 'achievements' of CIRT are noteworthy. Despite open skirmishes and alleged incompatibility between 'realist' and 'liberal' understandings of the international, there is considerable convergence between the two that has given Western IR its distinctive character. From particular notions of political community to ideas of authority, citizenship and modern subjectivity, the commonalities exceed the scope of divergences. CIRT's principal achievement is not only its repudiation of the imperialism of positivist methodology but its appreciation of problem-solving theory as ideology. CIRT has also allowed access to alternative imaginaries not bound by Westphalian conceit (Linklater 1998) or the primacy of state worship that has continued to nurture unfreedoms and exclusions. In the defence of the realm, violence and war have been perpetuated as have projects of pacification or intervention presumably targeted to spread democratic values and civilization. CIRT's normative commitment has rendered the world more accessible to scrutiny than lame rationalizations of immutability.

The limitations of CIRT, as some critics stress, are not merely a natural product of its reliance on Enlightenment rationality. These charges provoke a much wider engagement. The commitment to emancipation also cannot be taken as a deformity measured against an unstated, yet, essential, ideal of *critical* theory. Too often, the measure of purity can incite internecine battles over what is the preferred highway towards the attainment of Truth.

Despite acknowledgements of the collapse of metanarratives, the yardstick of purity can only produce exclusionary spaces of praxis. Recognition of injustice and inequality requires judgement. CIRT cannot be faulted if it welds analysis with judgement. The problem, as this commentary suggests, lies elsewhere: in the singularity enclosed within the idea of emancipation and a conception of the subject of the emancipatory project that refuses to step outside a particular (Protestant) cosmology.

Redemptive logic rests invariably on the assumption of original sin. Within a secularized discourse, the latter can appear as cognitive, cultural or civilizational immaturity (Kant 1976). The only viable escape routes from original sin are repentance and grace. The modern world guarantees neither. As a substitute, it throws up the notion of development. CIRT embraces that notion but only partially, avoiding the enchantment of materiality, but retaining the teleological element appended to its temporal horizons. Teleology takes the form of a civilizing process, both temporally and spatially. The subject of CIRT comes to self-awareness only in time. It also extends its wings in space, spreading enlightenment to other worlds hitherto bereft of reflexivity and critical awareness.

Unable to recognize its place within a wider cosmological world of difference and divergences, the subject of CIRT becomes increasingly dependent on its own cognitive resources. The greater the impulse for self-reflexivity, the greater the void that begins to separate this subject from unfamiliar zones inhabited by alternative desires and commitments. Reflexivity offers few solaces, but larger grief. To the degree that the subject of CIRT takes as its point of reference only what it knows and seeks to know only what its cognitive capacities compel it to know, it cannot embrace zones of otherness. The limits of CIRT are, therefore, not derivative of unawareness of other worlds, but of its own capacities. In this context, its world view may not be so radically different from mainstream sentiment.

Bibliography

Adorno, T.W. and Horkheimer, M. (1979) *The Dialectic of Enlightenment*, London: Verso.

Alker, Hayward (2005) 'Emancipation in the Critical Security Studies Project', in K. Booth (ed.) *Critical Security Studies and World Politics*, Boulder and London: Lynne Rienner.

Asad, T. (1993) *Genealogies of Religion: Discipline and Reasons of Power in Christianity and Islam*, Baltimore: Johns Hopkins University Press.

Ashley, R. and Walker, R.B.J. (1990) 'Reading Dissidence/Writing the Discipline: Crisis and the Question of Sovereignty in International Studies', *International Studies Quarterly* 34(3): 367–416.

Booth, K. (2005) 'Emancipation: introduction to Part 3', in K. Booth (ed.) *Critical Security Studies and World Politics*, Boulder and London: Lynne Rienner.

Bronner, S. (1994) *Of Critical Theory and Its Theorists*, Oxford: Blackwell.

Cox, R.W. (1981) 'Social Forces, State and World Order: Beyond International Relations Theory', *Millennium* 10(2): 126–55.

Devetak, R. (1995) 'The Project of Modernity and International Relations Theory', *Millennium* 24(1): 27–51.

Fraser, N. (1989) *Unruly Practices: Power, Discourse and Gender in Contemporary Social Theory*, Cambridge: Polity.

Habermas, J. (1985) *The Theory of Communicative Action: Reason and Rationalization of Society*, trans. Thomas McCarthy, vol. 1, Boston: Beacon Press.

___ (1987) *The Theory of Communicative Action: Lifeworld and System – A Critique of Functionalist Reason*, trans. Thomas McCarthy, vol. 2, Boston: Beacon Press.

Hoffman, M. (1987) 'Critical Theory and the Inter-Paradigm Debate', *Millennium* 16(2): 231–49.

Honneth, A. (2009) *Pathologies of Reason: on the Legacy of Critical Theory*, trans. James Ingram and others, New York: Columbia University Press.

Horkheimer, M. (1972) 'Traditional and Critical Theory', in *Critical Theory: Selected Essays*, trans. Matthew J. O'Connell *et al.*, New York: Herder and Herder.

Inayatullah, N. and Blaney, D. (2004) *International Relations and the Problem of Difference*, New York and London: Routledge.

Jahn, B. (1998) 'One Step Forward, Two Steps Back: Critical Theory as the Latest Edition of Liberal Idealism', *Millennium* 27(3): 613–41.

Kant, I. (1976) 'An Answer to the Question: What is Enlightenment?' in *Critique of Practical Reason, and Other Writings in Moral Philosophy*, translated and edited with an introduction by Lewis White Beck, New York: Garland.

Lapid, Y. (1989) 'The Third Debate: On the Prospects of International Theory in a Post-Positivist Era', *International Studies Quarterly* 33: 235–54.

Linklater, A. (1992) 'The Question of the Next Stage in International Relations Theory: A Critical-Theoretical Point of View', *Millennium: Journal of International Studies* 21(1): 77–98.

___ (1996) 'The Achievements of Critical Theory', in S. Smith, K. Booth, and M. Zalewski (eds) *International Theory: Positivism and Beyond*, Cambridge: Cambridge University Press.

___ (1998) *The Transformation of Political Community: Ethical Foundations of the Post-Westphalian Era*, Cambridge: Polity Press.

___ (2001) 'The Changing Contours of Critical International Relations Theory' in R. Wyn Jones (ed.) *Critical Theory and World Politics*, Boulder and London: Lynne Rienner.

___ (2005) 'Dialogic Politics and the Civilising Process', *Review of International Studies* 31: 141–54.

Mendieta, E. (ed.) (2005) *The Frankfurt School on Religion: Key Writings by the Major Thinkers*, New York and London: Routledge.

Neufeld, M. (1995) *The Restructuring of International Relations Theory*, Cambridge: Cambridge University Press.

Pasha, M.K. (2005) 'Islam, "Soft" Orientalism and Empire: A Gramscian Rereading', *Critical Review of International Social and Political Philosophy* 8(4): 543–58.

Pensky, M. (ed.) (2005) *Globalizing Critical Theory*, New York: Rowman & Littlefield.

Price, R. and Reus-Smit, C. (1998) 'Dangerous Liaisons? Critical International Theory and Constructivism', *European Journal of International Relations* 4(3): 259–94.

Rengger, N.J. (1988) 'Going Critical? A Response to Hoffman', *Millennium: Journal of International Studies* 17(1): 81–9.

Shani, G. (2007) '"Provincializing" Critical Theory: Islam, Sikhism and International Relations Theory', *Cambridge Review of International Affairs* 20(3): 417–33.

Siebert, R. (1976/1977) 'Horkheimer's Sociology of Religion', *Telos* 30: 127–44.

Steinman, C. (2005) 'Beyond Eurocentrism: The Frankfurt School and Whiteness Theory', in M. Pensky (ed.) *Globalizing Critical Theory*, New York: Rowman & Littlefield.

Taylor, C. (2007) *A Secular Age*, Cambridge: Belknap Press of Harvard University Press.

Walker, R.B.J. (1997) 'The Subject of Security' in Keith Krause and Michael C. Williams (eds) *Critical Security Studies: Concepts and Cases*, Abingdon: Routledge.

_____ (1999) 'The Hierarchization of Political Community', *Review of International Studies* 25: 151–6.

Wyn Jones, R. (2001) 'Introduction: Locating Critical International Relations Theory', in R. Wyn Jones (ed.) *Critical Theory and World Politics*, Boulder and London: Lynne Rienner.

_____ (2005) 'On Emancipation: Necessity, Capacity, and Concrete Utopias', in K. Booth (ed.) *Critical Security Studies and World Politics*, Boulder and London: Lynne Rienner.

7

VICO CONTRA KANT

The competing critical theories of Cox and Linklater

Richard Devetak

Introduction

This chapter juxtaposes the work of Robert W. Cox and Andrew Linklater. Both are regarded as leading critical theorists of International Relations, as this edited collection attests, but both offer very different accounts of what such a critical international theory might entail. This is largely a result of their contrasting intellectual heritages. Despite sharing a common inheritance from Karl Marx, Linklater and Cox draw upon vastly different literatures. Rather than survey and analyse the full range of similarities and differences in the critical theory programmes elaborated by Linklater and Cox, I shall focus on one aspect: their approach to history. Unlike many other critical international theorists – who tend to limit their temporal horizons to the very recent past, the present and, quite often, distant speculative futures – Linklater and Cox both engage seriously with history. However, as we shall see, they adopt very different approaches. Linklater's approach to history is informed and guided primarily by the philosopher of Königsberg, Immanuel Kant, and Cox's by the Neapolitan professor of rhetoric, Giambattista Vico. The rival understandings of history offered by these two eighteenth-century thinkers lead our twenty-first century thinkers to develop divergent critical theories.

Reflecting on his identity in the context of International Relations as a discipline, Robert W. Cox, in the interview published in this volume (Chapter 2), recalls Susan Strange's description of him as an eccentric (this volume, 17). Among the reasons Cox concurs with Strange's judgement is that in IR he is almost alone in writing about Vico, Sorel or Collingwood (this volume, 18). This is undoubtedly true when considering the work that currently passes under the banner of 'critical theory'. Unfashionably, Cox fails to engage with the intellectuals of Paris and Frankfurt who have dominated various strains of 'critical theory' in International Relations. Engagement with the writings of Jacques Derrida, Michel Foucault and Emmanuel Levinas are entirely absent.

Still more surprisingly, Cox neglects to engage even with the Frankfurt School of Critical Theory – there is no mention of Max Horkheimer, Theodor Adorno, Walter Benjamin, or Herbert Marcuse, nor even Jürgen Habermas. Indeed, the only times Cox seems to mention Frankfurt School thinkers is to explain that he has never read them, and that his work developed independently, and in ignorance, of the work carried out at the Institute of Social Research in Frankfurt (this volume, 18). So although Cox has used the term 'critical theory' and is often aligned with the Frankfurt School, there is little substance to the alignment, a point recently emphasized by Anthony Leysens (2008). This accounts for Cox's apparent eccentricity when placed alongside Linklater, Mark Hoffman and Richard K. Ashley, all of whom paid large intellectual debts to the Frankfurt School. To gain a better understanding of the divergence within critical theory represented by Cox on one side and Linklater on the other, it will be instructive to reflect on the thinkers upon whom they draw, and the kinds of conceptual and historiographical resources they supply. But before attending to the divergent intellectual histories, it is necessary first to outline the conventional understanding of critical international theory's sources.

Conventional narratives of the origins of critical international theory

Critical Theory finds its origins in the Institute of Social Research, which was established under the Directorship of Max Horkheimer in 1923 (Jay 1973). Critical Theory's research programme, to summarize, was concerned with understanding and critically analysing the central features of the modern social condition. In addition to highlighting the pathological features of modernity, Critical theorists were also at pains to identify and recover sources of potential social change. Through a method of immanent critique, Critical Theory conducted philosophical and sociological enquiries guided by an interest in emancipation or, to put it differently, the dismantling of social structures of domination and oppression. The dominant intellectual influences of the thinkers associated with the Institute include Kant, Hegel and Marx, as well as late nineteenth and early twentieth-century thinkers such as Nietzsche, Weber and Freud. It was from this array of German philosophers, social theorists and psychoanalysts that Critical Theory took its direction.

Although Max Horkheimer and Theodor Adorno would write a withering critique of the Enlightenment in *Dialectic of Enlightenment* (1972), they did not entirely forsake it or the forms of critical reasoning improvised by Kant in his three critiques. Their point was that one form of Enlightenment reason – instrumental or technical reason – had become dominant, and in colonizing vast areas of social and private life had introduced numerous modern pathologies. The end result was that the Enlightenment turned on itself, becoming totalitarian (Horkheimer and Adorno 1972: 6). The will to dominate nature had expanded and transformed into a general will to exercise domination over men, they argued.

Writing in the aftermath of two World Wars, the Gulag and the Holocaust, it is perhaps unsurprising that the leading figures of the Frankfurt School should indict the Enlightenment as its pathological instrumentalization of reason became 'an instrument of rational administration by the wholly enlightened as they steer[ed] society toward barbarism' (Horkheimer and Adorno 1972: 20). Although the *Dialectic of Enlightenment* may have left little space for a reconstruction of Enlightenment reason and the 'project of modernity', elsewhere, especially in the writings of Habermas, the Frankfurt School engaged in a critique of reason intended to transform and reconstruct it for the practical moral and political purposes of replacing forms of domination with more just, free and democratic forms of society. According to Habermas (1983; 1987), the 'project of modernity' was formulated by eighteenth-century Enlightenment thinkers who sought to release progressive social potentials capable of redeeming reason and reconciling it with notions of universal freedom and justice.

Central here is Kant. He has been at the heart of Habermas's effort to reconstruct the project of modernity (Habermas 1997), just as he has to efforts by critical international theorists (Devetak 1995; Linklater 1990: 21; Neufeld 1995: 14–15; Shapcott 2010: 26ff). Of particular importance here are Kant's historico-political essays written late in his life: 'Idea for a Universal History with a Cosmopolitan Purpose' (1970a), 'An Answer to the Question: "What is Enlightenment?"' (1970b), 'Perpetual Peace: A Philosophical Sketch' (1970c). There is no need here to provide a close contextual reading of Kant's argument; it suffices to make three points. First, that Kant conceives of Enlightenment as intimately tied up with the freedom to make public use of critical reason (Kant 1970b; Habermas 1989: 102–17). Second, that history is governed by the cosmopolitan purpose of perfecting republican civil and global constitutional orders capable of achieving 'the supreme political good – perpetual peace' (Kant 1970c: 175).[1] Third, that Kant envisioned his philosophical history as a propaedeutic of the cosmopolitan constitutional order. As Habermas observed, 'by virtue of the fact that its insights entered into the public's processes of critical reflection, the philosophy of history itself was to become a part of the enlightenment diagnosed as history's course' (1989: 115–16). For Kant, the cosmopolitan end enjoined by the Enlightenment project is the moral construction of a kingdom of ends wherein humanity, through the public articulation of a philosophical history, achieves universal freedom based on the universal principle of right.

Linklater's Kantian critical theory of International Relations

Linklater's Kantian programme of critical international theory has been, from its first formulation in *Men and Citizens in the Theory of International Relations* (1982), crucially supplemented by Marx. Linklater's attempt to combine Kant and Marx in a critical theory of international relations was highly original. Its originality was perhaps heightened by the fact that it came at a time when International Relations, especially in the US, was enamoured of the realist and positivist theory programme set out by Kenneth Waltz in *Theory of International Politics* (1979).

By contrast, Linklater's *Men and Citizens* laid the foundations for an ambitious research agenda concerned to recover a 'critique of the international states-system', and to establish 'a non-rationalist foundation' for moral and political obligations to humankind (1982: x–xi). If Waltz exhorted International Relations scholars to cultivate an intellectual persona committed to a positivist conception of knowledge and an analytical conception of method aimed at providing an explanatory theory of international relations, Linklater countered with an exhortation to cultivate an intellectual persona committed to a critical conception of knowledge and a method of philosophical history aimed at providing a normative or emancipatory theory of international relations. Kant and Marx were to provide the intellectual resources for this explicitly critical and emancipatory theoretical programme.

While Linklater has drawn upon both Kant and Marx, there can be little doubt that Kant has provided the moral compass for Linklater's employment of Marx. Marx may provide indispensible categories and concepts of social theory, yet they remain in need of normative orientation by the cosmopolitan purpose elaborated by Kant. In other words, Kant provides the normative framework within which Marx's theoretical resources are reconstructed. It is on the Kantian normative framework that I want to focus because it supplies a philosophical history that not only combats the historiographical assumption of recurrence and repetition that defines Waltz's neorealist theory of international relations, but also distinguishes it from the historicist mode of critical theory advocated by Robert Cox.

Cosmopolitan Enlightenment: Kantian philosophical history

As Linklater explained in the 'Preface' to *Men and Citizens*, the 'principles of a universal history' underpinning his critical international theory are 'exemplified in, but not completed by, the Kantian theory of international relations' (1982: xi). It is in this context then that Linklater has pursued, across three books (1982; 1990 and 1998), a sophisticated attempt to complete Kantian and post-Kantian forms of moral and political theory by the addition of Marxist and post-Marxist forms of social theory and historical sociology. Although the details of Linklater's integration of Kant and Marx have changed over the years, what has not changed is Linklater's commitment to a Kantian philosophy of history.

In *Men and Citizens,* Linklater employs a 'philosophical history' to suggest that the conflict at the heart of modern international life – the tension individuals experience by simultaneously bearing the personae of 'man' and 'citizen' – may only be capable of resolution if 'the human capacity for self-determination can be expressed more perfectly' (Linklater 1982: 138). Inspired by Kant, Linklater argues that '[t]he enhancement of the condition of civility within the state is but one step within a much more broadly conceived historical process which culminates in the granting of political expression to the idea of humanity' (Linklater 1982: 55). This is Linklater's way of expressing the Kantian hope that the persona of 'citizen' will eventually give way to 'man' in the projected 'kingdom of ends', thus overcoming the extant tension at the heart of modern international life.

Of particular interest for our purposes is Linklater's reliance on Kant's philosophy of history. What Linklater (1982: 116) finds attractive in Kant is the progressivist reading of history whereby states, like individuals, learn to overcome their ethical particularity in order to bring into existence a universal kingdom of ends where universal justice and perpetual peace will prevail. This historical movement towards perpetual peace rested on a particular conception of history which Kant had previously sketched in his essay on the 'Idea for a Universal History with a Cosmopolitan Purpose' (1970a).

Philosophical history, as proposed by Kant, demonstrates and promotes the movement towards the 'completion' or 'perfection' of humankind's 'natural' or 'original capacities'. This, he believed, depended on the transformative effects achieved by perfecting domestic and international political constitutions, thereby realizing 'the highest purpose of nature, a universal *cosmopolitan existence*' (Kant 1970a: 50–51). While Linklater clearly eschews the notion of nature's purposiveness and downplays the notion of perfecting humankind's natural capacities, he remains committed to a philosophical history that, by describing and supporting the progressive realization of human freedom, participates in the cosmopolitan transformation of political community.

This philosophical history operates at two levels: the level of theory and the level of empirical history. At the level of theory, Linklater posits a dialectical passage from the moral and political thought of Pufendorf, through Vattel, to Kant. 'Each [thinker] progresses beyond the other' (Linklater 1982: 60), overcoming weaknesses and correcting inconsistencies, culminating in Kant's theory of international relations. Even if Kant's theory remains to be completed by Hegel and Marx, or Habermas and Norbert Elias, it represents something like the crowning moment in this philosophical history.

At the level of empirical history, the task of philosophical history is to track the progress of universal human freedom in the phenomenal world, to identify obstructions as well as positive developments. In the absence of this Kantian philosophical history, critical international theory would lack a philosophical benchmark, such as the cosmopolitan 'kingdom of ends', against which to judge international history. It is for this reason that Linklater affirms that '[t]he philosophy of history creates the basis for a critical theory of international relations' (1982: 165). It makes possible an international theory from the moral point of view; a theory not just capable of critique, but of pointing the way to 'realising the moral life in an international system of states' (Linklater 1990: 138).

That said, Linklater was well aware that Kant needed a social-theoretical supplement if philosophical history were to contribute to an understanding of empirical rationalization processes. For Linklater, the work of Karl Marx was decisive, offering the methodological means of analysing the social, economic and technological forces driving history and shaping the boundaries of political community. In *Beyond Realism and Marxism* (1990) Linklater proposed a theory which would integrate the multiple logics of modernity: the geopolitical logics of war and state-building, the capitalist logics of production and accumulation, and the normative and civilizing logics of international society.

To reconstruct the development of this third set of logics, Linklater has engaged closely with the writings of two distinct bodies of literature: English School writings on the historical evolution of rules, norms and institutions in the society of states (Bull 1977; Wight 1977; Linklater and Suganami 2006), and the writings of Norbert Elias on civilizing processes (Elias 2000; Linklater 2004; Linklater and Mennell 2010). Linklater argues that Elias and the English School complement each other by virtue of Elias's focus on processes of internal pacification and civilization, and the English School's focus on external civilizing processes. In both cases, the emphasis has been on how restraints on violence have been historically developed and cultivated. This has led Linklater to embark on an ambitious, three-volume, historically and sociologically-informed study of the way that different states-systems have conceptualized harm and devised norms, rules and institutions for its minimization.

Paralleling Kant's 'Idea for a Universal History with a Cosmopolitan Purpose' (1970a), Linklater recently titled an article 'Towards a Sociology of Global Morals with an "Emancipatory Intent"' (2007). This suggests that his move to write longer-term histories should be read as an attempt to reconstruct, rather than abandon, Kantian philosophical history by rendering it more empirical. To summarize, Linklater's critical international theory approaches history through a Kantian philosophical history. This historiographical genre encourages a critical theory characterized by a normative philosophy with a cosmopolitan or emancipatory intent. History is put to the service of normative philosophy, tracing the gradual realization of reason and freedom.

Cox's Vichian critical theory of International Relations

Cox, as we have seen, disavows the Frankfurt School as an intellectual source for his critical theory. Interestingly, in the interview here and elsewhere, Cox (1996) also disavows any intellectual debts to the Enlightenment. This again will surprise many, since Linklater, Ken Booth and others take their orientation from the eighteenth-century Enlightenment, especially the cosmopolitan moral and political project of Kant. Instead, Cox mentions thinkers more commonly characterized as anti-Enlightenment: Edmund Burke, the great critic of the French Revolution, and Giambattista Vico, whose emphasis on culture so interested Johann Gottfried Herder (1744–1803), the ex-pupil of Kant.

If this were not bad enough, Cox also acknowledges debts to writers assigned to the traditions of political realism and historicism – traditions usually considered anathema to critical theory. Among the names Cox lists are E. H. Carr, Friedrich Meinecke and his student Ludwig Dehio, as well as the 'diabolical' figurehead of realism, Niccolò Machiavelli. To be sure, Linklater makes good use of realists and historicists too, but always through a Kantian philosophical history that claims to supersede them. Of course, Cox also recognizes the large debt he owes to Antonio

Gramsci, who, as is well known, informs a good deal of Cox's theory of historical materialism (Cox 1983; Bieler and Morton 2004). It may be the case that Cox's long-term engagement with the sickly Sardinian hunch-backed Communist Party leader is enough to outweigh his affection for the realists; but if we hope to gain a better appreciation of Cox's critical theory and its distinctiveness from other critical international theories, such as Linklater's, we need to understand the reasons for his interest in realism and historicism.

In the remainder of this chapter I want to suggest that Cox's version of critical international theory inherits a critical attitude and method derived from a tradition of early modern political thought which has remained distinct from Kantian-inspired or Enlightenment-forged philosophical history. This alternative form of critical method was designed to historicize and 'detranscendentalize' the way people think and write about politics, not to disclose the unfolding of reason and freedom in history. This form of political criticism first originated in the Renaissance courts of secularizing princely authorities who were determined to develop critical humanist methods for analysing history. In other words, it was designed to defend the state (and the prince) against attack by moralists as much as by internal insurgents or external foes.

A full account would require exposition of the Renaissance revival of *studia humanitatis* (humanist studies) and of its anti-scholastic tendencies – all of which cannot be undertaken here. For Renaissance humanists influenced by Cicero, the hypertechnical logic of Christian-Aristotelian scholasticism was a barbarism lacking any practical application (Copenhaven and Schmitt 1992: 29). A major deficiency, according to humanists, was its unhistorical method. For scholastics, the classical philosophical texts were to be read as if they were outside historical time; they were wrenched from the particular time and place of their production and transported to the higher plane of transcendental philosophy where they could be examined as intricate assemblages of propositions (Grafton 1999). Classic texts were thus little more than disembodied statements which could yield insight, or not, according to their capacity to answer questions in an unchanging present (*nunc stans*), against universal principles of reason and justice.

Against scholasticism's universalistic and moralistic approach to politics, humanism sought to develop a historically-contingent approach which recognized and preserved the autonomy of the political. In the sixteenth and seventeenth centuries, humanism began to draw more heavily upon Cornelius Tacitus than Cicero as a source of inspiration (Tuck 1993: 39ff). The Roman senator, whose histories recount Rome's bloody civil wars, became one of Europe's most fashionable intellectual influences – with intellectuals such as Justus Lipsius combining Tacitism with scepticism and reason of state to furnish an approach to politics which resolved to sacrifice Christian moral ideals for the end of civil peace (Tuck 1993: 45–64). In the context of Europe's fractious religious wars, the moral politics offered by scholasticism seemed too abstract, too detached from history and political practice, and insufficiently detached from the confessionalism driving the violent conflict. By bringing politics down to earth, humanists from Machiavelli and Francesco

Guicciardini to Lipsius and Paolo Sarpi were bent on treating the Church just like any other political actor, unmasking its mundane political interests and denying it any transcendental privileges.

It is out of this Renaissance humanism that seventeenth-century absolutist theorists of natural law such as Samuel Pufendorf and Christian Thomasius developed their anti-metaphysical historiographies (Hunter 2001). The critical historiographical methods forged by Renaissance humanists and further developed by absolutist natural law theorists were taken up in the eighteenth century by historians composing what J. G. A. Pocock (1999) called 'Enlightened narratives'. These histories – narrated by Pietro Giannone, David Hume, John Robertson and Edward Gibbon among others – shared with Renaissance humanist histories the historicizing urge and with the absolutist theorists of natural law the secularizing urge. Politics, as understood by exponents of this humanist, anti-metaphysical approach to history, was a mundane civil matter incapable of resolution by appeal to higher moral norms. Political orders, domestic and international, were to be founded on procedures, practices and institutions compatible with civil government. The key to understanding these procedures, practices and institutions lay with history rather than philosophy.

I want to suggest that it is in this intellectual context that Cox's interest in Vico makes sense. In both the interview published here and elsewhere, Cox repeatedly expresses an interest in historiography and historical modes of understanding. Indeed, in the interview he goes so far as to equate critical theory with an 'historical mode of thinking' (this volume, 20).

Neapolitan Enlightenment: Vico's civil historical method

If we accept – with Pocock (1999), Ian Hunter (2001, 2004) and others – that there are multiple Enlightenments, we may yet conceive Vico as an Enlightenment thinker. After all, like the humanist and Enlightenment historians discussed above, he insists on non-transcendental civil history as the most appropriate context for understanding human society. This, I believe, may explain why Cox finds Vico so attractive and so useful for the kind of critical international theory he proposes.

A long way from the French and German centres of Enlightenment thought that were so fashionable in his day, Vico was a participant in the Neapolitan Enlightenment (Robertson 2005: ch. 5). Among the various reasons Cox takes an interest in Vico we may consider two: first, Vico's *New Science* (2001) offered a critique of the dominant form of philosophical reasoning in his day, Cartesianism; and second, the *New Science* emphasized the changing historical forms of 'human civil institutions'. Each of these Vichian features is present in Cox's critical theory. Like Cox (1981), Vico reacted strongly to the privileging of naturalistic philosophy (positivism in Cox's case) by advocating a historicist approach. Similarly, Cox (1981; 1983) adopts an approach to world orders that, like Vico, takes them as civil institutions interacting with ideas, and susceptible to modification over time.

Cox's (1981; 1985) critique of positivism echoes Vico's rejection of Cartesian philosophy. In both cases, a philosophy that abstracts human consciousness from the world is indicted. It is in this context that Vico posited his *verum-factum* doctrine (the true is the made) as an alternative approach to knowledge. This 'maker's knowledge' doctrine implies that making something gives the maker a special knowledge or insight into what is made. The upshot is that humans are better positioned to gain knowledge of history rather than nature, since they have made the former but not the latter. Only God, the argument goes, can know nature. As Vico (2001: 119–20) explains:

> *The civil world is certainly the creation of humankind.* And consequently, the principles of the civil world can and must be discovered *within the modifications of the human mind.* If we reflect on this, we can only wonder why all the philosophers have so earnestly pursued a knowledge of the world of nature, which only God can know as its creator, while they neglected to study the world of nations, or civil world, which people can in fact know because they created it.

Cox (1996: 29) glosses the *verum-factum* doctrine's applicability to history by saying that 'history is the most appropriate form of human knowledge, since history was made by men and therefore men are capable of understanding what they have made'. By emphasizing the constitutive human elements in civil history, Vico's historiographical method may thus be considered a continuation and adaptation of the humanist methods improvised by Renaissance historians, absolutist natural law theorists, and Enlightenment civil historians.

Two and a half centuries after Giambattista Vico improvised his 'new form of criticism' to undermine fashionable Cartesian natural philosophy, Robert Cox set out an agenda of critical theory to undermine the positivism of mainstream international relations. In both cases, an historical mode of knowledge was deployed to combat scientific pretensions and to historicize human civil institutions. For Vico, writing the history of the civil world required a method capable of understanding changing cultural, legal, and political conditions, for these conditions form the contexts within which civil institutions such as nations or states rise and fall. Vico rejected Cartesian natural philosophy because its scientific method extinguished history and denied the constitutive role played by ideas in making human civil institutions. Ultimately, it remained incapable of grasping the interplay of ideas and institutions, and thus could not contribute to an understanding of 'the world of nations in its historical reality' (Vico 2001: 84).

For neither Vico nor Cox does history have to answer to normative philosophy. History's purpose is not governed by the cosmopolitan intent to trace the progressive unfolding of reason and freedom that characterizes Kantian philosophical history. Rather, it is to make sense of the changing ways in which civil institutions have shaped human experience. This historiographical genre encourages a critical theory characterized by an empirical intellectual history with mundane or civil intent. Even though it may contribute to understanding the potentials and limits of human reason and freedom, such a history makes no claim to reach for higher moral purposes.

Conclusion

This chapter has attempted to provide a brief account of two leading exponents of critical international theory: Andrew Linklater and Robert W. Cox. It carried out its task by historiographically redescribing the approach to history embodied in each version of critical international theory. In appealing to such radically different thinkers as Kant and Vico, it can be no surprise that Linklater and Cox cultivate such different approaches to history, and, in the end, elaborate such divergent programmes of critical international theory. Against the dominance of Kantian philosophical history in critical international theory, there is a case to make for accepting Cox's claim that Vico's historical approach is also 'that of critical theory' (1981: 133). The purpose of this chapter has not been to pass judgement on either approach, or to choose one over the other, but to clarify some points of difference that arise from these rival conceptions of history, and to encourage further reflection on the historiographical assumptions underpinning contemporary expressions of critical international theory.

Note

1 See also Bohman and Lutz-Bachmann (1997), Cronin (2003) and Schmidt (1992).

Bibliography

Bieler, A. and Morton, A.D. (2004) 'A Critical Theory Route to Hegemony, World Order and Historical Change: Neo-Gramscian Perspectives in International Relations', *Capital and Class* 28: 85–113.
Bohman, J. and Lutz-Bachmann, M. (eds) (1997), *Perpetual Peace: Essays on Kant's Cosmopolitan Ideal*, Cambridge: MIT Press.
Bull, H. (1977) *The Anarchical Society: A Study of Order in World Politics*, London: Macmillan.
Cox, R.W. (1981) 'Social Forces, States and World Orders: Beyond International Relations Theory', *Millennium* 19(2): 126–55.
_____ (1983) 'Gramsci, Hegemony and International Relations: An Essay in Method', *Millennium* 12(2): 162–75.
_____ (1985) 'Postscript 1985', in R.O. Keohane (ed.) *Neorealism and its Critics*, New York: Columbia University Press.
_____ (1996) 'Influences and Commitments', in R.W. Cox and T.J. Sinclair, *Approaches to World Order*, Cambridge: Cambridge University Press.
Copenhaven, B.P. and Schmitt, C.B. (1992) *Renaissance Philosophy*, Oxford: Oxford University Press.
Cronin, C. (2003) 'Kant's Politics of Enlightenment', *Journal of the History of Philosophy* 41(1): 51–80.
Devetak, R. (1995) 'The Project of Modernity and International Relations Theory', *Millennium* 24(1): 27–51.

Elias, N. (2000) *The Civilizing Process: Sociogenetic and Psychogenetic Investigations*, revised edn, Oxford: Blackwell.

Grafton, A. (1999) 'The Humanist as Reader', in G. Cavallo and R. Chartier (eds) *A History of Reading in the West*, trans. L. Cochrane, Amherst: University of Massachusetts Press.

Habermas, J. (1983) 'Modernity – An Incomplete Project', trans. S. Benhabib, in H. Foster (ed.) *The Anti-Aesthetic: Essays on Postmodern Culture*, Seattle: Bay Press.

____ (1987) *The Philosophical Discourse of Modernity: Twelve Lectures*, trans. F.G. Lawrence, Cambridge: Polity Press.

____ (1989) *The Structural Transformation of the Public Sphere: An Inquiry into a Category of Bourgeois Society*, trans. T. Burger, Cambridge: Polity Press.

____ (1997) 'Kant's Idea of Perpetual Peace, With the Benefit of Two Hundred Years' Hindsight', in J. Bohman, and M. Lutz-Bachmann (eds) *Perpetual Peace: Essays on Kant's Cosmopolitan Ideal*, Cambridge: MIT Press.

Horkheimer, M. and Adorno, T. (1972) *Dialectic of Enlightenment*, trans. E. Jephcott, London: Allen Lane.

Hunter, I. (2001) *Rival Enlightenments: Civil and Metaphysical Philosophy in Early Modern Germany*, Cambridge: Cambridge University Press.

____ (2004) 'Multiple Enlightenments: Rival *Aufklärer* at the University of Halle, 1690–1730', in M. Fitzpatrick *et al.* (eds) *The Enlightenment World*, London: Routledge.

Jay, M. (1973) *The Dialectical Imagination: A History of the Frankfurt School and the Institute of Social Research, 1923–1950*, Boston: Little, Brown.

Kant, I. (1970a) 'Idea for a Universal History with a Cosmopolitan Purpose', in H. Reiss (ed.) *Kant's Political Writings*, trans. H.B. Nisbet, Cambridge: Cambridge University Press.

____ (1970b) 'Answer to the Question: "What is Enlightenment?"', in H. Reiss (ed.) *Kant's Political Writings*, trans. H.B. Nisbet, Cambridge: Cambridge University Press.

____ (1970c) 'Perpetual Peace: A Philosophical Sketch', in H. Reiss (ed.) *Kant's Political Writings*, trans. H.B. Nisbet, Cambridge: Cambridge University Press.

Leysens, A. (2008) *The Critical Theory of Robert W. Cox: Fugitive or Guru?*, London: Palgrave.

Linklater, A. (1982) *Men and Citizens in the Theory of International Relations*, London: Macmillan.

____ (1990) *Beyond Realism and Marxism: Critical Theory and International Relations*, London: Macmillan.

____ (1998) *The Transformation of Political Community: Ethical Foundations of the Post-Westphalian Era*, Cambridge: Polity Press.

____ (2004) 'Norbert Elias, the "Civilizing Process" and the Sociology of International Relations', *International Politics* 41(1): 3–35.

____ (2007) 'Towards a Sociology of Global Morals with an "Emancipatory Intent"', *Review of International Studies* 33, Special Issue: 135–50.

Linklater, A. and Mennell, S. (2010) 'Norbert Elias, The Civilizing Process: Sociogenetic and Psychogenetic Investigations – An Overview and Assessment', *History and Theory* 49(3): 384–411.

Linklater, A. and Suganami, H. (2006) *The English School of International Relations: A Contemporary Assessment*, Cambridge: Cambridge University Press.

Neufeld, M. (1995) *The Restructuring of International Relations Theory*, Cambridge: Cambridge University Press.

Pocock, J.G.A. (1999) *Barbarism and Religion, Volume Two: Narratives of Civil Government*, Cambridge: Cambridge University Press.

Robertson, J. (2005) *The Case for Enlightenment: Scotland and Naples 1680–1760*, Cambridge: Cambridge University Press.

Schmidt, J. (1992) 'What Enlightenment Was: How Moses Mendelssohn and Immanuel Kant Answered the *Berlinische Monatsschrift*', *Journal of the History of Philosophy* 30(1): 77–101.

Shapcott, R. (2010) *International Ethics: A Critical Introduction*, Cambridge: Polity Press.

Tuck, R. (1993) *Philosophy and Government, 1572–1651*, Cambridge: Cambridge University Press.

Vico, G. (2001) *The New Science of Giambattista Vico*, translation of the third edition (1744), trans. David Marsh, Harmondsworth: Penguin Books.

Waltz, K. (1979) *Theory of International Politics*, New York: Random House.

Wight, M. (1977) *Systems of States*, Leicester: Leicester University Press.

PART III

Debating the Limits

8

ORIENTALISM AND THE POVERTY OF THEORY THREE DECADES ON

Bringing Eastern and subaltern agency back into Critical IR Theory

John M. Hobson

Introduction

While I shall draw on some of the points made in the interviews, my main objective is to provide a sympathetic-critical engagement with Critical IR Theory (CIRT). In essence, I seek to cast the critical gaze back onto CIRT to appraise the direction that it has taken in the last three decades so that CIRT might be reformed in the coming years. Note that this is not simply a task undertaken so as to think about possible future trajectories; for I believe that CIRT would not be living up to its name were it to be focused only on criticizing orthodox or problem solving theory. Indeed, failure to open itself up to a critical self-reflexive gaze would at the very least flirt with the proposition that CIRT has ossified into a new orthodoxy.

My argument will be that to date CIRT has fulfilled properly only half of its mandate. For while it has succeeded admirably in revealing structures of power in the world, it has largely, though not completely, failed to follow through with an analysis of how the agency of subaltern and non-Western actors have had an impact on shaping both the West as well as global politics/economics more generally. Overcoming this lacuna is particularly important for at least two reasons. First, in the current conjuncture, which spans the post-1989 era in general and especially the post-9/11 period in particular, it is all the more urgent for CIRT to pay special attention to the role of non-elite and non-Western agency within world politics. For we are living in a time when international theory – whether developed by liberals, neo-Conservatives, or certain types of realists – is preoccupied with the need for the West to intervene in the non-Western world, either to remake it along 'progressive' Western lines (as in broadly paternalist liberalism and neo-Conservatism), or as a means of containing the East in order to secure world order within a configuration that maintains the supremacy of Western civilization, as in more realist-inspired works.[1] Without an analysis of Eastern agency we are left merely with the Eurocentric representation of the West's monopoly of progressive agency; an idiom that underpins the 'new imperialism'.

Second, it is insufficient merely to reveal structures of power within world politics without also following through to consider the agency of non-elite actors. For in both cases, the upshot is to present a pessimistic picture, if not one of despair, since it leads to a reification of top-down power processes, whether these be in the form of structures of power (hyper-structuralism) or elite actors (hyper-elitism). Here the demands of one critical theorist, who is sensitive to the issue of subaltern agency, are pertinent. He argues for the need to

> bring [subaltern] people back in …as the agents at the centre of historical change. Otherwise, we are left with socially barren formulations that strip people and agency from history, leaving only 'structure' as the over-determining 'reality'. When globalization implies 'the death of politics', it feeds on political cynicism, defeatism, and immobilism.
>
> *(Gills 2000: 6)*

Bringing non-elite agency back in, I would argue, starts to redress this intellectual imbalance not for reasons of intellectual niceties but as a means of galvanizing politics from below, not least so as to challenge the new imperialism. For it is a common strategy of imperial elites to portray resistance as futile – indeed, it was the very leitmotif of British imperialism. And equally, one of the key pre-requisites for the decolonization thrust was the need to first regain a sense of dignity for the colonized (Césaire 2001, Fanon 2004) – something which, in the current conjuncture of a revivified politics of Western neo-imperialism, can be promoted by revealing moments of Eastern agency.

When viewed through this agentially-sensitive lens, and when we simultaneously reverse our critical gaze on CIRT, a set of scholars and publications different from the 'usual suspects' emerge in the foreground. For it is just over three decades now since three key publications emerged that cast a critical gaze on social, philosophical, developmental and IR theory in both their orthodox and especially critical manifestations. First and foremost was E.P. Thompson's magisterial text *The Poverty of Theory* (1995), which provided a robust and indeed caustic critique of Althusserian Marxist philosophy. Second, Robert Brenner's 'The Origins of Capitalist Development: a Critique of Neo-Smithian Marxism' (1977), which provided an equally robust and caustic critique of world-systems theory (WST).[2] Third and finally, Edward Said's *Orientalism* (2003), which provided a critique of both orthodox and critical (Marxist) theory by revealing their Eurocentric roots.

Although these were aimed at different intellectual audiences, the lowest common denominator that links them concerns the critique of structuralism in critical theory – especially Marxism – and the associated elision of subaltern agency. Both Thompson and Brenner sought to bring the agency of class struggle back into focus in order to transcend the rigid structuralism of Althusserianism and WST respectively, while Said was, or at least became later on in his life, interested in the process and effects of Eastern subaltern agency in shaping the West and global politics (Said 1994 and 2004) – a theme that has been marginalized, denigrated or simply denied by the Eurocentrism of orthodox- and Marxist-theory. A key part of my argument here is that CIRT's not infrequent elision of subaltern agency within the West finds its corollary in its Eurocentrism and dismissal of Eastern agency. Thus, given that the two elisions are inter-connected, it makes sense to treat these three scholars' contributions together.

When viewing CIRT in the last three decades I identify three inter-related fetishisms that have plagued this body of literature: hyper-structuralism, hyper-elitism, and hyper-Westernism (or simply Eurocentrism). That CIRT, of which Marxism is a particularly important contributor, has fallen prey to these traps is particularly ironic. For while Gramscianism superseded WST – not least because of the latter's structural determinism – nevertheless the former has, more often than not, fallen into the very trap that Brenner accused WST of falling into. Second, the extreme irony emerges insofar as I can think of no better thinker than Karl Marx who succeeded in making structures of power entwined with bottom-up subaltern agency a core theoretical theme; something that was revealed in his famous quote from 'The Eighteenth Brumaire' – that 'men make their own history but not under conditions of their own choosing' (Marx 1950: 225).

My aim is not simply to reveal these fetishisms but to point out the need for CIRT to go beyond them so as to provide fresh directions that might be undertaken in the coming years. My claim is not that *all* of the representatives of these critical theories have fallen into these traps – and I will signal various examples that have avoided them – but rather to suggest that much, if not the majority, of CIRT has reproduced these fetishisms. My critique, however, is offered as a constructive means to offer ways of emancipating CIRT from its current limitations.

Half way there . . .

My key criticism of CIRT is that while it has succeeded in revealing structures of power within world politics, it has nevertheless failed to follow through on this so as to reveal sites of non-elite agency. Why this is the case is worth briefly reflecting upon. First, Gramscianism has generally viewed the conjuncture of world politics since 1979 in highly pessimistic terms. Thus, although the era of US hegemony broke down in the 1970s, the hegemony of capital was reinstated after 1979 by the neoliberal revolution that was instigated within the West – especially Britain and America – as well as across the world by the anti-revolutionary vanguard parties of the Washington Consensus, the IMF and the World Bank, as they imposed neoliberal conditionality and structural adjustment programmes. And, of course, the IMF was wheeled back into playing a prime role in the global economy during the era of the Third World debt crisis. Moreover, the prime role of the transnational capitalist class and the formation of a new historic bloc under post-US hegemonic globalization are also deemed to be important (Cox 1987; Gill 1990; Van der Pijl 1984). It is presumably this that Cox has in mind when, in his interview in this volume, he justifies his pessimism on the grounds that it enables an appreciation of the considerable obstacles to change – using the dashed hopes of the new Obama administration as an example (this volume, 24). Similarly, when pressed upon the question of the possibility of progress, Cox retreats further into an almost Nietzschean-type rejection of progressive Enlightenment thinking.[3]

However, at the same time I want to suggest that this pessimistic predisposition also emanates from the Eurocentrism of much of Gramscianism. Because I have dealt with this issue in relation to Cox's work elsewhere (Hobson 2007: 95–99 and 2012: ch. 10), I shall not repeat all the details here. In essence, the Eurocentric traces can be located in a number of areas which comprise: an excessive focus on the hyper-agency of Western hegemons (British and American but also, on occasion, Dutch and Venetian) in the making of the global political economy;[4] an excessive focus on the Western origins of globalization in historical perspective, coupled with an elision of Eastern agency either in the making of globalization in the first place, or in shaping and resisting Western neo-imperialist domination in the last 60 years more generally; and a general tendency to ignore the role of subaltern Western agency, either in the re-making of the West or in the making of world politics more generally.

Of course, the immediate response would be that Gramscianism places a great deal of emphasis upon counter-hegemonic movements. But when one scans many of the principal representatives it appears that what is thought of as solid in effect simply melts into air. Thus, when one scans Cox's major writings, even when there is a discussion of counter-movements (in this case, Western ones), it is clear that the prospects for successful counter-hegemony are portrayed as extremely poor, with the Western working class appearing as all but overwhelmed by the hyper-power of the dominant capitalist elites (Cox 1987: 368–91; 1996: 191–207, 364–6, 471–90).

Again, in a key 1995 volume edited by Bjorn Hettne, a series of largely Gramscian authors set out to merge a Polanyian conception of the 'double movement' with a Gramscian analysis of hegemony and counter-hegemony. However, on closer inspection, it turns out that the emphasis on the first hegemonic movement is overplayed while the second (counter-hegemonic) movement is heavily downplayed. Thus, for example, Eastern counter-hegemony is accorded a one-page discussion in Stephen Gill's 34-page chapter, and a two-page discussion in Yoshikazu Sakomoto's 14-page chapter. One can similarly scan through Stephen Gill's (1993) edited volume with similar results.

Overall, the Gramscian emphasis on the overwhelming power of the transnational capitalist class (e.g., Cox 1996; Gill 1990), as well as the power of the West over the East more generally, means that Marxists seem all too frequently much more at home in talking about the power of the powerful than they do with the 'power of the powerless'.[5] In this way, they tend to blend the problems of hyper-elitism and hyper-structuralism at the expense of subaltern agency in general and Eastern agency in particular. Indeed, the problem of Western hyper-structuralism leads directly into the trap of *Eurofetishism*. For while Marx talked about 'commodity fetishism', which had the ultimate effect of naturalizing and eternalizing capitalism insofar as it failed to reveal the underlying social relations of production, so Gramscianism unwittingly naturalizes and *eternalizes* Western domination since it ignores the relations of civilizations and obscures the resistance and agency that non-Western movements and states invoke.

These problems of hyper-elitism, hyper-structuralism and Eurocentrism/ Eurofetishism are also found in much of postmodern theory, the effect of which is to write out of the script of world politics the contributions of subaltern and non-Western agents.[6] Here, the tendency is to exaggerate the power of the West to contain and repress the East, with the latter all too often appearing as a mere passive object of the former. And it is of course deeply ironic that postmodernists such as Baudrillard, Lyotard, Mouffe, Deleuze and Foucault have tended to reify the West as a self-contained entity while failing to recognize the interactive relationship between East and West, precisely because Said's conception of Orientalism/Eurocentrism rests on the Self/Other identity-formation process that Foucault first emphasized. Indeed, it is noteworthy that Said later criticized Foucault for ignoring the role of Eastern resistance in the making of global politics (Said 1994: 29–30, 335–6). Accordingly, Thompson's critique of Althusserianism can be applied to much of postmodernism and Gramscianism insofar as they not infrequently constitute a 'structuralism of stasis' (Thompson 1995: 6), thereby returning us to the problem of Eurofetishism once more.

A recent thrust of CIRT has seen the emergence of an *everyday life* approach, which draws much of its inspiration from Michel Foucault's (1980) concept of *governmentality*, as well as from the Marxist scholar Henri Lefebvre (1976). Three key critical IR theorists of note here are Paul Langley (2008), Matt Davies (2005) and Matthew Paterson (2007). As I have argued in detail elsewhere, this approach focuses on a 'logic of discipline' (Hobson and Seabrooke 2009). Here, the aim is to reveal how structures of power discipline, and are translated into, the practices of everyday life in order to denaturalize that which appears as natural and as 'common-sense'. Thus Langley, for example, shows how the transformation of pensions from 'defined benefits' to 'defined contributions' has transformed the practices of everyday life. In this case, while the individual perceives himself to be a 'free investing subject' who engages in financial self-discipline in order to accumulate long-term savings for his future pension, such a predisposition internalizes the repressive neoliberal politics and the idiom of the 'ownership society' that was first proclaimed by Margaret Thatcher. Similarly, Matthew Paterson (2007) critically interrogates the idea of the car as enhancing individual autonomy, arguing that the expansion of the car-owning public leads not to greater freedom but to greater environmental damage and ultimately to exacerbated levels of global injustice.

My problem is not with what has been done – for these approaches undoubtedly produce all manner of excellent insights – but with that which has not been considered. Such approaches take the initial first step of critique but do not fully follow through by revealing modes of subaltern agency in the making, not only of everyday life but also of the West and of world politics. The bigger point here is that much of CIRT's critical *modus operandi* is to reveal structures of power, with this being seen as an inherently emancipatory (intellectual) praxis. In his interview in this volume, Robert Cox echoes this tendency when he argues that critical theory's prime purpose is to critique existing power structures in order to open up an emancipatory space (this volume, 20). My purpose is by no means to undermine the importance of this move but rather to argue that we need to go one step further and follow through on this by considering how subaltern and everyday actors exercise agency in the making of their own lives, as well as those of others around and beyond them. For it seems to me that failure to do so leads back into the hyper-elitist, hyper-structuralist and Eurofetishist traps of rendering subaltern and Eastern agents, in the phraseology of Thompson, as but 'mere *träger* or vectors [ie., passive victims] of ulterior structural determinations' (Thompson 1995: 2–3). The route out of this *cul de sac*, then, requires revealing the bottom-up Eastern agential practices that also shape the West and world politics.

One small step for man … one necessary leap for Critical Theory?

I want to suggest that simply critiquing power and social inequality is a necessary but insufficient process for achieving a satisfactory critical theory. My case begins by returning to Karl Marx. It is certainly true that Marx believed that the proletariat was alienated under capitalism and that it could not necessarily recognize its own dire predicament. A Marxist critique of the exploitative nature of capitalism was an important means by which the proletariat could be brought to recognize this and thereby launch the transition of the proletariat from a class-in-itself to a class-for-itself. This much is consistent with CIRT as it is currently configured. But the key point is that for Marx, the dominant class was always challenged by the resistance of the working class – which is, of course, what he was alluding to in his famous claim that 'the history of all hitherto existing society is the history of class struggles' (Marx and Engels 1967: 79).

In my view, the key to Marx's approach – indeed what made it critical – is not simply that it reveals structures of power, crucial though this clearly is, but that it paints a picture of subaltern agency and resistance, not simply in the making of a better future but also in terms of how social history has been generated hitherto. This claim is, of course, the very same point that Thompson sought to make in his critique of Althusserian structuralism, a theme that underpins his brilliant book *The Making of the English Working Class* (1966). For what lies at base here is the notion that structures of power and the power of elites can only be properly understood by an accompanying focus on the actions of the subaltern classes within a structurationist approach that, in spirit at least, is congruent with Marx's statement in 'The Eighteenth Brumaire'. But what I find perplexing is that CIRT – in its Marxist and non-Marxist guises – has, for the most part in the last three decades, rigged the scales of structure/elite power and subaltern agency to such an extent that the former now hangs suspended permanently in mid-air, while the latter is grounded with few or no prospects of rising up. Accordingly, the question now becomes how we might go about following through by bringing subaltern and non-Western agency back in to critical theory's purview.

What I find problematic about Marx's conception of subaltern agency is that it is constrained within an overly narrow definition that necessarily diminishes and delimits the many spaces in which it is articulated and exercised. Like neorealism's definition of state struggle, so Marxism's key concept of class struggle is essentially conceived of within a 'billiard ball' framework. As Michael Mann originally argued, within Marxism classes are thought to meet only in *head-on conflict*, and merely clash like billiard balls on a billiard table. This is problematic, not for what it does say but for what it excludes. For I want to argue that classes and other forms of agents do not only meet in head-on conflict but also entwine in highly complex and promiscuous ways (Mann 1986: Chapter 1). Although, of course, this conception forms a major canon of Mann's neo-Weberian theory, when coupled with the concomitant concept of 'retracking' it can also form the basis of a critical theory of global politics. Ironically, an excellent example of this is found in the work of the postcolonial Gramscian writer Mustapha Pasha, when he talks of 'elective chains of affinities' (Pasha 2006: 153), or equally when the postcolonial Gramscian scholar Randolph Persaud asserts that

> resistance and counter-hegemony are too often seen as *responses* to … interests already formed, rather than theorized as dialectically defining the conditions which make hegemonic practices historically 'necessary' in the first place.… As such, counter-hegemonic practices must be seen as a fluid and unstable *engagement*, rather than a settled response to hegemony.
>
> *(Persaud 2001: 49, his emphases)*

This notion of 'promiscuous' relations between East and West simultaneously provides a counter to a further limitation of CIRT's conception of agency. Thus, the conception of head-on conflict entails situating agency within an either/or, winner/loser framework. This severely delimits the space within which subaltern agency resides in much of CIRT's imagination. For the assumption is that agency can only be recognized or declared when subaltern actors *win* their battle with the dominant. Thus, working class agency is often limited to those rare moments when the working class engages in a revolutionary praxis and overthrows the state. Given that these moments are by definition extremely rare, so working class agency becomes the exception rather than the agential rule. And given that neoliberal capitalism has become entrenched since 1979 across the world under the impetus of 'Western-led globalization' and the Washington Consensus, so the upshot is that the prospects for subaltern agency are diminished almost to the vanishing point. The point here is that subaltern agency has pretty much blipped off the critical theoretical radar screen, as the dominant elites within the West in effect sit back and enjoy the victories of hyper-elitism … Game over!

As an alternative to the pessimism of much of CIRT, I want to sketch the barest outlines of a larger picture of non-elite agency, which begins with the proposition that agency is not necessarily about winning or defeating various elites but is about shaping and re-shaping, tracking and retracking the Western dominant elites. Thus, in an alternative, more expansive vision of non-elite agency, I point to the example of the processes by which East and West have tracked and retracked each other's inner natures, which in turn have retracked the paths that they follow in the international or global system; a scenario that takes Eastern and Western agency as its ontological point of departure. The net result is the production of hybrid civilizations, rather than ones that are defined in pure and exclusive ways.

To capture this I talk about the 'dialogues' and 'dialectics' of civilizations. The dialogues refer to the ways in which all manner of inventions – ideational, technological and institutional – are pioneered in the East and West and are then assimilated or copied by each other in order to achieve development. In the period between roughly 500 and 1800, the predominant influence went from East to West, and I have traced this as a means of explaining the rise of the West (Hobson 2004). After about 1800, the predominant line of influence runs clearly from West to East – even if the latter refracts incoming influences and pressures through cultural filters, much as Europe did *vis-à-vis* the incoming influences from the East during its rise.

Moreover, after about 1800 the *dialectics* of civilizations cuts in (Pieterse 1990). This refers to the imperialist/neo-imperialist process whereby the West has sought to dominate the East and where the latter resists in all manner of ways – which leads on to changes within the Western countries. This retracks the direction that the Western countries undertake as they seek to find news ways of dominating the East – which, in turn, leads onto changes within Eastern societies. This occurs as a constant feedback loop, in the process retracking Eastern and Western societies in both their inner and outward trajectories. All in all, this is important for it serves to 'activate' what is commonly viewed as the 'passive' East, revealing it or its component societies as exercising forms of agency which impact on the development of the West, on the one hand, and on the conduct of world politics on the other. Moreover, I would argue that this process has been sustained right down to the present day in a variety of ways.

By means of an example here, I shall relate some of the basic outlines of the 'dialectics of civilizations'. After about 1800, Western imperialism in Afro-Asia gained in intensity before signs of Eastern resistance emerged through the 1865 revolt in Morant Bay in Jamaica and the so-called 1857 Indian Mutiny. Significantly, the shock that the 'Mutiny' caused among the British imperial elites, both at home and abroad, was such that the British subsequently imposed a harsher form of imperial control. At the same time, the 'Mutiny' provided a fertile context for the entrenching of scientific racism that had begun to emerge after about 1850 within Britain. By the end of the century, and especially after the Japanese defeat of Russia in 1905, Eastern resistance grew in strength and confidence (Aydin 2007: chapter 4). The years 1919–1922 in particular saw a major increase in the tempo and intensity of Eastern resistance, even though the imperial powers responded by upping the intensity of imperialism.

The nationalist movements continued to agitate to such an extent that the ending of the Second World War saw them successfully challenge the structure of empire. Critically, although some nationalist movements resisted through engaging in military actions, the majority sought more peaceful means. Their principal weapon was far less dramatic than open military defiance, taking the form of 'mimetic challenge' or rhetorical entrapment. Such a conception is far more subtle than traditional 'heroic' forms of defiance, though no less powerful – and arguably far more so. How did this play out and what is its significance?

The strategy of Eastern mimesis or *mimetic challenge* saw the nationalist movements appropriate Western civilizational rhetoric as a means to delegitimize empire (Hobson and Seabrooke 2009). They used, for example, the key third point of the Atlantic Charter, which asserted that the signatories (Roosevelt and Churchill) 'respect the right of all peoples to choose the form of government under which they will live; and they wish to see sovereign rights and self-government restored to those who have been forcibly deprived of them'. Although Churchill believed that this should apply to countries *outside* of Britain's empire, the opinion leaders in the colonies used this to push for emancipation. The attack on racism was pivotal, even though there were moves within the West that were also subverting this discourse (Hobson 2012: chapter 13). All in all, the nationalist movements pointed out that while the West stood for democracy, human rights, self-determination and political equality, it nevertheless failed to live by these principals in its imperial conduct.

In the end, the Eastern nationalist movements successfully prosecuted the West in a Western 'social court of justice' and, having hoisted the West on its own petard, won the case for decolonization by de-legitimizing empire. The ultimate significance of this for my discussion of Eastern agency is, first, that it undermines the point that the colonies had merely endogenized Western ideals for freedom; and, second, that it reveals the agency of Eastern peoples in breaking down the walls of empire through the deployment of a subversive form of mimesis.

Critical theory often views decolonization in highly Eurocentric terms, with many Marxists explaining it as but the handing over of the baton of global power from the formal imperialism of the British to the informal neo-imperial system of the Pax Americana. But this elides one of the greatest triumphs of collective Eastern resistance-agency the world has seen in the last two centuries. Of course, many critical theorists, including postcolonialists, portray the postcolonial era as merely the substitution of informal for formal imperialism. My point is not to take issue with this, but to note that Eastern peoples have also resisted this imposition in all manner of ways, many of which have reacted back on the West with deep consequences. Examples of this would include the OPEC oil shocks and the attack on the Twin Towers, both of which have had massive consequences for retracking the inner and outer trajectories of the West. Ultimately, then, my key point is that Eastern and subaltern agency needs to be understood in more expansive ways than much of extant critical theory envisages if we are to move away from the politics of despair to a more optimistic one that promotes emancipation.

Notes

1 See Hobson (2010 and 2012: chapters 11–12).
2 To this we could add the complementary, though less famous, critique of WST/dependency theory that was made by Ernesto Laclau (1971).
3 See Cox (this volume, 23–28). Of course, such a position is at the very least curious in the light of Marx's progressive evolutionary schema that reflected a strong Enlightenment mode of thought.
4 For the former two cases, see Cox (1986 and 1987), and for the latter two see Arrighi (1994).
5 But for excellent exceptions see Colás (2002) and Morton (2007).
6 This problem has been highlighted by a range of scholars. See, for example, Ling (2002) and Krishna (1993).

Bibliography

Arrighi, G. (1994) *The Long Twentieth Century*, London: Verso.
Aydin, C. (2007) *The Politics of Anti-Westernism in Asia*, New York: Columbia University Press.
Brenner, R. (1977) 'The Origins of Capitalist Development: a Critique of Neo-Smithian Marxism', *New Left Review* 104: 25–92.
Césaire, A. (2001) *Discourse on Colonialism*, New York: Monthly Review Press.
Colás, A. (2002) 'The Class Politics of Globalisation', in M. Rupert and H. Smith (eds) *Historical Materialism and Globalization*, London: Routledge.
Cox, R.W. (1986) 'Social Forces, States and World Orders: Beyond International Relations Theory', in R.O. Keohane (ed.), *Neorealism and Its Critics*, New York: Columbia University Press.
_____ (1987) *Production, Power and World Order*, New York: Columbia University Press.
Cox, R.W. with Sinclair, T.J. (1996) *Approaches to World Order*, Cambridge: Cambridge University Press.
Davies, M. (2005) 'The Public Spheres of Unprotected Workers?', *Global Society* 19 (2): 131–54.
Fanon, F. (2004) *The Wretched of the Earth*, New York: Grove Press.
Foucault, M. (1980) *Power/Knowledge. Selected interviews and other writings 1972–1977* (edited by C. Gordon), New York: Pantheon Books.
Gill, S. (1990) *American Hegemony and the Trilateral Commission*, Cambridge: Cambridge University Press.
_____ (ed.), (1993) *Gramsci, Historical Materialism and International Relations*, Cambridge: Cambridge University Press.
Gills, B.K. (2000) 'Introduction: Globalization and the Politics of Resistance', in B.K. Gills (ed.), *Globalization and the Politics of Resistance*, Houndmills: Palgrave.
Hettne, Bjorn (ed.), (1995) *International Political Economy: Understanding Global Disorder*, London: Zed.
Hobson, J.M. (2004) *The Eastern Origins of Western Civilisation*, Cambridge: Cambridge University Press.
_____ (2007) 'Is Critical Theory always for the White West and for Western Imperialism? Beyond Westphilian towards a Post-Racist Critical International Relations', *Review of International Studies* 33(SI): 91–116.
_____ (2010) 'Back to the Future of Nineteenth-century International Thought?', in G. Lawson, C. Armbruster, and M. Cox (eds) *Global 1989*, Cambridge: Cambridge University Press.

_____ (2012) *The Eurocentric Conception of World Politics: Western International Theory, 1760–2010*, Cambridge: Cambridge University Press.

Hobson, J.M. and Seabrooke, L. (2009) 'Everyday International Political Economy', in M. Blyth (ed.), *Routledge Handbook of International Political Economy*, New York: Routledge.

Krishna, S. (1993) 'The Importance of Being Ironic: A Postcolonial View on Critical International Relations Theory', *Alternatives* 18(3): 385–417.

Laclau, E. (1971) 'Feudalism and Capitalism in Latin America', *New Left Review* 67: 19–38.

Langley, P. (2008) *The Everyday Life of Global Finance*, Oxford: Oxford University Press.

Lefebvre, Henri (1976) *The Survival of Capitalism,* London: St. Martin's Press.

Ling, L.H.M. (2002) *Postcolonial International Relations*, Houndmills: Palgrave Macmillan.

Mann, M. (1986) *The Sources of Social Power*, Vol. I, Cambridge: Cambridge University Press.

Marx, K. (1950) 'The Eighteenth Brumaire of Louis Bonaparte', in K. Marx and F. Engels, *Selected Works*, vol. I, Moscow: Foreign Languages Press.

Marx, K. and F. Engels (1967) *The Communist Manifesto*, Harmondsworth: Penguin Books.

Morton, A.D. (2007) 'Peasants as Subaltern Agents in Latin America: Neoliberalism, Resistance, and the Power of the Powerless', in J.M. Hobson and L. Seabrooke (eds) *Everyday Politics of the World Economy*, Cambridge: Cambridge University Press.

Pasha, M.K. (2006) 'Islam, "Soft" Orientalism and Hegemony: A Gramscian Rereading', in A. Bieler and A.D. Morton (eds) *Images of Gramsci*, London: Routledge.

Paterson, M. (2007) *Automobile Politics: Ecology and Cultural Political Economy*, Cambridge: Cambridge University Press.

Persaud, R.B. (2001) *Counter-Hegemony and Foreign Policy*, New York: SUNY Press.

Pieterse, J.N. (1990) *Empire and Emancipation*, London: Pluto.

Said, E.W. (1994) *Culture and Imperialism*, London: Vintage.

_____ (2003) *Orientalism*, Harmondsworth: Penguin Books.

_____ (2004) *Power, Politics, and Culture*, London: Bloomsbury.

Thompson, E.P. (1966) *The Making of the English Working Class*, London: Vintage.

_____ (1995) *The Poverty of Theory*, London: Merlin Press.

Van der Pijl, K. (1984) *The Making of an Atlantic Ruling Class*, London: Verso.

9

UNCRITICAL THEORY[1]

Brooke Ackerly

Introduction

In 2001 Jacqui True and I undertook to write a paper that articulated the methodological core of diverse feminist contributions to International Relations (IR) and the key features of a critical feminist IR theory (Ackerly and True 2006). Andrew Linklater and Robert Cox were early and engaged commentators on that paper. Their critical engagement was directly with the substance of the paper and thinking through their comments greatly improved the project, so it is a thrill for me to be invited to comment on their work.

There was also a shadow to their commentary, and this shadow will be the focus of my engagement with these interviews. At one point, Linklater gave voice to that shadow when he asked between panels during a conference about feminisms' engagement with the Critical and post-structuralist theories of IR, 'is feminism a branch of Critical Theory, or something else entirely?'

In the first part of this commentary I partially answer this question by discussing the use and challenges of two theoretical methods that I have in common with some of the interviewees: skepticism and humility. These twin tools are at the heart of great intellectual partnerships across the 'critical theories'. By 'critical theories' I mean feminism, post-modernism, post-structuralism, post-colonialism, critical race theory, and the 'Critical Theory' of Gramscian-inspired and Frankfurt School-inspired scholarship. I use skepticism to reflect on the privilege of humility and therefore on the import of using humility in partnership with other critical tools.

In the second part of my commentary, I apply these tools to the concept of 'emancipation' and its role in security. The import of my engagement is *not only* with the meaning of the concept of emancipation, but also with the *methodology* we use in developing and reflecting on our concepts. In a longer commentary, I would extend this reflection to the concepts of struggle used by Cox or of harm developed by Linklater. The discussion of emancipation in the second part of the paper should not be interpreted to apply to the concept of emancipation uniquely, but rather should be read as a *methodological* criticism of Critical IR Theory. If we use our methods well, they should draw us to question the import even of concepts that seem indisputably central to Critical Theory.

Critical theories

Together, the interviews in this volume give Critical IR Theory's answer to the shadow question, 'Is feminism a branch of Critical Theory, or something else entirely?' Feminist IR is not a branch of Critical IR Theory; Feminist IR is concerned not just with a subset of issues which interest Critical IR theorists, but rather Feminist IR is a broader critical theory that is concerned with the issues and theoretical lenses of Critical IR theory, *and so much more*.[2]

First, Critical IR theory does not lead any of the four to a critical feminist theory. By their own accounts, the theoretical work of none of the authors brought him to think that gender was theoretically interesting to international security. By contrast, for feminists, 'gender is an integral, not accidental, feature of the worldwide structure of diplomatic, military and economic relations' (Parpart and Zalewski 2008: viii). The study of international relations without the study of gender underestimates the amount of power in the system and misunderstands its nature. In a possible exception among the Critical IR theorists, Booth offers a personal reason for his interest in feminism, but does not tie that concern back to his objective of answering mainstream IR's questions *better* using Critical IR Theory. Feminists have a broader understanding of the field of IR because they have a broader understanding of oppression, and in this sense, Critical IR Theory is a subset of Feminist IR Theory (not the other way around). In informal dialogue between panels, they may very well share the same concerns or acknowledge the import of the forms of oppression that feminists raise in their scholarship, but the substance of the papers on the panel, like the content of these reflective interviews, illustrate that these are not as important to their scholarship.

Second, Feminist IR scholars are more attentive to their methodologies than Critical IR theorists. Though both have a normative interest in scholarship that reveals oppressive ideologies, feminists are methodologically attentive to the ways in which a theoretical approach to scholarship itself can be an ideology that can be exclusionary or oppressive. Feminist critical theory, like Cox's Critical IR Theory, takes into account 'prevailing institutions, the material conditions and the prevalent ideas and ideologies' (Cox, this volume, 20). However, feminist critical theory does more; it has a methodology for doing so.[3] Feminist critical theory shares Cox's normative goal: 'achievement of greater equity in people's material life, a greater sense of understanding and tolerance of differences in culture and ideas and a means of moderating conflict among peoples' (this volume, 20). Furthermore, it has the tools for studying the intersectional dimensions of the range of power dynamics that affect the equity in people's material lives.[4]

Again, between the panels, feminists and critical theorists acknowledge the depth and importance of thinking about the ways in which particular political, economic and social forces intersect to cause oppression. I am particularly interested in how these forces intersect such that the oppression itself is rendered invisible or even 'natural'. I give a lot of theoretical and methodological attention to the ways in which we can study not just the fact that certain groups are marginalized or oppressed, but also the *ways in which* oppressive forces function in relation to one another. Feminist scholarship on intersectionality is essential to these inquiries.[5]

Even more importantly, the tools of feminist critical theory enable it continually to improve its tools and work to understand the complex ways in which intersecting political forces affect life on the ground in the areas of interest that feminists and Critical IR theorists share: political and economic justice, emancipation, oppression, systems of power, and the epistemological bases of authority. These are complex problems whose dimensions are difficult to enumerate and delimit. Complex problems such as those that interest critical theorists are never 'completely understood'. Our ambition is merely to understand them *better*.

In this brief commentary, I will discuss two of my own theoretical methods – skepticism and humility – and the ways in which it may be fruitful to notice how the interviewees in this volume refer to these in their own work. Skepticism is essential to humility. Without it, humility is an uncritical perspective of privilege. That privilege can be an ontological liability for a critical theorist. The methods of feminist critical theory are designed to engage continually with that liability. Decades of feminist self-criticism through movements regarding race, gender, sexuality, worker justice, immigrant justice, neo-colonialism, indigenous rights and disability have provided feminist critical theory with a more modest ontology, one with less confidence in the completeness of any author's view of global justice than Cox, Linklater, Booth, and Wyn Jones exhibit.

Skepticism

For feminists, skepticism – 'skeptical scrutiny' as I have called it – is part of a critical methodology.[6] It is the device that reminds us to revisit regularly ideas and approaches that we have previously considered settled. We might revisit the goals of 'achievement of greater equity in people's material life, a greater sense of understanding and tolerance of differences in culture and ideas and a means of moderating conflict among peoples' (Cox, this volume, 20) and, while not rejecting any piece of these, realize that we need a more rich study of the formation of desire[7] and political economy to render visible the international security dimensions of sex economies and reproduction.[8]

Skeptical scrutiny is a methodological application in research of what Abdullahi An-Na'im (1990: 341) calls 'a universal rational principle to the effect that strong evidence of a contrary view should induce a person to reexamine her or his position'. The challenge is in determining what constitutes 'strong evidence'.

Skeptical scrutiny leads us to be careful about giving too much meaning to concepts or allowing any meaning to become ossified. For example, Cox cautions against the use of 'emancipation' and 'progress'. These are words that 'can mean everything and nothing much' (Cox, this volume, 25). (I will return to the meaning of emancipation.) Skeptical scrutiny can also be directed at our methodological tools and I give an example of that next.

Humility

Humility may be the universal social science methodology.[9] Modesty in the face of all we do not know leads us to ask difficult questions and to pursue questions in terrain where we thought we knew all of the answers. Booth's appreciation of personal luck demonstrates an element of humility. Additionally, humility leads us to approach scholarship as always collaborative, always in progress with others either directly or indirectly, and always incomplete.[10]

Humility is behind Cox's pessimism. On Cox's view pessimism and optimism are not opposites. Pessimism is the 'keen sense of obstacles' and 'an appreciation of all of the difficulties inherent in making significant change' (Cox, this volume, 24). This form of humility is appropriate with regard to our subject of study but also to our methods. If the topic is changing, we will need to adapt our methods to study it.[11]

Humility can also be seen in Booth's crediting the Frankfurt School with his approach to critical thinking:

> To be specific, the key ideas of Frankfurtian-style thinking that appealed so much at the time were the recognition of the historical nature of knowledge in the social world (rejecting hubris about 'objectivity'); the importance of reflexivity (including being critical of Critical Theory); the relative merits of holistic as against reductionist thinking; the inseparability of politics and ethics; the practicality of understanding theory as constitutive; the pragmatic idealism of immanent critique; and the anchoring of theorizing in a notion of emancipation.
>
> *(Booth, this volume, 65)*

And we can see humility in Wyn Jones's revisiting realism in its nuance.

While obviously important to Cox, Booth, and Wyn Jones, humility needs to be deployed *with* skepticism. Those who need to cultivate humility are those with privilege. Humility as a tool of critical thinking or social science research is a tool of privilege. By saying this, I do not mean to suggest that those academics with privilege should abandon their use of this tool. Rather, in recognizing that humility is a tool of the privileged we remind ourselves that we must approach its use and findings with *skeptical scrutiny*. Alone, humility is not a strong enough tool for revealing injustice due to privilege.

Emancipation and security

Working together, humility and skeptical scrutiny encourage us to find questions and answers in the work of those in struggle. For academic critical theorists this means 'encouraging situations where peoples are able to think through their own way, and maybe make changes that they consider better in the knowledge that the world is a composite and plural entity', as Cox says (this volume, 31). Let us apply this to reexamining 'emancipation', a critical concept made central in Booth's writings and important to Wyn Jones. This assessment of emancipation uses the tools of humility and skeptical scrutiny and should also be addressed to Cox's work on struggle and Linklater's on harm, but space considerations have encouraged me to focus on emancipation.

Booth seeks to define and use emancipation in a locally appropriate, yet universal way: '[r]ight across the world, folk tales and histories recognize iconic struggles against oppression: struggles for material necessities ("bread"), struggles for truth in the face of dogmatic authority ("knowledge"), and struggles to escape from political and economic tyranny ("freedom")' (this volume, 70). This understanding of emancipation is certainly consistent with my own feminist work, which centres on women's struggles and how they define them.[12] However, the Critical IR theorists' approach to these is different.

Booth argues that emancipation requires 'removing those brutal, demeaning, and determining constraints on peoples' lives such as poverty, racism, patriarchy, war and so on' (this volume, 71). I certainly think that these are constraining. But they are not constraints, they are relations and processes that function in complex ways not structures that merely constrain agency.[13]

The activists who inform my work have not used the idea of emancipation to talk about their struggles with poverty, racism, patriarchy, and conflict. They do explicitly struggle for the enjoyment of their rights and against injustice and deprivation (Ackerly 2000). This is not to say that they might not use 'emancipation', but it does make me ask why, in all the re-reflection that their activism has gone through over the past three decades, across a changing global political economy, among terms that could mean 'everything and nothing' (Cox, this volume, 25), they prefer ideas like 'empowerment' and 'rights' rather than 'emancipation', which so cleanly evokes the end of a totalizing form of injustice.

According to Iris Marion Young, who describes her own project as one of Critical Theory, there are five faces of oppression, 'exploitation, marginalization, powerlessness, cultural imperialism, and violence' (1990: 40), which affect different groups differently. Emancipation from these forms of oppression requires humility in understanding the complexity of the causes and skepticism about whether we have fully identified all of these, so that we can transform them.[14]

The insecurity of women requires transforming the relations of production, representation, recognition and reproduction, and the practices associated with them including diplomatic, military, and economic relations. Does the concept of 'emancipation' entail this transformation, or is emancipation in fact *part of* a system of oppression? From a post-structuralist perspective, any attempt to broaden our inclusiveness necessarily draws a new line of inclusion and exclusion,[15] such that 'emancipation' is not transformative but always part of the system of oppression.[16]

Interestingly enough, in the historical practice of slavery, emancipation has always been a part of slavery; it does not engender a transformation from slavery.[17] In a 1996 essay, Guyora Binder argues that manumission of slaves did not abolish the practice of slavery. The argument is that the practice of slavery as described in new scholarship on slavery by Patterson (1982) and others shows that the promise of emancipation was an *essential practice of the institution of slavery*. In fact, with the abolition of the slave trade and the concurrent difficulty in replacing escaped slaves, the prospect of manumission became in increasingly important tool for keeping slaves in slavery.[18] Through informal agreements between slaves and owners, the terms of which the owners controlled, the prospect of manumission for themselves or loved ones created incentives for slaves not to try to escape.

Further, individual manumission changed the economic relationship between freed slave and citizens, but not the political or social relationship. Binder suggests that even the United States' Thirteenth Amendment, understandably interpreted as ending the practice of slavery – 'Neither slavery nor involuntary servitude ... shall exist within the United States, or any place subject to their jurisdiction' – in practice only manumitted the slaves, it did not transform the social or political relations between former slaves and citizens. The Fourteenth Amendment and subsequent civil rights legislation attempted to change those relations. Binder argues that without transforming those relations, 'emancipation' was not a sufficient goal.

From the perspective of feminist and critical race inquiry, security and emancipation are complementary, but not in a way that promotes 'achievement of greater equity in people's material life, a greater sense of understanding and tolerance of differences in culture and ideas and a means of moderating conflict among peoples' (Cox, this volume, 20). Security requires 'protection' etc. It is hierarchical and patronizing except between the two poles of a bi-polar international system. Those in struggle for their security and their freedom cannot feel 'secured' if their enjoyment is dependent on others.

Ironically, 'emancipation' is not empowering on the face of it. If political power, security and rights are privileges that can be granted and taken away, then emancipation is an act of privilege, not a transformation in political relations. If political power, security and rights are privileges, then the hierarchy underpinning their lack is not removed by their being granted.

Wyn Jones seems to take this up this concern:

> while I would insist on the centrality of emancipation, I would want to distinguish between taking emancipation seriously and defining security in terms of emancipation. While I still think the former is imperative, I am now much more dubious about the later, even if it was a pivotal argument in Ken's 'Security and Emancipation' piece as well as my own subsequent work.

We have been rightly critiqued on that score, and I think Ken moved away from his 'two sides of the same coin' image even before those criticisms were leveled. But while that initial impulse to equate security and emancipation may have been too crude, the concern with emancipation can and should remain absolutely central.

(this volume, 97; see also Wyn Jones 2001)

His backing off of the centrality of emancipation and of the notion that 'security and emancipation are two sides of the same coin' suggests that Critical IR Theory is becoming more influenced by the feminist concern about a broader list of sources of oppression and exploitable hierarchies. If tied too tightly to an uninterrogated notion of emancipation, Critical IR Theory is an entirely different inquiry from feminism.

Conclusion

We are now close to answering the question of the relationship between feminism and Critical IR Theory.

First, I rejected the idea that feminism was a branch of Critical IR Theory based on the latter's more narrow scope in both substantive and methodological senses. Second, I explored the possibility that feminist critical theory included Critical IR Theory. Approaches that use heavy doses of humility and skepticism would be compatible with feminist critical theory. While feminism is a broad theoretical umbrella, its methodological commitments give us lenses by which to assess feminist and other scholarship.[19] I argued that not all Critical IR Theory could be considered feminist because some Critical IR Theory does not deploy tools for examining its own key concepts. Booth and Wyn Jones's rethinking of the relationship between security and emancipation demonstrates a move toward a feminist critical theory; however, both focused their attention on the relationship between emancipation and security and less on the meanings of those concepts. The views of Critical IR Theory articulated in this volume do not fit within Feminist IR − broad as it is − because they lack sufficient application of the methodological tools to the key concepts of the theory.

Instead, in reflecting on this volume's restatement of the field of Critical IR Theory, I come to a different conclusion. Before I saw the interviews, I was flattered to be asked to comment on them as Linklater and Cox were early and engaged commentators on 'Studying the Struggles and Wishes of the Age: Feminist Theoretical Methodology and Feminist Theoretical Methods'. Each interview was interesting and engaging. I was interested in the intellectual journey of others. But I was sad that, with noted exceptions which were rare in the text, these key contributors to the field of IR were more interested in Critical IR Theory than in critical theories. Feminist and post-colonial theorists and the struggles that interested them were not inspiring interlocutors. Post-modern and post-structuralist interlocutors seemed to irritate rather than to provoke richer reflection (this volume, 59). In the drafts that were circulated for comment only one of these was named and I found my disappointment not intellectual, but academic. As an intellectual, I found something modestly interesting to say about the shared methods – humility and skepticism – of Feminist Critical Theory and Critical IR Theory and about how we could always learn more about even our central concepts – such as emancipation. But as an academic, I felt profoundly embarrassed, not just that this volume might perform an act of hubris and not humility, but also that when it was time to look back at thirty years of Critical IR Theory in world politics, so many of the struggles and wishes of the last thirty years era and the theoretical work that engaged those material struggles were not important to Critical IR Theorists' view of their own intellectual development.

I do not know what this means for Critical IR Theory. If I were writing a book review, I would probably characterize the book as a postmortem despite the obvious life in the work of the authors and so many who use Critical IR.[20] But it does make it very clear to me what the answer is to Linklater's question: 'Is feminism a branch of Critical Theory, or something else entirely?'

It is something else entirely: feminism is one of the critical theories.

Notes

1 Thank you to Jacqui True and Marysia Zalewski for their thoughtful comments on an earlier draft. I appreciate the broad engagement that they demonstrate in their scholarship and am grateful for their intellectual community.
2 An appropriate footnote here would cite a broad range of Feminist IR but would necessarily exclude as it includes; therefore, instead I will cite just one text that exhibits a feminist approach to developing the scope of Feminist IR research: Enloe (2004). Enloe's approach broadens the field and is a useful complement to other approaches which build a feminist research agenda from within the disciplinary paradigms of the field. See Caprioli (2000). Where research questions come from has been an important subject of feminist inquiry; see Blanchard (2003).
3 See Ackerly (2008a and 2009a) and Ackerly and True (2006; 2008b; 2010a and 2010b).
4 See Ackerly (2009b), Confortini (2009), Hancock (2007).
5 Ackerly (2011), Ackerly and True (2008a), Weldon (2006) and Yuval-Davis (2006).
6 See Ackerly (2000).
7 See Agathangelou (2004).
8 See Peterson (2003).
9 See Ackerly (2008b).
10 See Ackerly and True (2010b). Linklater discusses 'collective learning' in his contribution to this volume (this volume, 50).
11 See Ackerly and Attanasi (2009), Ackerly and True (2010b).
12 See Ackerly (2008a).
13 Some feminists use 'constraints' in a non-dynamic way, but reflections on the limitations of such an approach lead me to develop a more dynamic understanding of the ways that, along with structures, processes and behaviors are constraining.
14 See Bunch (1990), True (2003), Sampaio and Hermanas En La Lucha (2004).
15 See Mouffe (2000).
16 See Brown (1993 and 1995).
17 See Patterson (1982).
18 Additionally, this shift in the political economy of slavery also required the development of the field of gynecology to maintain the reproductive capacity of slave women. See Kapsalis (1997 and 2002).

19 Ackerly and True (2010b).
20 For two interesting reviews of this rich literature see Shepherd (2010) and Fierke (2010).

Bibliography

Ackerly, B. (2000) *Political Theory and Feminist Social Criticism*, Cambridge: Cambridge University Press.
____ (2008a) 'Feminist Methodological Reflection', in A. Klotz and D. Prakas (eds) *Qualitative Methods in International Relations: A Pluralist Guide*, London: Palgrave Macmillan.
____ (2008b) *Universal Human Rights in a World of Difference*, Cambridge: Cambridge University Press.
____ (2009a) 'Feminist Methods in International Relations', *Politics & Gender* 5(3): 409–10.
____ (2009b) 'Feminist Theory, Global Gender Justice, and the Evaluation of Grant-Making', *Philosophical Topics* 37(2). Available at <http://ssrn.com/abstract=1348902> (accessed 23 May 2011).
____ (2011) 'Human Rights Enjoyment in Theory and Activism', *Human Rights Review* 12(2): 221–39.
Ackerly, B. and Attanasi, K. (2009) 'Global Feminisms: Theory and Ethics for Studying Gendered Injustice', *New Political Science* 31(4): 543–55.
Ackerly, B. and True, J. (2006) 'Studying the Struggles and Wishes of the Age: Feminist Theoretical Methodology and Feminist Theoretical Methods' in B. Ackerly, M. Stern and J. True (eds) *Feminist Methodologies for International Relations*, Cambridge: Cambridge University Press.
____ (2008a) 'An Intersectional Analysis of International Relations: Recasting the Discipline', *Politics & Gender* 4(1): 156–73.
____ (2008b) 'Reflexivity in Practice: Power and Ethics in Feminist Research on International Relations', *International Studies Review* 10(4): 693–707.
____ (2010a) 'Back to the Future: Feminist Theory, Activism, and Doing Feminist Research in an Age of Globalization', *Women's Studies International Forum* 33(5): 464–72.
____ (2010b) *Doing Feminist Research in Political and Social Science*, London: Palgrave Macmillan.
Agathangelou, A. (2004) *The Global Political Economy of Sex: Desire, Violence, and Insecurity in Mediterranean Nation States*, 1st edn, New York: Palgrave Macmillan.
An-Na'im, A. (1990) 'Problems of Universal Cultural Legitimacy for Human Rights', in A. An-Na'im and F. Deng (eds) *Human Rights in Africa: Cross-Cultural Perspectives*, Washington: The Brookings Institution.
Binder, G. (1996) 'The Slavery of Emancipation', *Cardozo Law Review* 17: 2063–102.
Blanchard, E. (2003) 'Gender, International Relations, and the Development of Feminist Security Theory', *Signs: Journal of Women in Culture and Society* 28(4): 1289–312.
Brown, W. (1993) 'Wounded Attachments', *Political Theory* 21(3): 390–410.
____ (1995) *States of Injury: Power and Freedom in Late Modernity,* Princeton: Princeton University Press.
Bunch, C. (1990) 'Women's Rights as Human Rights: Toward a Re-Vision of Human Rights', *Human Rights Quarterly* 12 (November): 486–98.
Caprioli, M. (2000) 'Gendered Conflict', *Journal of Peace Research* 37(1): 51–68.
Confortini, C. (2009) 'Imaginative Identification: Feminist Critical Methodology in the Women's International League for Peace and Freedom (1945–1975)', PhD Dissertation, University of Southern California.

Enloe, C. (2004) *The Curious Feminist: Searching for Women in a New Age of Empire*, Berkeley: University of California Press.

Fierke, K. (2010) 'Critical Theory, Security, and Emancipation' in R. Denemark (ed.) *The International Studies Encyclopedia*, Oxford: Wiley-Blackwell.

Hancock, A. (2007) 'When Multiplication Doesn't Equal Quick Addition: Examining Intersectionality as a Research Paradigm', *Perspectives on Politics* 5(1): 63–79.

Kapsalis, T. (1997) *Public Privates: Performing Gynecology from Both Ends of the Speculum*, Durham: Duke University Press.

_____ (2002) 'Mastering the Female Pelvis: Race and the Tools of Reproduction' in K. Wallace-Sanders (ed.) *Skin Deep, Spirit Strong: The Black Female Body in American Culture*, Ann Arbor: University of Michigan Press.

Mouffe, C. (2000) *The Democratic Paradox*, London: Verso.

Parpart, J. and Zalewski, M. (eds) (2008) *Rethinking the Man Question: Sex, Gender and Violence in International Relations*, London: Zed Books.

Patterson, O. (1982) *Slavery and Social Death: A Comparative Study*, Cambridge: Harvard University Press.

Peterson, V. (2003) *A Critical Rewriting of Global Political Economy: Integrating Reproductive, Productive, and Virtual Economies*, London: Routledge.

Sampaio, A. and Hermanas En La Lucha (2004) 'Transnational Feminisms in a New Global Matrix', *International Feminist Journal of Politics* 6(2): 181–206.

Shepherd, L. (2010) 'Feminist Security Studies' in R. Denemark (ed.) *The International Studies Encyclopedia*, Oxford: Wiley-Blackwell.

True, J. (2003) 'Mainstreaming Gender in Global Public Policy', *International Feminist Journal of Politics* 5(3): 368–96.

Weldon, S. (2006) 'The Structure of Intersectionality: A Comparative Politics of Gender', *Politics & Gender* 2(2): 235–48.

Wyn Jones, R. (2001) 'Introduction: Locating Critical International Relations Theory' in R. Wyn Jones (ed.) *Critical Theory and World Politics*, Boulder: Lynne Rienner Publishers.

Young, I. (1990) *Justice and the Politics of Difference*, Princeton: Princeton University Press.

Yuval-Davis, N. (2006) 'Intersectionality and Feminist Politics', *European Journal of Women's Studies* 13(3): 193–209.

10

WHAT IS CRITICAL ABOUT CRITICAL THEORY REVISITED?

The case of four international relations scholars and gender

Jacqui True

In Tunisia, Egypt, Yemen and Bahrain, women and men have been taking to the streets to protest for political freedom and to shape their own emancipation from authoritarianism. Dispelling both Islamic and Western stereotypes, Arab women have taken up leadership roles in these incipient social movements in the streets and on the Internet. On International Women's Day – 8 March 2011, the centenary of this day celebrating women workers – in Tahrir Square, Cairo, hundreds of women, many of whom had participated in the protests that toppled Mubarak, chanted 'Now is the time; there is no freedom for men without freedom and equality for women'. In a counter protest, men objecting to the call for a new constitution allowing women to stand for the Egyptian presidency charged violently on the women while police and military stood by. Writing in *The Guardian*, Jumanah Younnis claimed 'this revolution will have achieved nothing if it does not recognise the basic right of the Egyptian women to exist, to demonstrate, to work, to live and walk the streets with dignity' (2011).

To feminist critical theorists, these events are telling. They are both evidence that women's activism is central to the transformation of some of the most oppressed societies globally and that women's struggles are multiple – not merely against political dictators but with respect to their gender oppression by men in every sphere of life. How far and in what ways could critical international relations theory contribute to clarifying and resolving this paradox at the heart of women's struggles in this region and globally?

There is something to be said for critical theory in the study of international relations. Its methods are compelling: analysing contradictions in the social, political and economic order, questioning underlying assumptions and biases of dominant perspectives and ideologies, searching for immanent emancipatory or democratic potentials within current social formations, considering more broadly the possibilities for alternative and more equitable futures and encouraging the development of 'organic intellectuals' who can make the leap from theory to practice, political vision to social movement, in order to progress such alternatives. The four critical international relations scholars in this volume, Cox, Linklater, Booth and Wyn Jones, have each contributed to developing these elements of the critical method in distinct ways.

And yet, as a feminist, I find myself continually let down by critical international theory. The texts of the interviews with the four have virtually nothing to say at all about – and do not seem informed by – the struggles and wishes of contemporary women in every country and globally for political voice, economic livelihood and independence, and freedom from men's violence. Women are two thirds of those in poverty in the world; and men's violence against women, including the most egregious forms, is estimated to affect 80 per cent of the world's women in peacetime, war, and after conflict or natural disaster – limiting their enjoyment of fundamental rights and freedoms.

Violence against women is only one aspect of women's struggle for freedom and equality, but it is a globalized struggle that is receiving increasing international attention, inter alia, as indicated by the several UN Security Council Resolutions that aim to end the strategic use of sexual violence in armed conflict. Moreover, the study of violence is at the heart of the study of international relations. If critical theory is worth its name in print – and its capitals in our field of study – then at a minimum its framework should be 'capable of foregrounding the evils of domination and subordination' including men's domination and women's subordination (Fraser 1989: 138). Where is the quest in the so-called 'critical theory of international relations' to understand half of humanity's struggles globally?[1] Is the failure to analyse multiple oppressions, including women's, and diverse emancipatory potentials, including within feminist movements, a problem of the critical theory method itself or the gender bias of the four thinkers in this volume? In this short commentary I will argue that the root of the problem lies both in the incomplete methods of critical theory – as I have argued with Brooke Ackerly elsewhere (Ackerly and True 2006) – and the persistent masculine gender bias of the scholars who deploy this method in the field of international relations.

To make this argument I assess the interviews, as one representation of each author's *oeuvre*, using critical theory criteria adapted from Scott Burchill and Andrew Linklater (2009), Robert Cox (1981) and Ackerly and True (2006; 2010). These criteria ask:

1. How *dialogic* is the interview? Does the scholar engage with other theories and theorists, including feminist theory?
2. Does the scholar *situate themselves* historically and within various social positions?
3. Are they *self-reflexive* about their work – its provisional truths and its effects of power/exclusion?
4. How *materially grounded* in empirical observation, aware of historical and contemporary change and continuity, is the theorist?

5. Does the theorist identify *emancipatory potentials* in existing practices and practice forms of emancipation through their research/scholarship?

For reasons of length, in this commentary I can only focus on the criteria in 1, 3 and 5 in interpreting the critical theory perspectives of Cox, Booth, Linklater and Wyn Jones. But the reader can assess 2 and 4 for themself.

Promoting dialogue

In his interview, Andrew Linklater argues that 'those who do align themselves with ethical standpoints need to engage with competing perspectives and confront what may be unpalatable facts' (this volume, 54). Robert Cox says in his interview that the role of the critical theorist is not merely 'to be aware of forces of opposition to the established order' but to highlight and engage these forces (this volume, 21). In the context of international relations theory I interpret both to mean that engaging with different theories, critical and problem-solving – and not just with those scholars and theories that subscribe to the same tradition, school or label – is fundamental for critical theorists.

As an example of such an attempt at dialogue, all four critical theory interviewees are asked in various ways about their relationship to postmodernism and almost all volunteer commentary on their relationship to realism. Curiously, none are asked about their relationship to feminism, which probably has more subscribers within the field of international relations than postmodernism. One can only surmise that feminism is not judged a rigorous or provocative enough dialogue partner. With respect to the engagement with postmodernism, however, the dialogue or lack of it is noticeable. Linklater attempts to assimilate postmodernism to his purpose, a synthetic critical theory of international relations despite his claim that 'dialogue between equals is central to cosmopolitanism' (this volume, 38): 'Critical Theory and postmodernism are not at odds, despite efforts to drive a wedge between the two ... both defend difference, redefine the relationship between inside/outside' (this volume, 53). Here, the distinctions between postmodern and critical theory perspectives are occluded and no contemporary international relations postmodernist is actually engaged with. Linklater's critical theory is sensitive to 'modes of discourse ... that marginalize and exclude' (this volume, 69), but he neither affirms differences that exist nor recognizes the problem of (liberal) inclusion rather than 'exclusion' as a central problematic in international relations and the cosmopolitan European Union that he defends.

A pluralist by admission, Ken Booth deploys a different strategy to dismiss rather than engage with postmodernism. He asserts that criticisms regarding 'metanarratives', 'western canons' or 'binaries' 'need to be turned back on post-structuralist thinking' (this volume, 69). Booth also claims that 'not all critical theories are equal'. He develops this specific point with respect to realism's explanatory power as a theory when it comes to the distribution of global power and its effects. This may also be a reason why he discusses poststructuralism and

Marxism but never feminism, which is apparently only relevant to Booth personally but not in terms of feminisms' implications for his theorizing. Booth recognizes the contribution of his wife to his thinking but not of feminist scholars of international relations.

Like Linklater, Richard Wyn Jones considers the differences between critical theory and postmodernism to be small in terms of their claims about international security, for instance.[2] Wyn Jones reduces theoretical differences to the Bourdieusian struggle for distinction in a context of academic capitalism. He exemplifies a stance of non-engagement, not assessing a single argument from postmodern international relations theory.

Cox, for his part, claims not to understand postmodernism, stating that 'overcoming "the other"', as opposed to recognizing the other for instance, 'is the primary goal of my critical thinking' (this volume, 26). But when he thinks about civilizations, Cox actually has the sensibility of a postmodernist: he does not essentialize differences or seek to assimilate different others to his way of thinking and being: 'you are not dialoguing with monoliths that have a fixed position, you are dialoguing with people who are undergoing a process of change' (this volume, 32). He talks about 'understanding each other without becoming each other' (this volume, 32). For Cox, 'this is a very personal level, of cosmopolitanism, of gradually expanding your understanding of the difference among people' (this volume, 33). However, these comments beg the question of why Cox does not seek to understand feminism or gender differences except in the briefest, most rudimentary way (see Cox 2002: 145)? That gender differences are largely ignored, even though they manifest at the level of everyday life, in the division of labour and structure of production and reproduction, doesn't give us much confidence in a critical theory that claims to be materially grounded.

Lastly, Wyn Jones uses feminists such as Carol Cohn on the 'rational' world of male defence intellectuals as a resource, and not a dialogue partner. When it comes to reading Frankfurt School influences, he cites Axel Honneth – who struggles to theorize about gender himself – rather than the critical feminist theorist Nancy Fraser. One cannot help but conclude that there is a loss of ideas here when men read men, men cite men … without scrutinizing what this loss says about (inclusive) community.

Practicing reflexivity

When most international relations scholars think about reflexivity, they recall Robert Cox's now famous aphorism 'theory is always for someone and for some purpose' (1981: 128). Of course, Cox is not the only critical scholar to have highlighted the importance of reflexivity, of being attentive to the way our scholarship exercises power and the effects of that power in the social and political world in which we live and theorize. Wyn Jones agrees with Cox that 'it matters what questions we ask'. He argues that 'there is an imperative on all of us to be ruthlessly self-reflexive about where we – as projects and individuals – fit into those structures of power we inescapably inhabit ... only on that basis can we hope to negotiate our way through them whilst maintaining some kind of integrity' (this volume, 93). So how do the four critical theorists interviewed in this volume exhibit this reflexivity in their own work?

Cox is notably humble. He sees himself as an 'underground author' rather than a leader of any school of thought, and admits that he 'did not anticipate the impact of that article' on critical compared to problem-solving theorizing about social forces and world order (this volume, 19). He is self-conscious about making intellectual abstractions removed from people's lives: 'but we are speaking in very abstract terms as behoves intellectuals!' (this volume, 21). He is aware of the effects of his conceptual language, preferring 'to think in terms of concrete forms of change' rather than to use terms like 'globalization' or 'democracy' since they have been 'used in many different ways, mainly supportive of the idea of gradual convergence toward a global free market economic, which would be dominated by the US' (this volume, 21). He does not reflect greatly, however, on the implications of deploying the highly abstract concept of 'civilizations' – although he clearly distinguishes his usage from the dominant, culturally-essentialist meaning present in Samuel Huntington and other's writings.

Booth makes some interesting comments on his situatedness as a theorist, discussing where his theory comes from and who it might be for. But reflection on one's social and political identity or location is not necessarily a practice of self-reflexivity (see Ackerly and True 2008). Booth recognizes the import of our personal behaviour in his comment that non-violence begins at home. But he does not push this insight further, to reflexively inform his theorizing about international relations. If non-violence begins at home, then pervasive and egregious violence against women – often seen as a 'private matter' – must affect state behaviour and the norms of international relations. Silence on the gendered dimensions of violence is not a neutral act by any international relations scholar. Booth states unequivocally, '[p]ower in all its forms need attention. We need to uncover it, to see how it works, who benefits and so on' (this volume, 68). What form of power is such silence on gendered violence? How does that silence work? Who benefits? What mechanism is there within critical theory to require theorists to reflect on not merely the power of ideas but the gendered power relations within which we are all embedded from the personal to the international realm?

Take Linklater's theory concerned with thinking through obligations to others on an ever increasing scale. How can we be sure that this ethical theorizing is not conducted through a biased, falsely universalizing set of values? What prevents this? Where is the reflexivity, the self/other questioning built into the critical method? From a feminist perspective, it is evident that critical theory (the capitalized version) does not interrogate all forms of power, or has a method for doing so. We are still waiting for the 'critical theory' analysis of the construction of masculine (and feminine) identity and/or the strategic use of sexual violence in projections of military power, for instance. Booth's identification of 'cruelty in the name of manliness' (this volume, 78), or manliness in the name of power, is one item in a long list of oppressive ideas that we must counter. But this is far from a theoretically adequate or nuanced conceptualization of the relationship between gender and international relations.

One expects a critical theorist to demonstrate reflexivity about the powerful creation of schools of thought that categorize and shape intellectual contributions and careers. And yet the four interviews contain little critical reflection along these lines. Wyn Jones observes that the emergence of critical security studies coincides with the end of the Cold War: '[i]ntellectual life … is so path dependent. If there is a debate that you can plug into then that makes it so much easier to get your voice heard' (this volume, 96). But what is the purpose and effects of the creation of capitalized critical theory or critical security studies (let alone the 'Welsh School' that Wyn Jones mentions)? Are there forms of exclusion, domination and coercive inclusion engendered by this naming? Similarly, what are the effects of deploying 'security' or 'emancipation' as anchors, replacements for realism (Booth), or as concepts along the way to a grand theory? Postmodernists have had much more to say here about securitization and the powerful, albeit depoliticizing, effects of constructing a problem as a security issue.[3] Emancipation remains the lynchpin concept for critical international theorists, but how is it theorized and practiced by the four scholars in this volume?

Exploring emancipation

Robert Cox states that critical theory 'requires thinking of alternatives' to the established order (this volume, 20). Cox considers the achievement of greater equity in people's material life, circumstances and opportunities, which could be seen as a proxy for emancipation, to be the normative purpose of that quest for social, political and economic alternatives. He sees economic crisis and inequalities as being at the root of civil and international conflicts, but recognizes that these inequalities are often expressed through different identities and loyalties. By contrast, Booth grasps the ideal of emancipation as a replacement for the realist struggle for power that dominated international relations during the Cold War. In so doing, Booth is not unlike those East Europeans who divested their communist loyalties for faith in ethnic nationalism after the fall of the Berlin Wall (Booth 1991). 'I knew what I was going away from in a theoretical sense – mainstream realism – but it was not yet clear where I was heading. The answer proved to be emancipation. Emancipation became an organizing principle, a way of trying to put it all together' (this volume, 67).

Like Linklater, Booth is a strong believer in the necessity of grand theories in solving the world's ills. Implicit within both Linklater and Booth's understandings of emancipation is an assumption of free choice, that human beings can be autonomous agents and throw off all oppressive or unnecessary constraints. For Booth, emancipation is equated to 'constructing a world of humane constraints that promise reasoned freedom' and his conception of insecurity is a determined life, a life not of choice. However, this definition relies on a particular, masculine account of human agency, rather than a relational notion of the human, connected and responsible to others, put forward by feminist critical theorists. Feminist scholars problematize the very dichotomy of choice/constraint (Hirschmann 2003; Pateman 1989; Benhabib 1987). Women's and men's choices operate within a larger set of oppressive patriarchal structures – thus our understanding of freedom must be concrete and contextual rather than abstract and universal. For instance, some women's choice to wear the veil may appear to be an oppressive, forced act when viewed from outside her context, rather than a practice of establishing identity as well as resisting patriarchy.[4] The dichotomy of choice versus constraint masks the culturally and historically-specific dynamics shaping men and women's agency and assumes we can act outside of prevailing social structures.

Booth's other definition of emancipation in the interview published here – 'the creation of the possibilities to explore what it might mean to be human' (this volume, 70) – is far more open to the wishes within any range of struggles, including women's struggles against oppression. But his comment that 'we should not only behave as if we have equality in a formal sense but from the understanding that we are the same' (this volume, 79) reveals the fatal flaw in the concept and historical experience of 'emancipation'. We are not all the same. Moreover, formulating visions or models for alternative social formations or world orders on the basis that we are all the same or should be all the same with respect to class, gender, race, sexuality, nationality has resulted in gross oppressions wherever it has been tried, in the Soviet Union/East Bloc, in Nazi Germany, in the ethnonationalism in the former Yugoslavia and in some Anglo-Saxon libertarian states, to name a few.[5]

Strangely, in the four critical scholars' rumination on emancipation or human betterment, as Wyn Jones puts it, we do not learn much explicitly about how they practice emancipation – conceived at a minimum as a conversation about what such an ideal might mean – through their scholarship. Wyn Jones considers social movements, in his case specifically the Welsh movement for self-determination 'to be as a practical locus for emancipation-oriented intellectual activity' (this volume, 90). It is clear also that Booth's scholarship has at various times been intended to inform strategy and emancipatory visions in anti-war/peace movements. Through their scholarship, Linklater and Cox seek to promote a more universal community and collective vision of the future by fostering appreciation for the significant differences between and among people as well as the 'shared vulnerabilities' (Linklater, this volume, 51) and 'common concerns' (Cox, this volume, 21). From a feminist perspective, neither goes far enough in recognizing and engaging – even at a theoretical/epistemological level – with the differences among critical approaches in the field of international relations, let alone with the differences among peoples, to be able to discern commonalities.

Conclusion

This exercise in evaluating the reflections of four critical international theorists from a feminist critical perspective reveals once more the overriding problem of 'gender neutral reification'. Fraser first identified this problem in the work of Habermas, although Habermas was, like the four scholars here, a critic of male domination. I have highlighted the four theorists' lack of reflexivity with respect to the effects of their own power and knowledge. Disappearing patriarchal social institutions and norms persist in structuring social reality; the social reality which international theorists have little 'critical distance' from (cf. Fraser 1989: 138). Unmasking power dynamics and exclusions within theory and practice is critical theory's purpose, yet international relations critical theory falls short on this mandate with respect to its own theorizing. I conclude that critical theory's method is insufficient in that it provides few mechanisms for practicing reflexivity.[6] By contrast, 'feminism offers a well-tested [critical] method relevant to the study of all important questions' (Ackerly and True 2006: 247).

A key challenge for all four critical international theorists is to develop collective ways of decision-making. In Booth's words, 'our duty as critical theorists is to change the collective consciousness of society, to challenge the ideas that made us' (this volume, 78). I would include in that gender as an idea and a social structure that has made us. And yet, the four authors seem remarkably inattentive to it.

Notes

1 My question here recalls Nancy Fraser's questioning of critical theory: 'How does [critical theory] theorize the situation and prospects of the feminist movement? Does it – or can it be made – to serve the self-clarification of the wishes and struggles of the contemporary women?' (Fraser 1989: 114). Twenty-five years ago Fraser had to construct her analysis mainly from 'absences' in Habermas' text: the task of the feminist theorist today is no different – leading one to wonder what social learning or dialogue has gone on between different forms of critical theory in the interlude.
2 Wyn Jones refers to the article authored by the c.a.s.e. collective on what counts as 'critical' in critical security studies (see c.a.s.e. collective 2006).
3 See Wæver (1995), Hansen (2000), Duffield (2001) and Balzacq (2005).
4 See McLeod (1991).
5 See, for example, Bock (1983), Kotkin (1997) and Korac (1998).
6 See Ackerly and True (2008).

Bibliography

Ackerly, B.A. and True, J. (2006) 'Studying the Struggles and Wishes of the Age: Feminist Theoretical Methodology and Feminist Theoretical Methods', in B. Ackerly and J. True (eds) *Feminist Methodologies for International Relations*, Cambridge: Cambridge University Press.

——— (2008) 'Reflexivity in Practice: Power and Ethics in Feminist Research on International Relations', *International Studies Review* 10(4): 581–600.

——— (2010) *Doing Feminist Research in Political and Social Science*, New York: Palgrave.

Balzacq, T. (2005) 'The Three Faces of Securitization: Political Agency, Audience, and Context', *European Journal of International Relations* 11(2): 171–201.

Benhabib, S. (1987) 'The Generalized and the Concrete Other: the Kohlberg–Gilligan Controversy and Feminist Theory', in S. Benhabib and D. Cornell (eds) *Feminism as Critique*, Minneapolis: University of Minnesota Press.

Bock, G. (1983) 'Racism and Sexism in Nazi Germany: Motherhood, Compulsory Sterilization, and the State', *Signs: Journal of Women, Culture and Society* 8(3): 400–21.

Booth, K. (1991) 'Security and Emancipation', *Review of International Studies* 17(4): 313–26.

Burchill, S. and Linklater, A. (2009) 'Introduction', in S. Burchill, A. Linklater, R. Devetak *et al.*, *Theories of International Relations*, Fourth Edition, Basingstoke: Palgrave.

C.A.S.E. collective (2006) 'Critical Approaches to Security in Europe: A Networked Manifesto', *Security Dialogue* 37(4): 443–87.

Cox, R.W. (1981) 'Social Forces, States and World Orders: Beyond International Relations Theory', *Millennium* 10(2): 126–55.

_____ (2002) 'Civilizations: Encounters and Transformations', in R.W. Cox and M. Schecter, *The Political Economy of a Plural World: Critical Reflections on Power, Morals and Civilization*, New York: Routledge.

Duffield, M.R. (2001) *Global Governance and the New Wars: The Merging of Development and Security*, London: Zed Books.

Fraser, N. (1989) 'What's Critical about Critical Theory: The Case of Habermas and Gender', in *Unruly Practices: Power, Discourse and Gender in Contemporary Social Theory*, Minneapolis: University of Minnesota Press.

Hansen, L. (2000) 'The Little Mermaid's Silent Security Dilemma and the Absence of Gender in the Copenhagen School', *Millennium* 29(2): 285–306.

Hirschmann, N.J. (2003) *The Subject of Liberty: Toward a Feminist Theory of Freedom*, Princeton: Princeton University Press.

Korac, M. (1998) 'Ethnic Nationalism, Wars and the Patterns of Social, Political and Sexual Violence against Women: The Case of Post Yugoslav Countries', *Identities: Global Studies in Culture and Power* 5(2): 53–81.

Kotkin, S. (1997) *Magnetic Mountain: Stalinism as a Civilization*, Berkeley: University of California Press.

McLeod, A.E. (1991) *Accommodating Protest: Working Women, the New Veiling, and Change in Cairo*, New York: Columbia University Press.

Pateman, C. (1989) 'Women and Consent', in C. Pateman, *The Disorder of Women: Democracy, Feminism and Political Theory*, Cambridge: Polity Press.

Wæver, O. (1995) 'Securitization and Desecuritization', in R. Lipschutz (ed.) *On Security*, New York: Columbia.

Younnis, J. (2011) 'Egypt's revolution means nothing if its women are not free', *The Guardian*, 9 March.

11

THE CONTINUING APPEAL OF CRITICAL SECURITY STUDIES[1]

Pinar Bilgin

Twenty years have passed since the publication of Ken Booth's seminal essay 'Security and Emancipation' (1991). It has been 16 years since Ken Booth and Richard Wyn Jones offered the first post-graduate level course on 'Critical Security Studies (CSS)' at Aberystwyth University (1995/96).[2] Since then, the critical body of work produced by Booth, Wyn Jones, their close collaborators and (by now many) students has come to be known as the Aberystwyth School of CSS. Twenty years on CSS is going strong.[3]

Over the years, CSS has made important inroads into the study of security in Western Europe, North America and Australia[4] – 'the West', for want of a better term.[5] Considering the growing number of courses offered at universities, seminars organized and/or sponsored by think-tanks, conference papers, journal articles, books and book chapters, the rest of the world has not remained indifferent to the appeal of CSS either.[6] This is in addition to a body of work produced by scholars located in 'the West' studying 'non-Western' insecurities from a CSS perspective.[7] Needless to say, these two sets of literatures have not developed in isolation from each other; there is plenty of jointly produced work.[8]

The standing CSS has reached outside the Western context must have come as a surprise to those who have viewed the centrality of emancipation to be a factor diminishing its potential for being picked up by scholars elsewhere in the world. In particular, the critics have pointed to the ideational origins of CSS, which is unmistakeably Western European, and argued that CSS is bound to have limited political impact.[9] These two points have shaped the debates on two interrelated issues: the relevance of CSS for understanding insecurities in the non-West, and what it means for CSS (as with other security scholarship) to have political impact. What follows takes each issue in turn and seeks to address the points made by the critics in light of both CSS scholars' writings and their reception outside Western contexts.

It is argued, first, that understanding why CSS has been remarkably well received in the non-West call for: (a) questioning our unacknowledged assumptions as to how and why theories and concepts travel from one context to another; and (b) recognizing that geo-cultural differences in security thinking are not pre-given (or immutable) 'facts of life', but themselves products of global dynamics.[10]

The second and related argument is about the supposed Eurocentrism of CSS. Without wanting to make too much of the fact that the critics sometimes fail the Eurocentrism test they set for the others, it is significant to highlight how CSS is often received in the non-West as an antidote to Eurocentrism. This is because non-Western scholars appreciate the refusal of CSS to limit the security agenda to those issues identified as security problems, and the emphasis put on those insecurities that are left unproblematized by the supposedly problem-solving theories. The point being that the potential of Critical Security Studies for political impact should be considered not only in terms of whispering practicalities into the 'Prince's ear' but also as 'challenging the ideas that made us' (the title of Ken Booth's interview in this volume).

The relevance of CSS for understanding insecurities in the non-West

Mohammed Ayoob (1995; 1997) is one of the most vocal critics of CSS. Over the years he has maintained that, while CSS may constitute a step forward in so far as it has moved away from mainstream approaches' almost exclusive focus on external threats, CSS scholars have made a crucial mistake by letting ethnocentrism in through the back door by linking security with emancipation.

On closer inspection, however, Ayoob's reservations seem to have less to do with the Western European origins of ideas about emancipation and more to do with their suitability outside 'the West'.[11] Emancipation-oriented approaches to security are not suitable for non-Western contexts, argues Ayoob, because those parts of the world are still going through a phase comparable to Europe's violent past, and therefore cannot (and should not) aspire to emancipation. Ayoob (1997: 127) writes:

> [T]o posit emancipation as synonym with security and the panacea for all the ills plaguing Third World states can be the height of naïveté. Emancipation, interpreted as the right of every ethnic group to self-determination, can turn out to be a recipe for grave disorder and anarchy as far as most Third World states are concerned.

It may be fine, Ayoob concludes, to consider emancipation as an aspect of security in the West, but 'it would be extremely far-fetched and intellectually disingenuous to do the same in the case of the Third World, where basic problems of state legitimacy, political order, and capital accumulation are far from being solved and may even be getting worse' (Ayoob 1995: 11).

CSS writings offer four sets of responses to such criticism. One is to say that Ayoob misjudges the CSS notion of emancipation. While emancipation eludes easy definition,[12] it is also 'a concept that has been associated with some of the great progressive struggles in modern history' (Wyn Jones 2005: 217). Depending on the context, self-determination may be one among many challenges encountered by individuals and social groups. As highlighted in the interview in this volume, Booth considers 'bread, knowledge, and freedom' as a comprehensive basis for thinking about emancipation worldwide.[13] The second and related response is to highlight the difference in the CSS approach to the politics of security/identity. From a CSS perspective, identity does not exist 'out there' prior to interaction. Accordingly, it is not accessible to security scholars independent of the particular political, social and historical context. As Bill McSweeney (1999: 73) has underscored, 'identity is not to be taken as an independent variable, *tout court*; it is often the outcome of a labelling process which reflects a conflict of interests at the political level'. Accordingly, insecurity need not be viewed as a product of identity differences; identity differences may well be products of insecurities (McSweeney 1999). Adopting a social constructivist and reflexive approach to security/identity dynamics as such allows CSS scholars to avoid the very risk that Ayoob has identified with linking security with emancipation – even if it were equated with self-determination.

The third response to Ayoob's critique is to clarify what emancipation entails from a CSS perspective. Defined in suitably flexible terms as the 'political–ethical direction' of security scholarship (Wyn Jones 2005: 217), emancipation is shared by most critical theorists even as they unambiguously distance themselves from the project of Enlightenment.[14] What is more, the very notion of emancipation adopted by Booth and Wyn Jones pushes the term beyond its Western European origins and conceptualizes it as 'political convergences on needs, not agreement on foundations', in Hayward Alker's turn of phrase (2005: 201).[15]

Finally, regarding the issue of emancipation's Western European origins, Booth has underscored that 'what matters is not where ideas come from but how well they travel' (Booth 2005a: 181). In his interview he elaborates on this point:

> I do not see the values of the Enlightenment as 'essentially' European, nor do I believe that 'we' are emancipated and 'they' need catch up. As it happens, at this moment in Western countries there is much moving away from what I consider to be the road to emancipation.
>
> *(Booth, this volume, 68)*

CSS scholars refuse to take ideas (such as emancipation) as products of a single geo-cultural setting. For that would amount to treating cultures as insulated containers of ideas and values. Indeed, CSS's reception worldwide suggests that what we take to be geo-cultural differences are themselves products of global political dynamics. The fact that the four key authors interviewed for this book have all their origins in the margins of their own geo-cultural setting (Booth from a mining village in Yorkshire; Wyn Jones from Wales; Linklater from Scotland; and Cox from an

Anglophone part of Francophone Quebec) underscore that the decisive divide is centre-periphery dynamics as products (and producers) of relations between the Global South and the Global North.[16]

While CSS scholars understand the relationship between geo-cultures and concepts as mutually constitutive, they have so far not paid close attention to the social and historical contexts in which concepts and theories travel from one place to another. Consider the case of China, where 'national security' has remained paramount in theory. This is partly because state security prevails over human security in practice. It is also partly to do with how some Chinese scholars consider 'national security' to be the conceptual framework through which the United States makes sense of the world (as with International Relations in general).[17]

Be it for reasons of rivalry or envy, US concepts and theories are adopted in China. Against that background, the geo-cultural explanation Yongjin Zhang (2007: 180) offers in explaining the apparent absence of CSS in the Chinese context (that it 'has no intellectual roots in China') is not entirely convincing. This is because, as Simon Dalby (2007: 253) reminds us, adopting CSS would not require too much of a theoretical stretch beyond 'reinventing their Marxist roots'. Contra Zhang, then, in China scholars seem to have made a choice for adopting a Western-originated body of concepts and theories for reasons less to do with job description of theory, or with the geo-cultural origins of ideas, but with the dynamics of global politics.[18] It follows that CSS's reception worldwide has less to do with geo-cultural origins of ideas and more with the (potential) practical implications of adopting one body of concepts and theories over another.

Consider Katrina Lee-Koo's reflection on this issue:

> It is not a revelation for critical feminists ... that political concepts designed ostensibly for a 'universal good' might be, for some, the source of oppression. Any political concept claiming universality is destined to silence the experiences, imaginings and goals of those who deviate from the mainstream construction of knowledge ... In this sense, emancipation is no different.
>
> *(Lee-Koo 2007: 242)*

Lee-Koo offers a two-fold strategy in an attempt to hold on to a notion of emancipation in re-thinking non-Western women's security. This strategy entails first, '[deconstructing] the gendered (which often simultaneously means oppressive) nature of the concept and to reconstruct it towards a feminist ethic that challenges *all* forms of domination for *all* women' (Lee-Koo 2007: 242). The second leg of Lee-Koo's strategy involves theorizing emancipation in such a way that it '[includes] the insights of an array of non-Western and post-colonial critical feminists working on issues of insecurity' (2007: 243). As such, Lee-Koo has identified a way of pushing emancipation beyond its geo-cultural origins, thereby avoiding the very dangers that the critics have warned against.

Haider Nizamani's (2008) analysis of South Asian dynamics from a critical perspective reaffirms the appropriateness of Lee-Koo's strategy. According to

Nizamani, adopting a critical perspective is a must because 'their' theories fail to account for 'our realities'. What is worth underscoring here is that Nizamani (2008: 91) considers 'their' theories to be those mainstream approaches that fail to account for (if not marginalize) South Asian 'realities'. At the same time, Nizamani embraces CSS 'as a more productive alternative to existing sterile Political Realism in various garbs'. He calls for 'synthesising Critical International Relations Theory and Subaltern Studies to analyse issues that are of concern to security analysts of South Asia' (Nizamani 2008: 106). In contrast to Zhang, then, Nizamani rejects categorizing theories in terms of geo-cultural origin but emphasizes their differences in terms their analytical and political appropriateness in the study of non-Western insecurities. Such a differentiation, in turn, corresponds to the problem-solving/critical theory distinction that CSS rests upon.

The potential of CSS for political impact

A second weakness the critics have pointed to is the limits of CSS in terms of political impact. Tarak Barkawi and Mark Laffey (2006) have located the roots of this problem in the Eurocentrism of Security Studies writ large. According to the authors, CSS is not immune from Eurocentrism as such and this limit defines the limits of its potential for political impact. Barkawi and Laffey characterize Security Studies as Eurocentric for two reasons. First, Security Studies has failed to grasp the full reality of global insecurity, partly due to its neglect of the Global South's experiences by virtue of security scholars adopting great power-centric lenses, and partly because of the limits of current categories of International Relations (IR), such as 'state', 'war' and 'terror'. Second, Security Studies has overlooked the linkages between 'the weak and the strong'; the 'Global South' and the 'Global North' and the constitutive relationship in between. Indeed, as they note, '[t]hat the weak play an integral part in shaping world politics is harder to deny when a Southern resistance movement strikes at the heart of Northern power' (Barkawi and Laffey 2006: 333).

The point that critical approaches are not immune from Eurocentrism was made previously.[19] What is distinctive about Barkawi and Laffey's critique is the way they link it up to mainstream Security Studies' failure to account for current and historical security dynamics, and the potential implications of such a failure for security policies worldwide. That said, the authors' labelling of CSS as Eurocentric (and therefore limited in terms of political impact), even as they highlight Ayoob's argument as appropriately non-Eurocentric (and therefore having more potential for political impact) is somewhat confusing.

Eurocentrism in IR could be defined as the practice of putting Europe at the centre of one's thinking about the past, present and future of world politics. Eurocentrism need not be reduced to conscious acts of putting Europe (and/or 'the West') and its interests first. One can be Eurocentric in an unthinking manner, by way of taking European experiences as the norm when considering international phenomena. What is characteristic to the latter form is a particular understanding of Europe and its experiences as unique and self-contained. It is this second form of Eurocentrism that Ayoob's analysis exhibits along with some other forms of critical IR. In contrast, from its earliest origins in Booth's book *Strategy and Ethnocentrism* (1979), CSS has sought to distance itself from Eurocentrism.[20]

To start with Ayoob, his criticism regarding mainstream approaches to security and their global relevance is that their notion of state does not fit the Third World where states 'happen to be at a stage of state making at which most industrial democracies were in the sixteenth and nineteenth centuries' (Ayoob 1997: 122). Formulated as such, Ayoob offers a crucial corrective to mainstream approaches that are built upon assumptions of states as uniform entities. However, Ayoob does not push his critique to its logical conclusion, stopping short of offering an assessment of mainstream conceptualizations of the state. What he offers instead is a critique of states in the Third World and how they do not fit Security Studies notions. Whereas, as debates surrounding 'state failure' have lain bare, the problem at hand is not only with the 'nature' of some states but also with prevalent notions of 'the state'.[21]

What is more, by way of buying into the 'stages of development' assumptions on which modernization theories are built, Ayoob exhibits a form of Eurocentric ethnocentrism that he otherwise wishes to do away with. This is because he adopts a certain understanding of Western European history as the norm and sketches a trajectory for the rest – his only reservation being that critical approaches should not impose contemporary 'Western' standards onto the rest of the world. However, it is historically inaccurate to argue, as Ayoob does, that '[t]erritorial satiation, societal cohesion, and political stability – all part of a successful state making – have determined the generally pacific nature of industrial democracies' relations with each other' (Ayoob 1997: 136). On the contrary, as Barkawi and Laffey (1999) have argued elsewhere, the 'pacific nature of industrial democracies' is an historical product of (often neglected) constitutive relations between the periphery and the core, including the role that the deployment and constitution of force elsewhere around the world has played in allowing 'peace' among democracies. Furthermore, as Sandra Halperin has shown, the Western European model against which the Third World is measured is 'more fiction than fact' and 'the pattern displayed in contemporary Third World development is analogous to the pattern of development in pre-1945 Europe' (Halperin 1997: viii–ix) – but not the sixteenth or nineteenth centuries as Ayoob argues. Then, contra Ayoob, who joins mainstream approaches in conceiving an insurmountable gap between the development trajectories of states in Western Europe and the Third World, Historical Sociology and Critical Theory accounts underscore synchronic *and* diachronic links between the two.[22] Further, they identify the mainstream notion of state as a product of this very relationship.

On closer inspection, then, Ayoob's notion of the state emerges to be problematic by virtue of its Eurocentrism that overlooks historical relationships of state formation and consolidation. These relationships are not merely those between the colonizers and the colonized, some which have survived de-colonization. Rather, these are relationships that result in the social production of insecurity in a variety of ways, involving the constitution of categories including state, democracy, success/failure, developed/developing. If it is the construction of a 'Western' identity as distinct from (if not superior to) the rest that has helped to obscure the 'Eastern origins of Western civilisation' (Hobson 2004) and 'Europe's colonial past' (Halperin 1997), the very categories through which we make sense of security dynamics in a synchronic manner are complicit in the (re)production of insecurities worldwide, including the Global South. Understanding insecurities as by-products of our own categories, in turn, demand both diachronic *and* synchronic scrutiny. Following Coxian Critical Theory, CSS offers both.

While offering a non-Eurocentric account does not immediately translate into political impact, the insight CSS provides into the historical (re)production of insecurities worldwide is testimony to its potential as such. For, as highlighted above, one reason why CSS is received well in non-Western contexts has to do with its focus on insecurities experienced in the Global South. While mainstream critics identify the origins of CSS in Critical Theory to be a major weakness, that critical edge transpires to be a source of strength in the eyes of non-Western scholars. In Booth's formulation, the job definition of CSS as a 'theory of world security' (Booth 2007) is different from that of mainstream approaches: not one of seeking to advise 'the Prince' but 'to stand outside the contemporary situation as far as possible and hold up a mirror – to try to show people what the world is like and what it will continue to be like if behaviour remains dominated by the traditional ideas that made us' (Booth, this volume, 76). This definition fits right into Cox's distinction between problem solving and critical theory. At the same time, it turns on their heads everyday understandings of what it means to 'solve problems' versus being 'critical'. In the interviews, Cox clarified the difference between problem solving and critical theories as follows: 'critical thinking is directed more toward historical change, whereas problem solving means thinking within the existing historical structure about how to overcome the difficulties that might arise' (this volume, 20).

While the distinction that Cox makes does not leave much room for confusion, it is often the case that everyday understandings of being critical (engaging in navel-gazing) versus problem solving (being useful) are imposed upon Coxian terminology. Hence Booth's clarification of the distinction between critical versus problem-solving theories of security. CSS, he writes, offers 'a security studies that goes beyond problem-solving *within* the status quo and, and instead seeks to help engage through critical theory with the problems *of* the status quo' (Booth 2007: 48).

To recap, Ayoob suffers from a form of Eurocentrism that Barkawi and Laffey would like to do away with. As such, the political and policy relevance of Ayoob's account is bound to be as limited as mainstream Security Studies. In turn, by virtue of the diachronic and synchronic analysis it offers, CSS does not fit the authors' definition of Eurocentrism. Furthermore, its focus on producing critiques of the structures that produce problems (as opposed to solving those problems defined in the narrow terms of mainstream approaches) need not hinder the potential of CSS for political impact. For, political impact need not be reduced to advising the policy-maker alone. CSS seeks to make an impact by refusing to engage with 'the world as it is, because we have to live in it' (Waltz quoted in Booth, this volume, 81), and instead calling for a discussion '[f]ocusing on the meaning of "the world as it is" and whether trying to "live in it" under contemporary conditions with traditional ideas is a recipe for disaster' (Booth, this volume, 75).

Conclusion

From 1991 to 2011, CSS has developed into a wide-ranging subfield of Security Studies with many students. Significant steps have been taken in terms of elaborating on certain key concepts and a lot remains to be done on some others. The appeal of CSS beyond the West has clearly surpassed the presumptions of the critics. It could be surmised that it is because CSS constitutes an instance of post-Eurocentric Security Studies that it is so well received in non-Western contexts. While few CSS scholars explicitly draw upon Post-Colonial Studies,[23] Booth's individual and joint work with Peter Vale on Southern Africa (1995) and Eli Stamnes' studies on peacekeeping (2004) offer insight into the dynamic relationships between the weak and the strong, including notions and practices of security in the Global South (Thomas and Wilkin 1999 and Whitworth 2004).

The critics of CSS often suggest that while it may be fine to try and change the world, this is the world that we have to live in. We should seek to address problems first, they argue, and perhaps later we can try and change the world! Or, as Booth has neatly summarized, 'Hobbes today, Kant tomorrow' (1991: 321). One response to such caricaturized representations of critical versus problem-solving theory is to highlight the relationship between short-term (1–12 months), medium-term (2–3 years) and long-term (3–15 years) policy-making and the need to avoid 'short-termism (the preference for approaching security issues within the time-frame of the next election, not the next generation)' (Booth 1999a: 4). For Hobbesian practices of today may make it impossible to follow Kantian policies tomorrow due to the potentially counter-productive implications of short-termist policies (as witnessed in US policy-making toward Afghanistan during the 1970s, 1980s and in the post-9/11 era) (Bilgin and Morton 2004).

Another response to the critics would be to remind them that what renders CSS attractive in the non-West is not the promise of Kantian 'Perpetual Peace' as is often presumed, but the fact that non-Western insecurities cannot be reduced to Hobbesian fear alone. CSS presents a theory of security that better explains *and* offers a way out of insecurities encountered in/by the Global South. From a non-Western perspective, critical theory of security as offered by CSS *is* a more promising framework for solving problems in so far as it problematizes, seeks to understand and tries to address those issues that are left unproblematized and unaccounted for by mainstream Security Studies.

Notes

1 I would like to thank Ali Bilgiç, Paul D. Williams and the Editors for feedback.
2 Nicholas J. Wheeler had joined Booth and Wyn Jones on the teaching team during the 1995/96 academic year. I was among the five students taking the course.

3 Critical Security Studies (CSS) refers to the Aberystwyth School approach whereas critical security studies (css) is the umbrella term inclusive of a variety of approaches critical of mainstream Security Studies.

4 See Alker (2005), Booth (1997; 1999a; 1999b; 2004; 2005b and 2007), Booth and Wheeler (2007), Burke (2001 and 2007), McSweeney (1999), Neufeld (2004), Wyn Jones (1999 and 2005).

5 Throughout the chapter, I will use the terms 'developed/developing', 'West/non-West', 'Europe/non-Europe', 'First World/Third World', 'core/non-core', 'South/North' interchangeably not because I am not aware of the problems involved, but because I want to talk about a set of problems that are tied up with these binaries. Following Spivak, I have made a choice for 'strategic essentialism', that is 'using a clear image of identity to sight a politics of opposition (which would not be possible if all the aspects of identity were to be incorporated)' (cited in Sharp 2008: 114).

6 See Behera (2004), Bilgic (2010), Bilgin (2002; 2004; 2005 and 2007), Burke and McDonald (2007), Messari (2002), Nizamani (2008), Swatuk and Vale (1999), Vale (2003).

7 See Davies (2004), Kennedy-Pipe (2004), Parnwell (1998), Stamnes (2004 and 2009), Stamnes and Wyn Jones (2000), Thomas and Wilkin (1999), Williams (2000 and 2007), Williams and Bellamy (2005).

8 In this respect see Bilgin and Morton (2002 and 2004), Booth and Vale (1995), Burke and McDonald (2007).

9 See, for example, Ayoob (1995) and Barkawi and Laffey (2006).

10 See Bilgin (2009a), cf. Vaughan-Williams and Peoples (2009).

11 After all, Ayoob (2002) favours an English School perspective in understanding international relations of the Third World and beyond.

12 As with others, such as power, security and culture. Also note that in the interviews, Cox (this volume, 23) starts out with a narrow definition ('emancipation from slavery') but then goes on to argue that 'the idea of being critical is bound with the concept of emancipation, since, after all, you are criticizing the established way of thinking. The established way of thinking is usually something that works to the benefit of an established power or social structure, so that if you are writing critically you are writing with the implication of some kind of change that can be made to the social structure' (Cox, this volume, 24).

13 See Booth (this volume, 70; 2008: 110–11).

14 See Cox (this volume, 25) and Linklater (this volume, 54–5).

15 See also Booth (2007: 60–61).

16 I would like to thank the Editors for highlighting this dimension.

17 See Wang (2009).

18 See also Bilgin (2009a and 2010).

19 See, for example, Halperin (2003 and 2006) and Hobson (2004 and 2007).

20 See Booth (this volume, 69; 1997).

21 See Milliken and Krause (2002), Bilgin and Morton (2002 and 2004).

22 Cox distinguishes between synchronic and diachronic analysis in terms of their usefulness for problem solving and critical theory, respectively. He makes an argument for their combined use in analysing world politics (Cox, interview: 12).

23 But see Bilgin (2008a; 2008b; 2008c and 2009b) and Bilgin and Morton (2002).

Bibliography

Alker, H. (2005) 'Emancipation in the Critical Security Studies Project' in K. Booth (ed.) *Critical Security Studies and World Politics*, Boulder: Lynne Rienner Publishers.

Ayoob, M. (1995) *The Third World Security Predicament: State Making, Regional Conflict, and the International System,* Boulder: Lynne Rienner Publishers.

Ayoob, M. (1997) 'Defining Security: A Subaltern Realist Perspective', in K. Krause and M. Williams (eds) *Critical Security Studies: Concepts and Cases*, Minneapolis: University of Minnesota Press.

____ (2002) 'Inequality and Theorizing in International Relations: The Case for Subaltern Realism', *International Studies Review* 4: 27–48.

Barkawi, T. and Laffey, M. (1999) 'The Imperial Peace: Democracy, Force and Globalization', *European Journal of International Relations* 5: 403–34.

____ (2006) 'The Postcolonial Moment in Security Studies', *Review of International Studies* 32: 329–52.

Behera, N. C. (2004) 'A South Asian Debate on Peace and Security: An Alternative Formulation in the Post-Cold War Era', paper presented at the Fifth Pan-European Conference, The Hague, Netherlands.

Bilgic, A. (2010) 'Security through Trust-Building in the Euro-Mediterranean Cooperation: Two Perspectives for the Partnership', *Southeast European and Black Sea Studies* 10: 457–73.

Bilgin, P. (2002) 'Beyond Statism in Security Studies? Human Agency and Security in the Middle East', *Review of International Affairs* 2: 100–18.

____ (2004) 'Whose Middle East? Geopolitical Inventions and Practices of Security', *International Relations* 18: 17–33.

____ (2005) *Regional Security in the Middle East: A Critical Perspective,* London: Routledge Curzon.

____ (2007) 'Making Turkey's Transformation Possible: Claiming "Security-Speak"–Not Desecuritization!', *Journal of Southeast European and Black Sea Studies* 7: 555–71.

____ (2008a) 'Securing Turkey through Western-Oriented Foreign Policy', paper presented at the 7th International Relations Conference of Middle-East-Technical-University, Ankara, Turkey.

____ (2008b) 'The Securityness of Secularism? The Case of Turkey', *Security Dialogue* 39(6): 593–614.

____ (2008c) 'Thinking Past "Western" IR?', *Third World Quarterly* 29: 5–23.

____ (2009a) 'The International Political "Sociology of a Not So International Discipline"', *International Political Sociology* 3: 338–42.

____ (2009b) 'Securing Turkey through Western-Oriented Foreign Policy', *New Perspectives on Turkey* 40: 105–25.

____ (2010) 'The "Western-Centrism" of Security Studies: "Blind Spot" or Constitutive Practice?', *Security Dialogue* 41(6): 615–22.

Bilgin, P. and Morton, A. (2002) 'Historicising Representations of "Failed States": Beyond the Cold War Annexation of the Social Sciences?', *Third World Quarterly* 23: 55–80.

____ (2004) 'From "Rogue" to "Failed" States? The Fallacy of Short-Termism', *Politics* 24: 169–80.

Booth, K. (1979) *Strategy and Ethnocentrism,* New York: Holmes & Meier.

____ (1991) 'Security and Emancipation', *Review of International Studies* 17: 313–26.

____ (1997) 'Security and Self: Reflections of a Fallen Realist' in K. Krause and M. Williams (eds.) *Critical Security Studies: Concepts and Cases*, Minneapolis: University of Minnesota Press.

____ (1999a) 'Nuclearism, Human Rights and Constructions of Security (Part 1)', *The International Journal of Human Rights* 3: 1–24.

____ (1999b) 'Nuclearism, Human Rights and Contructions of Security (Part 2)', *International Journal of Human Rights* 3: 44–61.

Booth, K. (ed.) (2004) Special Issue on Critical Security Studies, *International Relations* 18.

_____ (2005a) 'Emancipation' in K. Booth (ed.) *Critical Security Studies and World Politics*, Boulder: Lynne Rienner Publishers.

_____ (ed.) (2005b) *Critical Security Studies and World Politics,* Boulder: Lynne Rienner Publishers.

_____ (2007) *Theory of World Security,* Cambridge: Cambridge University Press.

Booth, K. and Vale, P. (1995) 'Security in Southern Africa: After Apartheid, Beyond Realism', *International Affairs* 71: 285–304.

Booth, K. and Wheeler, N. (2007) *The Security Dilemma: Fear, Cooperation, and Trust in World Politics,* Basingstoke: Palgrave Macmillan.

Burke, A. (2001) *Fear of Security: Australia's Invasion Anxiety,* Annandale: Pluto Press.

_____ (2007) *Beyond Security, Ethics and Violence: War against the Other,* New York: Routledge.

Burke, A. and McDonald, M. (eds) (2007) *Critical Security in the Asia-Pacific,* Manchester: Manchester University Press.

Dalby, S. (2007) 'Conclusion: Emancipating Security in the Asia-Pacific?', in A. Burke and M. McDonald (eds) *Critical Security in the Asia-Pacific,* Manchester: Manchester University Press.

Davies, S. (2004) 'Community Versus Deterrence: Managing Security and Nuclear Proliferation in Latin America and South Asia', *International Relations* 18: 55–72.

Halperin, S. (1997) *In the Mirror of the Third World: Capitalist Development in Modern Europe,* Ithaca: Cornell University Press.

_____ (2003) *War and Social Change in Modern Europe: The Great Transformation Revisited,* New York: Cambridge University Press.

_____ (2006) 'International Relations Theory and the Hegemony of Western Conceptions of Modernity', in B. Jones (ed.) *Decolonizing International Relations,* Lanham: Rowman & Littlefield.

Hobson, J. M. (2004) *The Eastern Origins of Western Civilization,* Cambridge: Cambridge University Press.

_____ (2007) 'Is Critical Theory Always for the White West and Western Imperialism? Beyond Westphilian Towards a Post-Racist Critical IR', *Review of International Studies* 33: 91–116.

Kennedy-Pipe, C. (2004) 'Whose Security? State-Building and the "Emancipation" of Women in Central Asia', *International Relations* 18: 91–107.

Lee-Koo, K. (2007) 'Security as Enslavement, Security as Emancipation: Gendered Legacies and Feminist Futures in the Asia-Pacific' in A. Burke and M. McDonald (eds) *Critical Security in the Asia-Pacific,* Manchester: Manchester University Press.

McSweeney, B. (1999) *Security, Identity and Interests: A Sociology of International Relations,* Cambridge: Cambridge University Press.

Messari, N. (2002) 'The State and Dilemmas of Security: The Middle East and the Balkans', *Security Dialogue* 33: 415–27.

Milliken, J. and Krause, K. (2002) 'State Failure, State Collapse, and State Reconstruction: Concepts, Lessons and Strategies', *Development & Change* 33: 753–74.

Neufeld, M. (2004) 'Pitfalls of Emancipation and Discourses of Security: Reflections on Canada's "Security with a Human Face"', *International Relations* 18: 109–23.

Nizamani, H. K. (2008) 'Our Region Their Theories: A Case for Critical Security Studies in South Asia', in Behera, N. C. (ed.) *International Relations in South Asia,* Delhi: Oxford University Press.

Parnwell, M. J. (1998) 'Tourism, Globalisation and Critical Security in Myanmar and Thailand', *Singapore Journal of Tropical Geography* 19: 212–31.

Sharp, J. P. (2008) *Geographies of Postcolonialism: Spaces of Power and Representation*, London: SAGE Publications.

Stamnes, E. (2004) 'Critical Security Studies and the United Nations Preventive Deployment in Macedonia', *International Peacekeeping* 11: 161–81.

_____ (2009) '"Speaking R2P" and the Prevention of Mass Atrocities', *Global Responsibility to Protect* 1: 70–89.

Stamnes, E. and Wyn Jones, R. (2000) 'Burundi: A Critical Security Perspective', *Peace and Conflict Studies* 7: 37–55.

Swatuk, L. and Vale, P. (1999) 'Why Democracy Is Not Enough: Southern Africa and Human Security in the Twenty-First Century', *Alternatives – Social Transformation and Humane Governance* 24: 361–89.

Thomas, C. and Wilkin, P. (1999) *Globalization, Human Security, and the African Experience*, Boulder: Lynne Rienner Publishers.

Vale, P. (2003) *Security and Politics in South Africa: The Regional Dimension*, Boulder: Lynne Rienner Publishers.

Vaughan-Williams, N. and Peoples, C. (2009) *Critical Security Studies: An Introduction*, London: Routledge.

Wang, Y. (2009) 'China: Between Copying and Constructing', in A. Tickner and O. Wæver (eds) *International Relations Scholarship Around the World*, London: Routledge.

Whitworth, S. (2004) *Men, Militarism, and UN Peacekeeping: A Gendered Analysis*, Boulder: Lynne Rienner Publishers.

Williams, P. D. (2000) 'South African Foreign Policy: Getting Critical?', *Politikon: South African Journal of Political Studies* 27: 73–91.

_____ (2007) 'Thinking about Security in Africa', *International Affairs* 83: 1021–38.

Williams, P. D. and Bellamy, A. J. (2005) 'The Responsibility to Protect and the Crisis in Darfur', *Security Dialogue* 36: 27–47.

Wyn Jones, R. (1999) *Security, Strategy, and Critical Theory*, Boulder: Lynne Rienner Publishers.

_____ (2005) 'On Emancipation: Necessity, Capacity and Concrete Utopias' in K. Booth (ed.) *Critical Security Studies and World Politics,* Boulder: Lynne Rienner Publishers.

Zhang, Y. (2007) 'Discourses of Security in China: Towards a Critical Turn?', in A. Burke and M. McDonald (eds) *Critical Security in the Asia-Pacific*, Manchester: Manchester University Press.

PART IV
Future Directions

12

BEYOND (WESTERN) IR THEORY

The post-colonial tradition and the restructuring of (critical) IR theory

Mark Neufeld

> Part of intellectual work is understanding how authority is formed ... And if you can understand that, then your work is conducted in such a way as to be able to provide alternatives to the authoritative and coercive norms that dominate so much of our intellectual life, our national and political life, *and our international life above all.*
>
> *(Said 2001a: 366–7)*

Introduction

A few years after the publication of my book *The Restructuring of International Relations Theory* (1995), which focused on modernist (neo-Gramscian), postmodernist and feminist critical variants, I encountered a review that caught my attention in that it reflected a theoretical orientation – post-colonial theory – with which I was only vaguely familiar:

> Mark Neufeld's recent writings replicate this problem [of Western-centrism]. [His work] is also an example of Western reflection upon Western theorizing. There is no room for postcolonial reflection on postcolonial theorizing. The silencing of the voice of the 'other' here is just as total as anywhere else in IR. Consequently, [the solution advocated] ends up being merely a 'corrective' to Western discourses and not their transcendence.
>
> *(Ahluwalia and Sullivan 2001: 353)*

Engaging the themes and issues raised in the interviews featured in this volume provided me with an ideal opportunity for exploring the theme of post-colonial theory and its relationship to critical International Relations (IR) theory. My particular focus here will be the question of what critical IR theory can learn from an engagement with post-colonial theory.[1]

A couple of caveats are in order. First, although I will be referring to post-colonial theory generally, it is the figure of Edward Said who will figure most prominently here. For reasons that I hope will become clearer as I proceed, I think Said in particular offers invaluable insights that are very relevant to any discussion of a 'restructuring' of critical IR theory in a less Western-focused direction. I shall proceed by organizing my thoughts around three key theses.

Thesis one: post-colonial theory is not all of a piece

I began my exploration of post-colonial theory by engaging the work of current theorists such as Spivak and Bhabha – and especially Said – and their precursors such as Fanon, Memmi and Guevara. One thing that became immediately apparent is that, notwithstanding important commonalities, there are also important differences in flavour, emphasis, and even basic position. Said, for example, lays much greater stress on theory needing to be wedded to concrete praxis if it is to have critical purchase; Spivak and Bhabha, on the other hand, are more willing to see certain kinds of theorizing as critical practices sufficient in themselves.

There is no reason that post-colonial theory should be all of a piece, of course. So-called Western critical theory, notwithstanding certain commonalities, also contains important internal differences – modernist, post-modernist, and feminist forms of theorizing are not 'the same thing'. It does raise the question, however, of how useful it is to speak of 'post-colonial theorizing' – or, for that matter, 'Western critical theory' – as homogenous monoliths that can be opposed one against the other. In other words, plurality would seem to mark both theoretical families, and the more interesting question would seem to be how to conceptualize and respect that plurality.

Thesis two: post-colonial theory offers important insights regarding pluralism

One does not have to read very far into Fanon or Guevara before one encounters Marx. One does not have to read very far into Said before one encounters Gramsci. Nor does one have to read very far into Spivak or Bhabha before one encounters Foucault. The ways the latter are taken up by the former are distinct, of course. But if it is an overstatement to say that post-colonial theory and, for example, Gramscian theory are the 'same thing' (and I believe it is), it also misrepresents post-colonial theory to represent it as *sui generis*, separate and distinct from Western theoretical traditions. In other words, one should, of course, respect differences; however, constructing and representing a theoretical tradition as 'wholly other' is a problematic move, even when the intent is a worthy one – i.e. presenting a body of work as original, authentic and not merely derivative of existing work.[2] It is, arguably, exactly the kind of move the work of someone like Said is meant to challenge. The question, then, is how to promote meaningful dialogue in the light of commonalities and differences across a variety of critical traditions of which post-coloniality is unquestionably an important one – given that even where ideas are developed independently, striking parallels across independent traditions can be identified as readily as differences within them.

Let us focus, then, on Said. Interestingly for this argument on pluralism, music was a major source of inspiration for Said, intellectually as well as emotionally. Specifically, Bach's counterpoint, brought to life by the pianist Glenn Gould, had a major impact on Said's thinking about theoretical pluralism. As he notes in a discussion of his intellectual development, 'I had begun to write more about music, and most of my writing about music really focused on contrapuntal work [counterpoint]. I mean, that's what interests me the most … forms in which many things go on simultaneously' (2001b: 184). From this, Said developed a distinct methodology – contrapuntal reading: '[a]s we look back at the cultural archive, we begin to reread it not univocally but *contrapuntally*'.

A contrapuntal reading is one which tries to reproduce the multi-vocal sensitivity of counterpoint. As Said notes, (1994a: 59–60),

> [i]n the counterpoint of Western classical music, various themes play off one another, with only provisional privilege being given to any particular one; yet in the resulting polyphony there is a concern and order, an organized interplay that derives from the themes, not from a rigorous melodic or formal principle outside the work.

Chowdhry (2007: 105) makes this point as well:

> The goal of a contrapuntal reading is thus to not privilege any particular narrative but to reveal the 'wholeness' of the text, the intermeshed, overlapping, and mutually embedded histories of metropolitan and colonized societies and of the elite and subaltern. A contrapuntal reading is like a fugue which can contain 'two, three, four or five voices; they are all part of the same composition, but they are distinct'.

And, she argues, it does so in a way that avoids devolving into a 'plea for incipient liberal or postmodern plurality'.

I believe Chowdhry is right to distance a contrapuntal reading from liberal or post-modern conceptions of plurality. What should be stressed, however, is that the contrapuntal approach does not imply a distancing from the question of plurality *tout court*. What is distinctive – and instructive – about counterpoint is its *active* approach to the multivocality of the piece. To begin, counterpoint is first and foremost a way of *composing* music – as such, it is demanding in that it requires of the composer that multiple voices be introduced and held in a particular relation. On the one hand, the voices are not discordant – at the same time, they never resolve into the easy, banal harmony of elevator music. No one voice is privileged, but neither are the different voices left to exist in an interplay of 'defensive', 'polemical' or 'flabby' pluralism.[3] Rather, all voices are placed in creative tension which allows for a mutual testing of the authenticity – indeed, the 'truth' – of each. As such, counterpoint distinguishes itself as exemplifying a particular kind of pluralism – 'engaged fallibilistic pluralism'. As Bernstein (1992: 336) notes,

> Such a pluralistic *ethos* places new responsibilities upon each of us. For it means taking our own fallibility seriously – resolving that however much we are committed to our own styles of thinking, we are willing to listen to others without denying or suppressing the otherness of the other. It means being vigilant against the dual temptations of simply dismissing what others are saying by falling back on one of those standard defensive ploys where we condemn it as obscure, woolly, or trivial, or thinking we can easily translate what is alien into our own entrenched vocabularies.

Said's use of contrapuntality is a fruitful way of thinking how the kind of critical IR theory being promoted in this volume might relate to other critical traditions.

Let us turn to the question of the relationship of modernist to post-modernist critical IR theory. On re-reading the interviews above, I felt I detected a subtle sense of unease with post-modern IR theory; it is identifiable in Booth's contention that post-modernism erroneously equates emancipation with 'Eurocentrism' and 'Enlightenment metanarratives' and charges those who advocate emancipation with 'cultural imperialism';[4] in Wyn Jones' perceptible frustration that post-modernists (along with constructivists) have shown a 'marked reluctance' to engage in dialogue around the theme of emancipation (this volume, 98); or simply in Cox's admission that 'I don't think I ever really understood the post-modern criticisms of [modernist] critical theory'.[5]

There is no question that one can think of reasons to be wary of at least parts of the post-modern tradition. One can, for example, raise the question of whether at least some post-modernists are scholars drawn to the tradition because they are fundamentally uncomfortable with truly radical forms of thought and action. In their case, post-modernism may provide a way to dress up their preferred mode of theorizing – traditional/problem-solving theory – as a form of critical-*sounding* theory. As such, they derive such benefits that may accrue to those who appear to be 'cutting edge' *so long as*, of course, their work is not perceived as part of the truly radical traditions they and their target audiences abhor. Such views help to make sense of, for example, recent efforts associated with some post-modern theorists to purge modernist critical thinkers of any link to the Marxian tradition, notwithstanding the fact that it is the Marxian tradition that provides the over-riding inspiration for their work. Efforts to strip Gramsci of his Marxist identity – to re-cast him as a much more palatable (much less threatening) 'post-modern Italian cultural theorist and theatre critic' – have prompted their own substantive counters.[6]

Of course, it would be wrong to tar all post-modern theorists with the brush of being problem-solving wolves in critical sheep's clothing. True criticality need not be expressed in Marxian language, of course, and scholars must be free to work within the tradition that speaks most clearly to them. To the degree that additional insights are thereby generated, theoretical pluralism should be welcomed by all. However, questions can be raised even in the case of those with truly radical political commitments. I have often wondered if a major part of the attraction of post-modern IR is that it offers a way for critically oriented IR theorists to express the impulse toward criticality without risking any association with the Marxian tradition – a tradition which still has the power to taint a thinker and undermine a career. I concede that this form of sociology-of-knowledge explanation is undoubtedly unfair to some, but it does have the merit of explaining why post-modernism is the dominant form of critical IR in the US (where the general culture of anti-Marxism is strongest) but only one of several strands of critical IR (including Frankfurt School and Gramscian-inspired forms) in countries like Great Britain and Canada, where Marxian intellectual and political traditions (including but not limited to social-democracy) were never so radically eradicated from the cultural landscape as they were in the McCarthy-ite atmosphere of the United States.

In sum, the challenge of coping constructively with multivocality and with pluralism is not just a politically correct affectation – it is central for the construction of a 'non-coercive and non-dominating knowledge' (Said 2001a: 367). And it is hard work: it means taking traditions like post-modern IR seriously enough to engage them: fairly, respectfully, but uncompromisingly critically. Accordingly, while I do not deny there may be grounds for some wariness with regard to the post-modernist tradition (and here I concede I am deviating from Said's rather more strident rejection of the tradition), I think it behooves modernist critical IR to reflect more deeply on how it is to relate to post-modern IR, not least of which because criticality is difficult to sustain in the best of circumstances, in the present context, we need all the help we can get.

Thesis three: post-colonial theory offers important insights regarding intellectuals

It comes as no surprise that the theme of 'intellectuals' is also common to the thoughts of the interviewees featured in this book. The conceptualization of the nature and role of intellectuals has been a major preoccupation of critical theorists from at least Gramsci onward.[7] And here, again, I believe the post-colonial tradition – and in particular the work of Edward Said – has much to offer. I will organize my thoughts by adding to the P of pluralism three additional Ps – passion, politics and praxis.

P stands for passion

I once tried to develop an analogy of critical and mainstream IR as follows: the thing with which mainstream intellectuals are most uncomfortable is the idea that, despite their best efforts at implementing value-free, neutral and objective research methodologies, the knowledge they produce has politico-normative content; in other words, that theory – including their theory – is always 'for someone and for some purpose'. Assuming this to be true, one might pose the following question: 'hidden, unacknowledged politico-normative content': mainstream theorists :: _____: critical theorists? Or, put otherwise: if mainstream theorists need to recognize the hidden, too-oft unacknowledged politico-normative content of their work, what is it that critical theorists need to acknowledge?

I would argue that the answer to that question is 'passion'. I have often had the feeling, when in the presence of other critical theorists – especially male critical theorists – that the very notion of passion was intellectually suspect. Reason, on the other hand – and sometimes a very non-dialectical, analytical form of reason at that[8] – remained very much in evidence. At the same time, acknowledgement of *passion* – understood as short-hand for what motivates us to do what we do, and what makes us care about what we care about – tends to be rather rare.

The reason we tend to eschew the P-word is something I am still unsure about. I have begun to suspect, however, that it is not unrelated to the fear that to admit to passion is to set ourselves up to be dismissed as un-*reasonable* and even ir-*rational*. That is, the presumption seems to be that one can be one or the other, but never both. I wonder too if there is not a gender dimension as well – after all, hegemonic masculinity's defining features include hyper-rationality and self-control (meaning control of one's emotions), while the devalued qualities of the feminine traditionally include an emphasis on 'feeling' over 'thinking'. In short, I wonder, do male critical theorists fear discussing their passion because they fear that in doing so they would be perceived as being too feminine?

This is another reason I find the work of Edward Said so refreshing. He is clearly a passionate individual. Nor is he any less 'rational' than other commentators on a myriad of subjects. But the significance of passion, for Said, goes further. He is one of the few to recognize that an absence of passion is not neutral; it is a significant weakness – a weakness which robs critically oriented theorizing of its power:

> [Secular critical theorizing] can't happen without some personal and intellectual investment. Intellectuals have to be moved, I think ... by a sense of justice; and that's what I find missing ... For intellectual discourse and for intellectual activity, one has to be stimulated ... [by] a kind of moral view, as you find it in Chomsky, or Bertrand Russell, and people like that. I feel that's the only hope.
>
> (Said 2001b: 205)[9]

P stands for politics

Politics is central for Said in relation to the question of intellectuals. We can best understand the significance of his position by placing it alongside the typology of intellectuals developed by Aronowitz and Giroux (1985: 23–45). In this typology, they follow Gramsci in distinguishing two kinds of conservative intellectuals. On the one hand, they talk of 'hegemonic intellectuals' who 'self-consciously define themselves through the forms of moral and intellectual leadership they provide for dominant groups and classes'. On the other hand, they identify 'accommodating intellectuals' who also 'stand firm within an ideological posture and set of material practices that support the dominant society and its ruling groups' but who do so less self-consciously, adopting the self-designation of 'free-floating [but who] function primarily to mediate uncritically ideas and social practices that serve to reproduce the status quo' (Aranowitz and Giroux 1985: 39–40).

Said's critique of mainstream intellectuals (2001a: 357–67) – both of the 'accommodating' and the 'hegemonic' variety – is well known and does not need to be repeated. What is worth noting is that his critical gaze is directed at intellectuals at the oppositional end of the spectrum as well. Again, the categories of Aronowitz and Giroux provide a useful way of contextualizing Said's position. In parallel to their two categories of intellectual on the right, they identify two on the left. To begin, there are 'critical intellectuals', who while 'ideologically alternative to existing institutions and modes of thought ... do not see themselves as connected either to a specific social formation or as performing a general social function that is expressively political in nature ... As individuals they are critical of inequality and injustice, but they often refuse or are unable to move beyond their isolated posture to the terrain of collective solidarity and struggle' (Aranowitz and Giroux 1985: 37).

These critical intellectuals stand in contrast to a second category. These are 'transformative intellectuals', who 'work with any number of groups ... including the working class' and who 'use the language of critique' to 'advance emancipatory traditions and cultures within and without alternative public spheres'. These 'transformative intellectuals' recognize that '[k]nowledge and power are inextricably linked in this case to the presupposition that to choose life, so as to make it possible, is to understand the preconditions necessary to struggle for it' (Aranowitz and Giroux 1985: 36).

It is interesting to observe that Said works with much the same categories. Particularly with regard to critically oriented intellectuals, he makes much the same point that politics – in the sense of commitment to and involvement with a specific and concrete historical community – is a vital part of bridging the gap between theory and practice. Significantly, he criticizes no less than Chomsky, whose reticence about becoming involved in the messy nitty-gritty of political coalition-building had led him to function as a more limited 'critical intellectual' than as the fully 'transformative intellectual' he might have been (Said 2001c: 141–2).

The problem, Said argues, is that in giving up 'a fundamental connection' to 'an ongoing political movement', one gives up 'the real game': 'communication with actual people and communities' (2001c: 141). It is this vital difference that distinguishes the merely 'critical' intellectual from the fully 'transformative' – and it is the latter that Said, with his insistence on the centrality of politics, aspired to be and to inspire.

P stands for praxis

> *Denn die einen sind im Dunkeln*   (There are some who are in darkness)
> *Und die andern sind im Licht*   (And the others are in light)
> *Und man siehet die im Lichte*   (And you see those in the light)
> *Die im Dunkeln sieht man nicht*   (Those in darkness you don't see)[10]

Said offers important direction as well on the kind of praxis appropriate to critically oriented intellectuals. There is an irony, however: while his praxis is consistent with a radical orientation, his mis-labelling of the kind of praxis he desires to promote serves to confuse as much as to elucidate.

Said refers to his praxis as 'speaking truth to power'. It is important to understand the origins and underlying assumptions of this form of praxis to understand why it is less than apt in Said's case. The origins of the phrase – and approach – are to be found in the Society of Friends (Quakers).[11] As a form of praxis, 'speaking truth to power' grew out of two fundamental assumptions. First, though people of faith, the Quakers believed God was also a God of reason – accordingly, through the right application of reason, God's truths could be established. It is important to note that the 'right application of reason' was generally a scientistic-positivistic form; and truths were logico-empirical in nature. The second assumption was that each person carries a piece of God within them. This holds for state leaders and policy-makers as well. And it is the piece of God within them, it was believed, that would make them receptive to hearing and responding positively to truths brought to their attention. Accordingly, within Quaker praxis, 'speaking truth to power' traditionally combined scientistic, policy-oriented research[12] with direct appeals to the conscience of those in positions of authority to comport themselves more morally.[13] Notwithstanding the admirable motives of many Friends, this form of practice must be understood for what it is: a form of 'problem-solving' theory.

Unfortunately, Said uses the same phrase to describe his praxis (1994b: 85–102). Nor is he alone. Valerie Kennedy, for example, concludes that Said can be seen 'as the embodiment of his own idea of an intellectual … the un-coopted oppositional intellectual "speaking truth to power"' (2000: 80). Happily, a closer reading shows that his praxis is of a much more Gramscian bent and, as such, actually stands in clear opposition to 'speaking truth to power'.[14] Said notes, for example, that he never writes 'for Power'. In response to the question of 'for whom do you write?', he responded as follows:

> I write most of the time for an occasion rather than for a person. *I certainly don't address policymakers*. In the US, I'm really considered outside the consensus. My readers tend to be people on the left who are themselves outside the consensus and looking for alternatives to the prevailing worldview.
>
> *(Said 2001d: 282, emphasis added)*

At another point, he speaks of Arab politics in terms very much reminiscent of Gramsci's strategy of the 'war of position':

> Then there's the other agenda, a 'slow politics' that takes place over a long period of time, which can allow for coalition-building …The necessary coalition would be between people in different parts of the Arab world who are actively involved in local struggles for democracy, economic justice, women's rights, human rights groups, university groups …What we really need is a critical language and a full-scale critical culture.
>
> *(Said 2001a: 363–4)*

It is also this concern with promoting a recasting of the imagination among the policy-takers rather than the policy-makers that lies at the foundation of Said's critique of post-modernism. In response to a question about the 'Responsibility of Intellectuals' (Chomsky 1967), Said pulls no punches:

> One would have to pretty much scuttle all the jaw-shattering jargonistic post-modernisms that now dot the landscape. They are worse than useless. They are neither capable of understanding and analyzing the power structure of this country, nor are they capable of understanding the particular aesthetic merit of an individual work of art. Whether you call it deconstruction or post-modernism or post-structuralism or post-anything, they all represent a sort of spectacle of giving back tickets at the entrance and saying, we're really out of it. We want to check into our private resort and be left alone.
>
> *(Said 2001a: 365)*

His alternative is equally clear:

> Re-engagement with intellectual process means a return to an old-fashioned historical, literary and, above all intellectual scholarship based upon the premise that human beings, men and women, make their own history. And just as things are made, they can be unmade and remade. That sense of intellectual and political and citizenly empowerment is what the intellectual class needs.
>
> *(Said 2001a: 366–7)*

In sum, critical theory's practice is not to engage those 'hiding in the darkness' with policy-relevant analysis twinned with pleas for more ethical behaviour − it is to expose them to their victims by shining the light of critique in their direction. Said understood this. So should we.

Conclusion

On the wall of my office hangs a poster − it is a drab, colourless poster, befitting its origins I suppose: I purchased it in the now extinct German Democratic Republic.

On the poster are the words to Brecht's poem *Der Zweifler* (*The Doubter*, my translation):

> Whenever it seemed
> We had found the answer to a question
> One of us untied the string of the old rolled-up
> Chinese scroll on the wall, so that it fell down and
> Revealed the man on the bench who
> Doubted so much.
> I, he said to us
> Am the Doubter.
> I am doubtful whether
> The work that devoured your days was done well
> Did it take the contradictions out of things?
> Is it too unambiguous?
>
> If so, what you say is useless.
> Your thing has no life in it.
> Who are you?
> To whom do you speak?
> Who finds what you say useful?
> And, above all.
> Always above all else:
> How does one act if one believes what you say?
> Above all: how does one act?
> Reflectively, curiously, we studied the doubting
> Blue man on the scroll, looked at each other and
> *Took up the task anew.*

Given the gap in time between my first encounter with post-colonial theory and my current engagement with it, I had expected to see its influences in current critically oriented IR theory. I was surprised to find how modest that influence continues to be.

There are exceptions, of course. When I looked to see who was engaging post-colonial theory in a serious way, I noticed a familiar pattern – and the names are not unfamiliar ones either, names like Chowdhry, Ling, Agathangelou, Nair.[15] In short, a good number of them are women and committed feminists. That cannot be just coincidence. And it serves as one more reason for critical IR to take, not just post-colonial theory seriously, but feminist theory seriously as well.

In conclusion, three decades is, arguably, not a long time in the life of ideas. Much has been accomplished, and it is good that we take this time to review and, yes, acknowledge critical IR's achievements. The themes treated here – pluralism, passion, politics and praxis – clearly have resonance with the work of Cox, Booth,

Linklater and Wyn Jones, whose scholarly contributions serve as an excellent jumping-off point for further discussions of the future of critical IR theory.

At the same time, there remains much to do. The reality is that modernist critical IR theory still has a long way to go in incorporating insights from other critical traditions (e.g., post-colonial theory, feminist theory) if its claims to criticality in perspective and to emancipatory ends in praxis are to be realized.

So let us celebrate today, and then, tomorrow, under the watchful eye of the Doubter, 'take up the task anew'.

Notes

1 Several excellent pieces have been published on the same theme. See, for example, Chowdhry (2007: 101–16).
2 Of course, acknowledging a debt to a pre-existing body of theory need in no way imply that the theory in question is therefore no more than a subsidiary and derivative effect of pre-existing theory. Post-colonial theory's debt to Marxism, for example, in no way means that post-colonial theory is a sub-set of Marxism any more than Marxism's debt to the Great Law and the political thought of the Iroquois means that Marxism is but a sub-set of Turtle Island's Indigenous Theory ... though it might be useful ideological-corrective to see it as such. For a discussion of the debt of Marx and Engels to the theory of the Haudenosaunee, see Wright (2005).
3 The terms are Richard J. Bernstein's, who defines 'defensive pluralism' as 'a form of tokenism, where we play lip service to others "doing their own thing" but are already convinced that there is nothing important to be learned from them'; 'polemical pluralism', where 'the appeal to pluralism doesn't signify a genuine willingness to listen and learn from others, but becomes rather an ideological weapon to advance one's own orientation'; and 'flabby pluralism' where 'our borrowings from different orientations are little more than glib superficial poachings' (1992: 335–6).
4 This volume, 69. It is also perceptible in his comment that 'I probably have read enough post-structuralist work for the moment; I know I have a long list of reading which is of far higher priority. I do not need to be persuaded that it is about time I re-read *War and Peace* after 40 years, but I do need persuading that I should read the next interpretation of Foucault, Derrida, Agamben and so on in an IR journal. I will need persuading that such work will tell me something of real usefulness in relation to the things I primarily want to know about – which, in brief, is how the dynamics of international politics shape the distribution of security, prosperity, and ideas across the world' (this volume, 73).
5 This volume, 25. Linklater seems the exception to the rule, with little in his comments suggesting a similar sense of unease with post-modernism.
6 See Thomas (2009). Regrettably, this tendency toward distortion through the 'sanitization' of the more embarrassing Marxist dimensions of leading thinkers is also manifest in some recent theorizing in post-modern IR. See, for example, the representation of Said as a Foucauldian (Salter 2010) – a particular problematic reading given Said's expressions of serious reservation about Foucault's theorizing, and his equally clear statements of his indebtedness to the Marxian tradition in general, and Gramsci in particular. In fact, Foucault's influence on Said was mainly negative; see in this respect Said's interviews (Viswanathan 2001: 53, 77, 79–80, 138, 160, 165, 168, 222 and *passim*). Tellingly, when asked what demarcated his more politically engaged, more optimistic approach from that of Foucault, Said responded as follows: 'if you wanted to put your finger on one particular thing and one particular style of thought, I think it's the Gramsci factor' (Viswanathan 2001: 170). As Said notes elsewhere (Viswanathan 2001: 80), in his case, it is Gramsci who serves to mediate between a strategic and geographical sense of knowledge, on the one hand, and a temporal one, on the other.

7 Indeed, Gramsci's entire *Prison Notebooks* output began as an outline for a book on the question of intellectuals.

8 See my discussion of forms of reason and critique below.

9 Critical IR theorists may also wish to take note of the fact that Said singles out the 'appallingly solemn' – i.e., passion-less – Habermasian tradition as having little to contribute.

10 Bertolt Brecht and Kurt Weil, 'The Ballad of Mack the Knife', *Threepenny Opera*.

11 While it has, at times, been attributed to the Society's founder, George Fox, it is more likely that its provenance is more recent.

12 Thus it was that Lewis Richardson, a mathematically oriented Quaker, committed himself to using his mathematical skills to model international conflicts in particular arms races. Similarly, Kenneth Boulding – an economist by training and a Quaker by conviction – oriented his work to the field of peace research.

13 On this, see Yarrow (1978).

14 Richard Wyn Jones also frames his practice in terms of the notion of 'speaking truth to power'. Once again, I would argue that, for critical theorists, it should not be. Happily, from what I know of Wyn Jones, it is not. And I say 'happily' for there is, arguably, no better way to leave oneself open to co-optation – what Gramsci calls *trasformismo* – than to orient oneself to gaining the ear of those with power and privilege. For an application to the analysis of foreign policy, see Neufeld (1999).

15 See, for example, Chowdhry and Nair (2004). There are, of course, men working in this field as well. See, for example, the contributions of Persaud and Beier in this volume.

Bibliography

Ahluwalia, P. and Sullivan, M. (2001) 'Beyond International Relations: Edward Said and the World', in Robert A. Crawford and Darryl S. L. Jarvis (eds) *International Relations: Still An American Social Science? Toward Diversity in International Thought*, New York: State University of New York Press.

Aronowitz, S. and Giroux, H.A. (1985) 'Teaching and the Role of the Transformative Intellectual' in S. Aranowitz and H.A. Giroux, *Education Under Siege: The Conservative, Liberal and Radical Debate over Schooling*, Westport: Bergin & Garvey.

Bernstein, R.J. (1992) 'Pragmatism, Pluralism and the Healing of Wounds', in R.J. Bernstein, *The New Constellation: The Ethical-Political Horizons of Modernity/Postmodernity*, Cambridge: MIT Press.

Chomsky, Noam (1967) 'The Responsibility of Intellectuals', *The New York Review of Books*, February 23.

Chowdhry, G. (2007) 'Edward Said and Contrapuntal Reading: Implications for Critical Interventions in International Relations', *Millennium* 36(1): 101–16.

Chowdhry, G and Nair, S. (eds) (2004) *Power, Postcolonialism and International Relations: Reading Race, Gender, and Class*, New York: Routledge.

Kennedy, V. (2000) *Edward Said: A Critical Introduction*, Cambridge: Polity Press.

Neufeld, M. (1995) *The Restructuring of International Relations Theory*, Cambridge: Cambridge University Press.

_____ (1999) 'Democratization in/of Canadian Foreign Policy: Critical Reflections', *Studies in Political Economy* 58: 97–119.

Said, E. (1994a) *Culture and Imperialism*, London: Vintage.

_____ (1994b) 'Speaking Truth to Power', in *Representations of the Intellectual*, New York: Vintage.

_____ (2001a) 'The Intellectuals and the War', in G. Viswanathan (ed.) *Power, Politics and Culture: Interview with Edward W. Said*, New York: Random House.

Said, E. (2001b) 'Culture and Imperialism', in G. Viswanathan (ed.) *Power, Politics and Culture: Interview with Edward W. Said*, New York: Random House.

_____ (2001c) 'Criticism and the Art of Politics', in G. Viswanathan (ed.) *Power, Politics and Culture: Interview with Edward W. Said*, New York: Random House.

_____ (2001d) 'I've always learned during the class', in G. Viswanathan (ed.) *Power, Politics and Culture: Interview with Edward W. Said*, New York: Random House.

Salter, M.B. (2010) 'Edward Said and post-colonial international relations' in C. Moore and C. Farrands (eds) *International Relations Theory and Philosophy: Interpretive Dialogues*, London: Routledge.

Thomas, P. (2009) *The Gramscian Moment: Philosophy, Hegemony and Marxism*, Boston: Leiden.

Viswanathan, G. (ed.) (2001) *Power, Politics and Culture: Interviews with Edward W. Said*, New York: Random House.

Wright, R. (2005), *Stolen Continents: Five-Hundred Years of Conquest and Resistance in the Americas*, New York: First Mariner Books.

Yarrow, C.H. (1978) *Quaker Experiences in International Conciliation,* Princeton: Yale University Press.

13

'COME IN, MAKE YOURSELF UNCOMFORTABLE!'

Some thoughts on putting Critical Theory in its place

Martin Weber

A significant aspect of academic activity in the social sciences is the cyclical recurrence of self-surveying images painted on a large canvas, which integrate scattered motives, snippets, or fragments into a collage, the parts becoming instantly smaller than the whole. The capacity to let the pieces fall into their place, to create coherence, and the sense of programmatic purpose of which such efforts are sublime expressions, are pervasive – and the stuff of which textbooks are made. Invariably, and perhaps inescapably, this activity leads straight into another, which is the business of differentiation. The whole in which the parts participate is not one in which any part may participate; some things must be kept outside the frame.

At this point, the reader may be forgiven for thinking that s/he is about to descend into another Jeremiad about the exclusionist attitudes adopted by some mainstream or other towards Critical Theory, and I must hurry to allay such fears. This is emphatically not the objective of this brief contribution. Rather, my purpose is twofold: one goal is to raise some questions about how critical theoretic work might be done in intersection with those for whom an investment in a disciplinary project called 'International Relations' is of much more central importance than anyone interested in Critical Theory would be able to accord. The other, and, as I will argue, far more important goal, is to suggest that Critical Theory, while it certainly has a place in the broad spectrum of heterodox scholarship seeking to make some sort of sense of the condition of the plurality of globally interconnecting people and peoples, also has to be 'put in its place'. This second aspect speaks to a growing sense of unease about where Critical Theory in International Relations might be headed; my sense here is that some of the lessons of critical theorizing, of which the interviews in this volume tell, are in danger of being obliterated.

In pursuing the two goals, I want to keep the image I have raised above in the background, in order to remind both myself and the reader of the kind of approach I want to avoid: the idea of outlining the critical theoretic project by way of painting it into a frame, and to suggest that it frames things more beautifully, completely, or convincingly than other frames.

If this now suggests that what follows advocates some sort of woolly version of epistemic relativism, let me rush to dispel this notion right away. Below, I do seek to at least imply that there are some basics to Critical Theory which, though often implicit in various contributions inspired by it, are all too often not considered either directly, or with the requisite clarity, or both. Thus, Critical Theory does have distinctive interests, approaches, and justifications for these, as well as questions around them; what I am questioning specifically is the tendency to assume exclusivity on any of these, and what I want to suggest is perhaps a way of imagining how its contributions relate to other, equally or perhaps more important, ones. Avoiding the frame, the programmatic project which defines what does and what does not belong to Critical Theory for the purpose of establishing 'its' claims to explanatory hegemony must, I think, be of paramount importance, lest much of what our four interviewees enunciate regarding the independent-mindedness of critical inquiry be just jettisoned by *fiat*.

I want to be very clear that the discussion below concerns Critical Theory as a theoretical project, which identifies as a research programme in International Relations. There is plenty of work in and around the discipline, which is critical, takes up the task of explicating struggles against domination and injustices, and does not use or need the conceptual inventories of the more 'self-consciously' Critical Theory identified works. Much of this sort of work is, in my opinion, richer, more relevant, and more challenging than most of what happens under the label of critical theorizing these days. While I do think, then, that Critical Theory has the genuine potential to make contributions, I would stress that the value of these will have to be established in a dialogue precisely with such work.

What is Critical Theory? The comfortable take

Critical Theory, understood broadly, offers a range of inspirational, fascinating, and occasionally truly revealing ontological, epistemological and methodological moves, which are quite attractive for thinking 'outside the box' about a number of challenges facing the social, political, and politico-economic organization of human affairs across global and local levels. The interviews in this collection provide ready back-up for such hunches, as do the increasing numbers of PhD projects yet again seeking to make critical theoretic inventories fecund for diverse projects covering human suffering, economic inequality and its implications, security policy or technological change – aside from those directly seeking to address theoretical and methodological concerns.

In one sense, this is perhaps all that Critical Theory in the context of International Relations is: a general point of reference, which provides a none-too-specific, justifying backdrop to heterodox scholarship, to the cultivation of both an inquisitive mind and a progressively inclusive analysis. Throw in a penchant for reading across disciplinary boundaries and an equally general commitment to be doing this work for someone or something and, with a suitably recognizable contingent of the usual suspects in footnotes, we have Critical Theory.[1]

In this one sense, we could leave it at that. There would be better and worse contributions in this general spirit, but it would both be sufficient to sustain an ongoing concern and open to a whole range of different approaches, flavours and even outlooks. This 'foggier' idea of Critical Theory has its fair share of exposure, not least in the works of its critics, whose efforts at identifying what they don't like about Critical Theory all too often culminate in generalizations, which only make sense as expressions of this vaguer 'mélange-perspective'. It is a valuable, perfectly defensible way of understanding a loosely connected set of commitments to scholarly inquiry and political outlooks. For the most part, this notion of critical theoretic activity offers relatively easy ways to self-identify, while providing some general markers for the disinclined to help with keeping themselves at a distance. It facilitates substantive non-engagement, where critical theorists are afforded the room to differentiate their work from other approaches through heroic generalizations, in the same way as others get to refer to Critical Theory in terms of stark outlines: the effect is one of mutual criticism, which remains external to the respective project(s) of others.

Lest all this sound too cryptic, think of the practices of short-hand use in debates over, for instance, relativism vs. foundationalism, utopianism vs. realism (or pragmatism), idealism vs. materialism, or any other of the mainstay dualisms with which clarity is achieved in positioning papers, articles, books, or conversational contribution in, for instance, the conceptual map of a 2×2 box-matrix. Textbooks are full of these, and their widespread usage underlines their usefulness in positioning different approaches. At the same time, however, such schematics are always a reminder, too, that the abstractions they involve require much prior agreement and shared interpretive practices among those to whom they appeal or make sense. There are, then, good reasons to be slightly uncomfortable with merely positioning a practice called 'critical theory' within International Relations debates, even if one were to, so to speak, merely hang that frame in a spirit of pluralism among all the others.

Becoming more uncomfortable

If, however, we find ourselves even only mildly discontent with this, the trouble starts. Here, my two goals come into play – and, as a reminder, this is also where the constant risk of being drawn into painting it all into a frame begins to loom large. The more ambitious answer to the essay question is communicated in at least two distinct directions, which map onto my two goals: in one instance, responsive to goal number one, this communication would be concerned with salient differences between Critical Theory and other theoretical approaches in International Relations; here, critical theorists are called upon to respond to criticisms and challenges presented by those who disagree with either premises, substantial analytical issues, or the politics of the project of Critical Theory (and, not infrequently, perhaps all three). For instance, in order to make sense of the claim of constructivists (see for example Price 2008) that Critical Theory is of limited value because its practitioners are invested in utopianism – understood to involve normative commitments which obstruct clear-headed and relevant analysis – reception practices will have to be probed, this position within constructivism reconstructed and its premises subjected to scrutiny and discussion. This kind of work points towards one of Critical Theory's common-place mainstays, namely immanent critique. Without appreciating lineage, function, and implications of this portrayal of Critical Theory by constructivists, any response from critical theorists to such a challenge will remain dedicated to juxtaposition as its dominant expository strategy, remain outside the constructivist imaginary, and result merely in asserting positional difference and disagreement. While there may be occasions when such gestures are not particularly problematic, as a form of engagement it fails Critical Theory's standards of comprehensiveness and circumspect analysis.

Immanent critique, in this context of intra- and trans-disciplinary divisions, requires a deep involvement with the substantive features of the position, approach, or constellation at which it is directed, as well as the provision of a reflectivist account of the critical theorist's own involvement in and with these. If anything, this kind of work – which, for instance, Richard Ashley's famous 'double reading' (1988) could be seen as an example of – has of late not seen much exposure.[2] There are, again, good reasons for this. On the one hand, it is a laborious process to engage in reconstructive work on a theoretical field other than one's own, and it carries some significant risks. What may be involved, to stick with my example, in engaging constructivist misconstruals of Critical Theory such as the one regarding the latter's utopianism? First, a reconstruction is needed of what kinds of sources constructivists do, or may, draw upon to sustain such claims. Second, an assessment is needed of how constructivists' reception practices in relation to 'utopianism' claims are enabled by the self-understanding of constructivist research practice; this involves, *inter alia*, the retrieval of ontological, epistemological and methodological precepts. Third, this requires an exposition of the critical theoretic alternative, any tendencies it might have towards the alleged commitments and a sympathetic retrieval of tropes, analyses or statements which may give rise to misunderstandings (occasionally by self-declared critical theorists themselves). Finally, it requires an in-depth discussion of the responses critical theorists have to the alleged problems, conducted in an idiom which is intelligible to the primary target audience (constructivist detractors).

All this, it seems, requires an awful lot of work and involves a great deal of strain, which one may easily avoid by sticking with the 'positioning' approach outlined above: the strategy of external criticism requires only to take note of what others are arguing from within one's own framework. 'For us', the critical theorist may then say, 'there is nothing utopian about expecting that increased, conflictual interaction among various actors in the world arena can potentially deliver emancipatory transformations; to us, all human interaction is morally inflected and contains the resources for challenge, critique, and the raising of claims according to which such transformation may be effected'. To which the constructivist will then retort (quite predictably): 'but there is in fact no unconstrained discourse, and hence no ideal speech situation, to pick just one of your ideals; the emancipatory principles you are seeking to defend are effective only to the degree that people or states themselves hold them, and there is just no evidence that they do so in significantly large numbers. By confronting the messy real world with your idealized versions of its potential normative ordering protocols, you therefore engage in unsustainable idealizations'. Repeat *ad nauseam*. A brief survey of the past decade of critical theoretic work in International Relations would, I think, lead us to see that this model of mutual criticism, which remains by and large external to one another, has had far too much of the upper hand (and obviously not just with regard to constructivism). It is this, rather than any sense that theoretical or conceptual work adds little value to analysis, which underpins the occasional sense of exasperation regarding International Relations' 'over-theorization'.[3]

There are, of course, motivating factors, which one may want to consider in the context of asking the question of why so much ostensible 'engagement' remains so heavily invested in the practice of external critique. That this is the case is even more puzzling in the context of a social science discipline, which devotes – as International Relations has over a number of years now – an ever-increasing share of its conceptual attention to questions of ontology. Political partisanship, a charge often directed at critical theorists by defenders of a 'value-free' social science (whether in the much more qualified Weberian sense or along neo-positivist lines), is an obvious candidate for such explanations. Likewise, one could look to the constitutive function of the negative framing of opposing positions for the purpose of consolidating an identifiable research programme, something in which the use of 'straw-persons' surely has a pertinent legacy. Another alternative would be to delve into the political economy of research production, where there may well be good reasons to suspect that 'positioning' carries a premium (not least in terms of career advancement) over reconstructive, problem oriented, immanentist approaches – both in terms of time-efficiency and the workings of the peer-review system.

But if we set these aside we are left with the more interesting question of what the implications are of this tendency to opt for 'external' rather than 'immanent' critical appraisal in the context of attempts to sharpen concepts and refine methods. Here, I only want to indicate one of these, which helps to articulate why there is a point in getting more uncomfortable and doing such conceptual and methodological work in direct engagement with the critics of Critical Theory, beyond the tendency to restate stereotypes.

The over-investment in positioning and external critique leads to a decline in tangible self-reflective activity. Some examples should help to highlight what is at stake here: in the contemporary research landscape, research in the disciplinary context of International Relations on political economy either belongs to broadly liberal or post-structuralist frames, with the odd pitch by structuralist Marxists (who, on the whole, tend to not have much time for Critical Theory as part of the legacy of Marx). The debate on the kinds of social theoretic inventories required to make sense of current constellations has been taken up within various strands of constructivism and developed in distinction from rationalist approaches, while moving International Relations much closer to functionalist sociology.[4] Post-structuralist research has taken over the task of the critique of modernity. Finally, the battle-ground over the role (or lack thereof) of normative theory is pretty much laid out between constructivist norm sociology and its English School interlocutors on the one hand, and critiques of normativity inspired *inter alia* by Foucault, Levinas, or Agamben (behind which lie Nietzsche, Heidegger and Schmitt) on the other. Critical Theory, once raised as a research project with transformative potential and initially so well set up within and for the discipline by, among others, the four interviewees, has by and large remained content to replay a few mainstays around notions of emancipation, a broadly democratic imaginary and the expansion of inclusive institutional arrangements by dialogic means. This is not nothing, but given the trans-disciplinary horizon in which Critical Theory was conceived, it is also quite probably not enough.

Making yourself really uncomfortable

While the desiderata put forward in the previous section would, I think, go a long way in getting Critical Theory as a distinctive project back on the road in ways much more consistent with the programmatic openings provided at the onset stage, they remain tied to limitations – which are ultimately even more problematic. These arise in the context of a debate framed by, and held within, an academic discourse called International Relations, which, despite being much more open to the 'import' of theorems and methodological inventories from cogent disciplines than from other social sciences, has *prima facie* much more reason to worry about some really big picture questions than most of the others.

For most of its existence as a scholarly pursuit, International Relations has, in one way or another, borrowed heavily into a set of constitutively assumed universals and facilitated debate and discussion on the implicit assumption of their salience. Insofar as Critical Theory partakes in these, it remains open to a range of political and analytical critical charges, which are, I think, much more serious than the disagreements with various International Relations schools of thought, as high-lighted above. I want to focus on three instances around which universal(ist) assumptions cluster, which should be profoundly problematic for critical theorists but are not routinely tackled explicitly. I want to argue that, as a result of the cultivation of such blind spots, Critical Theory is often rightly seen as quite irrelevant by perspectives of which its proponents like to see themselves as advocates. Where Critical Theory in International Relations advocates cosmopolitanism and difference-sensitive universalism, without concerning itself much more clearly with the constraints and problematic legacies to which it might remain dedicated inadvertently while doing so, it loses its capacity to make a distinctive contribution to the emergent study of world politics.

The first instance that I would like to highlight in this context concerns the problem of the philosophy of history. With the exception of Robert Cox's work on civilizations and John Hobson's explorations (2004) of the co-production of modernity out of subalternized encounters, Critical Theory in International Relations has been far too comfortable with what is essentially the script of modernization theory.[5] Measuring the distance between 'modernity' and the associated capacity for social orders based on universalizing reason on the one hand, and those societies and communities considered in such respects as 'not quite there yet' on the other, on a scale identifying relative emancipatory success with the degree of proximity to the top of a ladder at the end of which the pluralist, social-democratic welfare state located, should not even be implied unless one has gotten profoundly uncomfortable with this narrative in the first place. What may be an understandable shortcoming of approaches confining themselves deliberately to a Eurocentric perspective (and Habermas' would certainly qualify here) turns into a rather big problem when the former are unreflectively scaled up to the study of world politics. Critical Theory has always been concerned with understanding, analysing and working against relations of domination, and some of its conceptual inventory on these is extraordinarily rich and potentially helpful. However, this requires much more sensitivity to the kinds of critical investigations into the modern condition put forward forcefully, for instance, by Barry Hindess (2007), and echoed widely in post-colonial studies and decolonizing thought. The question of what kind of work is done by assumptions in the realm of the philosophy of history to sustain the progressivist orientations of Critical Theory is quite pervasive: for instance, whether critical theorists can and should accept without further ado a merely cosmetically updated version of the Kantian thought that reason operates behind the backs of people to deliver a properly cosmopolitan future should at least be part of an explicit debate in a context in which proponents of Critical Theory (rightly!) seek to distance themselves from the mainstream analytics of the 'democratic peace'. The distinction between traditional and post-traditional societies – a mainstay of Frankfurt School theory since Habermas at the latest – is another expression of a temporal politics potentially invested in practices of domination, whose urgency as a problem only increases with the very reach of the relations under consideration.[6]

The second set of concerns I would like to point out here is linked to the first and concerns the 'politics of difference'. Perhaps out of some well-founded reservations *vis-à-vis* post-structuralist approaches and the relativism these are imputed to entail, Critical Theory in International Relations has had a tendency to drift away from questions about identity and identification, and focused much more on issues linked traditionally to the concerns of political philosophy: equality, liberty, and justice. Now, there is nothing wrong with being profoundly interested in the latter. As Rob Walker reminds us in his recent challenge (2010), these may well be the crucial questions to be asking *en route* to world political transformation, however the latter is to be conceived. Nevertheless, they should figure precisely as questions, and the presumption for Critical Theory research ought to be that whatever answers the tradition has put forth should be investigated thoroughly, rather than made the basis for political analysis without further reflection. There is a difference between the struggle of a people in the idiom of human rights (think, for instance, of East Timor), and moves towards implementing frameworks for humanitarian intervention based on justifications based in human rights discourse. Registering injustices may yet have more interesting things to get across than formulating a, or any, fully-fledged theory of justice with the aim of comprehensive coverage. Not to be misunderstood, I am not suggesting that the latter is somehow profoundly pointless, but rather that our sensitivities as critical theorists ought, on balance, to be more attuned to the former, which registers for us what is missing, omitted, written out or dis-articulated.

This, I think, is even more pertinent and important when dealing ostensibly with world political questions, with the critique of the international order and with concerns regarding the limitations of the contemporary political imaginary, since the expansion of liberal modernity has clearly moved into overt crisis mode. Adorno's insistence on the work done by the negative, the non-identical, should help guard against all too quick and easy identifications – including his own.[7] Questions of race, the legacy of empire, latent or overt orientalism, dispossession and subalternization in and across different contexts are not anywhere near as central to critical theoretic work in International Relations as they ought to be. For a theoretical ideal conceived once in a transdisciplinary fashion, Critical Theory in International Relations has remained extraordinarily disinterested in the concerns associated with a culturally plural world through which 'liberalizing' socialization patterns reach, often in the name of development and equally often with devastating consequences.

This links to the third instance I would like to raise, which revolves around the place of political economy within Critical Theory. It is a telling shortcoming of Critical Theory in International Relations (and, perhaps in this case, more widely) that there has been little it has had to contribute over the years on some of the most blatant injustices committed in the name of 'advancing' an economistic paradigm, which looks distinctly implausible as a framework for global governance. When self-declared critical theorists in International Relations can pronounce on the desirability of WTO governance as an expression of an incremental advancement towards a cosmopolitan world order, while at local levels thousands die of the direct consequences of the privatization and commercialization of water supplies, the project of Critical Theory is rightly in trouble – and justifiably ignored by critical scholarship on and from what is misleadingly referred to as the Global South.[8] The problems associated with the spread and increasing reach of 'market' relations was the focus of critical attention already in Hegel's work, was central to Marx' thinking and received further attention by Gramsci. The interviewees in this volume have done much to commend this line of analysis as one of central importance. If anything, dealing with it has become more urgent, as new distributive battles loom over environmental resources and a blatant politics of dispossession takes hold again as if it were a matter of mere routine. The legitimacy crisis signalled over financial sector bail-outs and the socialization of costs has been felt with utmost urgency in non-Western parts of the world for the longest part of the history of 'development'. The latter – a regime in its own right – should have received the critical attention in Critical Theory; for this, there are some resources in the wider Critical Theory literature outside International Relations, but very few within it.

Postscript

This has been a 'crusty' essay and, I am sure, mostly quite unfair. It would certainly be unfair, were it seen as a criticism of the work of those who have done so much to establish Critical Theory as a going concern in International Relations, including the four interviewees in this volume. This was emphatically not my intention. Rather, I wanted to register what I thought was wrong with the way their opening has been taken up for further work. In the first part, I suggested that it would be desirable if Critical Theory engaged more and in more depth with its detractors than it has done. Some great work is actually under way here, and it is heartening to see that, after too long a lull, things are picking up in this respect.[9]

The second part of this essay contains, I think, the bigger challenge. Critical Theory has been far too comfortable with its inventory, with the frame it has painted full of pictures about the accommodation of difference and cosmopolitan possibilities – and an unreflective Eurocentric outlook. Where its appeal to dialogue has been a rightly attractive feature of its approach, it has neglected to pay attention to the expectations it has invested in the possibilities of dialogic politics, and hence dropped the crucial imaginary of what it means to be talked back at in a dialogue, and by whom. I picked only three tropes to suggest that Critical Theory is failing to answer important questions about its universalist aspirations; this was not to argue it should ditch these, but rather to suggest that it does not already have the answers there, and that working towards these requires it to be much more connective to critical work done elsewhere, in other idioms, and sometimes with other concerns in mind.

Seeking out these conversations, and having them, would be the end of Critical Theory as a 'position' in the disciplinary context of International Relations, and the beginning of a phase in which we find out how well (or how badly) some of the inventories gained mainly out of an immanent critique of very specific social and political constellations travel, when they reach out beyond these. To be sure, they *may* connect to the struggles already in some of these contexts, however, most likely in ways that have to first be understood. As the brief sketch on political economy suggested, the extension of social relations, their integration and fragmentation, reaches through the political architecture of International Relations with profound political implications; however, these implications play out with actors and contexts that we should not treat analogously to what we are already familiar with. Even if it is not paid enough attention, the relational imaginary is perhaps the strongest core in Critical Theory, although it is certainly not exclusive to it. In it lies the memory of a critique of liberal conceptions of freedom along republican lines, the associated principled discomfort with domination and the concern with human (and, perhaps, non-human) suffering and its enabling conditions, as well as the insight that the institutions through which suffering and domination are meted out are, in the last instance, not natural, but rather human-made – and hence, in principle, alterable. This primes Critical Theory for potential connectivity with other critical discourses on gender, race, indigeneity and cultural diversity in ways not open to liberal approaches – or, for that matter, to those approaches still invested in strong variants of nineteenth century Marxism.[10] In such contexts, however, Critical Theory has much more listening than pronouncing to do, and much more actual dialogue to engage in, rather than issuing demands for dialogue, or painting it into neat and elegant frames.

Notes

1 The textbook version of 'Critical Theory in International Relations' frequently supports such a framing.
2 Of course, at this stage Ashley had already left behind the inventories of post-Marxist thought and the influences of the Frankfurt School writings, which had informed his 'The Poverty of Neorealism' (1984).
3 See, for example, Owen (2002) or Der Derian (2009).
4 Among the constellations I have in mind here are, for instance, the societalization trends referred to (but under-analysed) under the label of 'globalization', with their attendant challenges to contemporary practices of legitimation and the heteronomies they entail or exacerbate.
5 A classical text here is, of course, W. W. Rostow's *Stages of Economic Growth – A Non-Communist Manifesto* (1960), if only because it states the subterranean temporalizing convictions of modern thought as unabashedly as possible.
6 Consider in this context S. Buck-Morss, *Hegel, Haiti and Universal History* (2009). I mention the book here only as a stand-in reminder for the problematic ways in which the tradition of Critical Theory, extending from Hegel through Marx to the twentieth century, has managed to keep itself away from questions of colonial domination, slavery and the denial of historical agency of whole worlds.
7 Eric Wolf's *Europe and the People without History* (1982) tells a critical story about Eurocentrism that extends nicely to some of the pronouncements Adorno made, for instance, in his lectures on history (see Adorno 2006).
8 See Roach (2007: 340). There are multiple cases of water-privatization which lead to impoverished households resorting to obtaining their supply from local rivers, with the result of deadly cholera outbreaks. For a critique of the 'meta-dialectical' resolution, which makes much more sense of the 'work of the negative', see Brincat (2009). It is an unfortunate side-effect of the rush to make Critical Theory-snippets work either with regard to empirical problems in international politics, or as offers of theoretical or conceptual alternatives, that little gets through of the *internal* debates, systematic (and 'de-systematizing') efforts among critical theorists outside the discipline. For instance, Axel Honneth's (2001) essay on the epistemology of recognition offers at least an occasion to begin to engage with race and racism, as well as with wider concerns regarding the scope and limits of the moral theoretic aspects of Critical Theory.
9 Indicatively, see Vij (2007), Pusca (2009) and Brincat (2010).
10 To be sure, this signals also that much remains to be done in the context of adapting critical theoretic conceptual and methodological inventories to the study of world politics. A much more comprehensive and systematic engagement with what is being written here outside the disciplinary context of International Relations will raise questions, for

instance, about Critical Theory's relation with liberal thought (Habermas' 'liberal turn' after the *Theory of Communicative Action* is a marker here), its differences in relation to late neo-Marxist approaches (one may think of Norman Geras' embrace of liberal tenets for Marxist thought), or, methodologically, its engagement with the limits of sociological approaches (topical for the debate with constructivist approaches). Something like this has been outlined, for instance, by Gillian Rose (1981).

Bibliography

Adorno, T.W. (2006) *History and Freedom*, Cambridge: Polity Press.

Ashley, R.K. (1984) 'The Poverty of Neorealism', *International Organization* 38(2): 225–86.

____ (1988) 'Untying the Sovereign State: A Double-Reading of the Anarchy Problematique', *Millennium* 17(2): 227–62.

Buck-Morss, S. (2009) *Hegel, Haiti and Universal History*, Pittsburgh: University of Pittsburgh Press.

Brincat, S. (2009) 'Negativity and Open-Endedness in the Dialectic of World Politics', *Alternatives–Global, Local, Political* 34(4): 455–93.

____ (2010) 'Towards a Social-Relational Dialectic for World Politics', *European Journal of International Relations*, available online at http://ejt.sagepub.com/content/early/2010/08/17/1354066110373838.abstract (accessed 10 April 2011).

Der Derian, J. (2009) *Critical Practices in International Theory: Selected Essays*, London: Routledge.

Geras, N. (2002) 'Marxism, the Holocaust, and September 11: An Interview with Norman Geras', *Imprints – Journal of Analytical Socialism* 6(3): 194–9.

Habermas, Jürgen (1984) *Theory of Communicative Action: Reason and the Rationalization of Society*, Boston: Beacon Press.

____ (1987) *Theory of Communicative Action: A Critique of Functionalist Reason*, Boston: Beacon Press.

Hindess, B. (2007) 'The Past is Another Culture', *International Political Sociology* 1(4): 325–38.

Hobson, J. (2004) *The Eastern Origins of Western Civilization*, Cambridge: Cambridge University Press.

Honneth, A. (2001) 'Invisibility: On the Epistemology of Recognition', *The Aristotelian Society – Supplementary Volume* 75(1): 111–26.

Owen, D. (2002) 'Re-orienting International Relations: On Pragmatism, Pluralism, and Practical Reason', *Millennium* 31(3): 653–73.

Price, R. (2008) 'Moral Limit and Possibility in World Politics', *International Organization* 62(2): 191–220.

Pusca, A. (2009) 'Walter Benjamin: A Methodological Contribution', *International Political Sociology* 3(2): 238–54.

Roach, S. (2007) 'Critical International Theory and Meta-Dialectics', *Millennium* 35(2): 321–42.

Rose, G. (1981) *Hegel Contra Sociology*, London: The Athlon Press.

Rostow, W. (1960) *The Stages of Economic Growth – An Anti-Communist Manifesto*, Cambridge: Cambridge University Press.

Vij, R. (2007) *Japanese Modernity and Welfare: Self, State and Society in Contemporary Japan*, Basingstoke: Palgrave Macmillan.

Walker, R.B.J. (2010) *After the Globe, Before the World*, New York: Routledge.

Wolf, E. (1982) *Europe and the People without History*, Berkeley: University of California Press.

14

THE POTENTIAL AND PERILS OF OPPOSITION

Michael C. Williams

Critical Theory is by definition and vocation oppositional. Standing apart from prevailing orders, it seeks, in Robert Cox's now famous formulation, to question the origins and interests of theoretical visions, and to reveal their connections to structures of power and dynamics of domination. As the evolution of Critical Theory in International Relations (IR) demonstrates, opposition can be as intellectually fruitful as it is politically essential. Identifying defining oppositions is not only a key mechanism of critique and a means of challenging orthodoxy, but it may also – by design or through more circuitous developments – hold powerful potential for the formation of relatively self-conscious counter-movements that can provide both the intellectual and institutional support necessary if critique is to develop an agenda beyond isolated individual scholarship and engagement.

Yet opposition also comes with perils attached. At one level, it brings with it the question of precisely what engagement means. Does the adoption of a 'critical' perspective mean to be fated always to being an outsider, or to be at best, like Horkheimer and Adorno, casters of 'messages in bottles' toward some future epoch when (supposedly or hopefully), the prospects for linking its theory to concrete practice will be more propitious? Without the comforting historical immanence of Hegel or Marx, the position of Critical Theory *vis-à-vis* the real or the actual that it stands outside remains as big a challenge for its position in IR as it does in any other part of intellectual, social, and political life.[1]

If this question is true of Critical Theory's relationship to 'real' practices (of historical actuality, to use Hegel's terminology), it is equally true of its relationship to other analytic positions or intellectual traditions – 'positivism', 'scientism', 'realism', etc. – toward which it seemingly by definition stands in opposition. Yet here, too, the question arises: is to be critical necessarily to stand 'outside' or against a prevailing orthodoxy? If so, how is one to engage this 'mainstream' without setting up hermetically sealed theoretical positions in which critique remains wholly external to and outside the terms of that it seeks to engage?

One of the most intriguing aspects of many of the interviews in this volume is the degree to which they can be seen as seeking to re-engage a form of immanent critique. Whether through Linklater's conception of harm, Booth's vision of security or Wyn Jones' questioning of rationality and reason in strategy and security, each shows a sensitivity to questions of engagement with the actual that puts paid to many caricatures of Critical Theory as inescapably abstract or purely normative. Yet, there seems to me little doubt that visions of Critical Theory in IR more broadly remain coloured by an oppositional vision of its history, agenda and imperatives that is both ambivalent and, at times, debilitating. It is this aspect of the perils of opposition that I would like to focus on in this brief commentary.

Opposition and critique

As in politics, opposition is the heart of intellectual life. Relationality is central to thinking at the level of concepts and it is the essence of academic endeavour. But as the Frankfurt School and its intellectual forbearers sought continually to remind us, relationality is not the same thing as direct opposition – the latter leads to dualistic rather than dialectical thinking, and to reification and ossification rather than engagement, dynamism and insight. It may well be that the perils of opposition in the form of the seductions of dualism and the potential for reification are intrinsic to thinking in itself. But be this as it may, there seems to me little doubt that it is a danger particularly prevalent in academic life, where stark oppositions and arresting contrasts are often the rhetorics most successful in gaining notoriety. This dynamic is frequently reinforced by a conceptual spiral disturbingly reminiscent of some theories of arms races, as subsequent critics find themselves tempted to caricature positions or individuals, and to further reify the terms of debate in order to stake out, defend or popularize their contending positions. And all of this is, of course, wrapped up in the collective aspect of academic life, the attractions of creating or becoming a 'school', or of being a prominent critic of one.[2]

Despite (or, perhaps, partly because of) its intellectual lineage, Critical Theory has been far from immune from these dynamics, and as I suggested earlier, this is by no means to be wholly decried: its vibrancy, energy and development no doubt owe much to them. Yet it also comes with considerable costs, and it may at this point in time be useful to consider briefly how some of these oppositions may in some ways have become hindrances to the further development of Critical Theory in IR.

One of the great merits of a volume such as this is that it facilitates such reflection. Thinking about theory through theorists, rather than as some wholly de-personalized and abstract activity, certainly presents analytic as well as expository challenges. Interviews lack the systematic structure of their subjects' carefully constructed writings, and they highlight with particular clarity the difficulties involved in adopting the deceptively straightforward maxim that 'theory is always for someone and for some purpose'. However, this form of expression also holds considerable rewards. As in the case of this book, interviews demonstrate the depth and diversity of Critical Theory in IR, often helping to rescue the ideas (and the individuals associated with them) from caricatures that reduce them to mere shadows of themselves, and demonstrating how their ideas go well beyond narrow (often mis-) construals to which critics have tried to reduce them.

A perfect illustration here lies in the seminal figure of Robert Cox, whose casting of himself as a Burkean conservative with often deeply pessimistic inclinations will, I suspect, come as something of a revelation to many of his supporters as well as his critics. At the same time, this connection seems also to open the way for a reconsideration of one of Critical Theory's defining oppositions: that toward realism. Conservatism and pessimism, after all, are positions more often associated in IR with realism than with any other position, and Burke was as deeply admired by many realists as he was loathed by many liberals and Marxists. How, then, might one reconcile this apparent tension? The first step might, of course, be to note that Cox does not see his version of Critical Theory as opposed to realism *tout court*. He embraces an historicist realism that he associates with E.H. Carr (and, possibly, parts of the English School more broadly), and which he distinguishes starkly from that connected with Hans Morgenthau and the rise of an 'American' social science of IR. Beneath this distinction, therefore, lies a defining divide between Critical Theory and 'American realism', which mirrors a wider divergence in the field between IR as a positivist American social science and the historicist and philosophical traditions found in earlier forms of realism. This, in turn, provides the basis for the construction of a scholarly geopolitical divide between 'European' (and some other) approaches, and the 'social scientific' theory dominant in the United States and spread via its influence. To caricature it only a little, to be critical thus comes to be defined as standing outside that which is 'American', 'positivist' and 'realist', with the three usually combined in one way or another.

To be sure, there is little doubt that this picture captures important parts of a whole, particularly at the time Cox first formulated it. There is little doubt, for instance, that the kinds of rationalist social science that Cox identifies with American realism often stand starkly at odds with the realism of Carr and those traditions of enquiry from which Critical Theory emerges. As Richard Wyn Jones points out, there is also little doubt that by the 1980s this form of realism had sometimes become a 'caricature of itself' (see this volume, 92), something that can no doubt still be found today and which is, as Booth pithily puts it, likely 'best kept in its box' (see this volume, 73).[3] The difficulty, however, is that Cox's divide also cuts off Critical Theory from crucial parts of its intellectual history and legacy in social theory and IR in the United States. As a consequence, it narrows our appreciation of the history and evolution of Critical Theory as a whole, of its relationship to the history of IR theory and to American social science, and of its potential relationships to other forms of theory today. In short, the defining opposition risks becoming dysfunctional for both intellectual clarity and engagement.

Two aspects of this narrowing seem to me particularly important. The first is that by identifying social science with both positivism and American realism, it risks creating a defining divide between Critical Theory and large parts of the social sciences. In this view, to do Critical Theory is, by definition, not to do 'American' social science, and to take a principled opposition toward forms of empirical method that by definition are seen as part of 'positivism'. This is unnecessarily constricting, both in terms of research and in terms of the relationship between Critical Theory and other parts of the social sciences. To be sure, there is no need to be naive in this regard – the critique of positivism at the core of the critical tradition remains vital, and attempts (and, to some degree, successes) of various theoretical positions to present as neutral methods what are in fact fundamental epistemic, ontological and political positions and commitments are not difficult to identify, and their influence is as perfidious as critical theorists have long insisted.

Yet it is also worth noting that, methodologically, the early Frankfurt School was by no means a wholly theoretical or conceptual enterprise; nor was it by any means opposed to empirical social science and its methods. Indeed, some of its most creative work, such as the Studies in Prejudice and even its inquiries into the Authoritarian Personality, involved extensive surveys, innovative forms of data collection and interpretation, and statistical analysis. Whatever one makes of the ultimate quality and multiple motives behind this research (reflecting in part as it did the émigré status of the Institute), there is ample evidence that many members of the Frankfurt School were interested in a variety of methods, and it serves a useful reminder that for even those most critical of 'positivism' in all its forms, these forms of social research were not necessarily positivistic in the strict sense. On the contrary, they could be remarkably revealing.

Thus, while the idolatry of quantitative methods found in much of political science and IR today is certainly facile and deserving of criticism, we should not fall into the unnecessarily constricting belief that all such methods are irredeemably 'positivist', and that a critical methodology is defined by its rejection of quantitative methods *per se*. Nor should it be defined by a complete rejection of 'policy relevant' research. While it is once again essential to resist the idea that only such research is valuable, 'real' or relevant, and while it is equally vital (as critical thinkers such as Ken Booth and Steve Smith have long pointed out) to be clear about the limitations and dilemmas of speaking 'truth to power',[4] it is surely debilitating to identify being 'critical' with an a priori eschewal of any such engagement. Richard Wyn Jones' comments in this book on his engagement with political 'science' in attempting to come to terms with Welsh politics in an era of devolved governance in the UK demonstrate the important directions that such an engagement can in fact take (see this volume, 89). In this context, it is also worth recalling that members of the Frankfurt School – including Kirchheimer, Marcuse and Neumann – worked in the American Office of Strategic Services during the Second World War, and that Marcuse continued (though not entirely happily) to be employed by the US State Department until 1951.[5] To put these issues back squarely on the agenda of Critical Theory is to reopen some of the difficult questions surrounding the relationship between theory and practice that have long bedevilled it, and which remain to be grappled with. Yet, as the dialogues in this book demonstrate, such a process remains essential.

In wide terms, then, it is essential that Critical Theory does not fall into the belief that American realism equals positivism, which equals social science, which must therefore be eschewed. To do so is to cut itself off from a range of attempts to combine carefully constructed empirical work with theoretically sophisticated analysis, and to place unnecessary barriers between itself and similarly attuned research, such as the critical sociology pioneered by Pierre Bourdieu.[6] It is also to risk becoming increasingly dominated by a philosophical turn that is haunted by the quite despairing negative dialectics that characterized the later thinking of Horkheimer and Adorno, or by turns such as Habermas' discursive ethics or the increasingly sociologically distanced forms taken by many variants of linguistic or post-modern theory. None of these directions, to be clear, is unproductive – the opposite is quite often the case, and there is a strong case to be made that the tendency of Critical Theory and post-modern-inspired positions to be been as inevitably in conflict is yet another deleterious symptom of the perils of oppositional thinking.[7] But they should not be mistaken for the only road that can be taken in the name of a misguided equating of all 'empirical' method with some kind of unreconstructed positivism.

A further, and to my mind most fertile consequence of reopening the opposition between Critical Theory and realism lies in its connections to classical realism. Here, Cox's choice of Morgenthau as the representative of American positivism was particularly unfortunate, for it actually put in place an opposition that has cut Critical Theory off from some of its most significant connections with the history of IR theory, from an engagement with some of its most sophisticated issues and interlocutors, and from exploring its relationship to intriguing dimensions of American thinking about politics and foreign policy.

Again, the history of the Frankfurt School provides a useful way into this question at a number of levels. As numerous historical appraisals have shown (Williams 2007b; Scheuerman 2009; Jutersönke 2010), Morgenthau and other so-called 'classical' realists were deeply engaged in Weimar political debates that intersected with the concerns of the early critical theorists. In Morgenthau's case, his work with the left-wing labour lawyer Hugo Sinzheimer provided a personal point of contact, and while there is limited evidence of any direct engagement between Morgenthau and the School, there is equally little doubt that he would have been aware of its existence and arguments (Scheuerman 2009: 12–24).

Substantively, his engagement with post-Weberian political theory, as well as with the legal controversies associated with Carl Schmitt, clearly discernable in works such as *Scientific Man versus Power Politics* and *Science: Servant or Master?*, echo concerns that were also central to Frankfurt School Critical Theory, including the nature of reason, the dangers of scientism, the paradoxical relationship between modern rationalism and irrationalism, and numerous other themes. Morgenthau and a number of the other realists with whom he came to be associated no doubt developed these themes and their responses to them in ways quite different from those (also widely divergent) associated with the Horkheimer circle, and I am certainly not suggesting that the these bodies of thought are directly analogous. But it is important to recognize that they are far from completely divorced, and that the theoretical issues raised by this shared lineage provide a very different reading of the relationship between Critical Theory and the developing theory of International Relations in its post-war American context.

The history of the Frankfurt School also reveals connections to other aspects of American political thought that not only call into the question a stark divide between American and Critical Theory, but also mean that the critical tradition resonates with contemporary developments and debates in important and often under-acknowledged ways. Here, as Thomas Wheatland has nicely shown, the location of the Frankfurt School 'in exile' in the United States through much of the 1930s and 1940s put it into contact with (if in often ambivalent relation to) some of the most dynamic intellectual movements in America at the time. Philosophically, perhaps the most interesting of these connections was with the controversial figure of Sidney Hook (memorably named by Wheatland as 'John Dewey's Pit Bull') and his ambitious, if idiosyncratic, attempt to fuse Marxism and that most American of philosophical positions, Deweyian pragmatism.[8] Indeed, the 'failure of nerve' (Wheatland 2009: 197–239) that Hook accused Critical Theorists (and others) of succumbing to in their scepticism toward science and reason has intriguing affinities to the analogous, if much less philosophically sophisticated, accusations made about critical theories by many rationalist theorists in IR today.[9] As both an historical marker and a theoretical problematic, this early encounter provides fascinating avenues for exploration, including American pragmatism's affinities with – and departures from – the philosophical foundations of realism. This background includes not only a shared debt to Nietzsche, but a self-conscious engagement with pragmatism by many of the émigrés and their associates – pre-eminently Reinhold Neibuhr – and suggests a relationship between 'European' realism and American intellectual traditions that goes well beyond the stale contrast between an American liberal idealism and post-war power politics.

Similarly fertile, and perhaps even more politically intriguing, are the resonances between the Frankfurt School and the leftist 'New York intellectuals' of the 1930s, 40s, and 50s, many of whom later went on to become key figures in American neo-conservatism (Wheatland 2009: 140–88). Although direct contacts between the émigrés and the radical thinkers in what was one of the liveliest parts of American intellectual life and political debate were limited, the affinities between their concerns and the different trajectories that they have taken deserve much closer scrutiny.[10] For the New York intellectuals, as for the Frankfurt School, the nature and fate of Marxism and capitalism, the dilemmas and dangers of liberal rationalism and atomism, the impact of aesthetics and the pernicious effects of the 'culture industry' were key issues in political modernity.

The directions in which figures such as Daniel Bell and Irving Kristol took these themes clearly differ radically from the ways in which they have been conceived in

Critical Theory (and, it must be admitted, in the extent of their influence on practical politics), and it may often seem today that Critical Theory and neoconservatism are about as far apart as it is possible for positions to be. However, casting a look backward reveals that there are numerous points of intersection that provide the basis for in-depth engagement and critique beyond a purely oppositional stance. Indeed, despite the gulf between them, Critical Theory may provide incisive tools for thinking about the genesis and impact of neoconservatism on American politics and foreign policy. One of the most significant innovations of neoconservatism, for instance, resides in the ways that it locates its policy positions self-consciously within a wider set of philosophical and sociological claims about the nature of modernity and its cultural and political dynamics. Rationalist theories in political science and most realist positions in IR lack the philosophical and theoretical tools and rhetorical resources to engage effectively with the themes and political strategies that were articulated initially by neoconservatives, and that have since become powerful across the American Right. These include not only specific mobilizations of cultural politics, but also the ability powerfully to connect domestic and international politics in ways that cut across the analytic boundaries defining much of IR, and enable political rhetorics and strategies that marginalize intellectual critique both conceptually and institutionally.[11] While it must be admitted that it is far from clear that Critical Theory has a compelling political response to these challenges, it does possess a philosophical legacy replete with resources capable of being mobilized to engage directly with them, and may even be able to contribute to cogent social and political analyses of their power and limitations.

In sum, while the contrast between Critical Theory and American realism in its rationalist forms is undoubtedly crucial, the specific framing that it has tended to take on in IR theory is unfortunate. It leads, and often has led, to a set of convictions about the relationship between Critical Theory, the evolution of realism and its place in 'American' political science that are frequently misleading – and to a set of categorical oppositions that actually prevent a fuller exploration of the important relationship that Cox initially seemed to open up. It has also allowed Critical Theory to be represented as outside the traditions of IR – and wholly external to its genesis as an 'American social science'. While this can be useful, it also allows its opponents to lay exclusive claim to both the realist 'tradition' and the 'legitimate' disciplinary evolution of IR, and to present Critical Theory as foreign to development and concerns of both, when the opposite is actually the case.

Perhaps even more strikingly, this tendency toward opposition has obscured the way that, as William Scheuerman (2011) has recently shown, much of post-war realism adopted a 'progressive' politics that has been written out of the history of the field as realism has in many ways been transformed into the kind of objectivist social science or conservative *realpolitik* that Cox assailed. Indeed, a closer look at classical realism reveals an often striking contrast to visions of realism today proffered by both its proponents and its critics. While there is no doubt that these thinkers adopted a hard-edged and sometimes brutal approach to political life that requires critical engagement, it is equally true that they expressed concern with a range of issues that might well today fit more comfortably under the rubric of Critical Theory than any other theoretical position in IR. For example, one need only read Morgenthau's *The Purpose of American Politics*, or Niebuhr's voluminous writings, to get a clear sense of the depth of their concerns with the state of democracy and the vitality of the public sphere – concerns that resonate with critical theories, including those of Hannah Arendt, if one wishes to stretch the label that far. Similarly, their engagement with (and frequent sympathy towards) supranational forms of governance, such as those they saw emerging in Europe, has long been ignored – as have their deeply critical views on nuclear weapons, and their (admittedly less than successful) attempts to think anew about international ethics.

From this perspective, the critical desire to put the normative back into IR theory again looks more complicated than the contrast between 'normative Critical Theory versus amoral realism' that has often structured debates. While important parts of Critical Theory have sought to place a recognisably Kantian ethic at the heart of its vision of IR in direct contrast to realism,[12] this concern was also far from absent in post-war realism. Indeed, it is possible to argue plausibly that one of the core concerns of these forms of 'classical' realism lay in attempting to work through the implications of Kantian and post-Kantian ethics for domestic and international politics. This was expressed in its engagement with legal categories crystallized around the work of Hans Kelsen (Koskenniemmi 2002; Jütersonke 2010); its implication in questions of social scientific method, power, modernity and political responsibility framed by the protean vision of Max Weber; and its intense engagement with diverse attempts to work through the consequences of Weber's vision of modern politics, including those of Carl Schmitt and the Frankfurt School. Political theology, as Nicolas Guilhot (2010b) has compellingly demonstrated, was central to 'classical' realism, and to the extent that much of Critical Theory[13] (as well as post-modern thinking, and much else besides) can be read as attempting to work through and against this legacy, it is working through a background it shares with some of the most prominent figures in the history of 'mainstream' IR theory.

My goal in this commentary has not been to 'defend' realism against Critical Theory. Even less has it been to suggest that realism provides a superior view, that it in any way managed satisfactorily to resolve its dilemmas, or that somehow these different theoretical orientations should be synthesized. That would pay insufficient respect to the strengths of each, as well as to the important divergences between them. What I have tried to suggest, however, is that Critical Theory can be well-served by a fuller engagement with classical realism rather than a straightforward opposition toward it. In a revealing statement, Hans Morgenthau (1959: 22)[14] wrote that

> [a] political science which is true to its moral commitment ought at the very least to be an unpopular undertaking. At the very best, it cannot help being a subversive and revolutionary force with regard to certain vested interests – intellectual, political, economic, social in general.

If one of the central tenets of Critical Theory lies in Adorno's famous aphorism that 'all reification is a forgetting', then remembering the relationship between realism and Critical Theory may help both to avoid this fate, and might even provide a means of developing their relationship in the future.

Notes

1 At one level, Linklater's conception of harm and perhaps Booth's vision of the universality of security can be seen as attempts to reframe the issue of immanence within less teleological assumptions that nonetheless avoid presenting critique as wholly external, and thus susceptible to the charge of idealism; indeed, much of the controversy that surrounds their views reflects these more basic questions.

2 These attractions need not by any means be wholly or even mainly nefarious: personal and intellectual affinities, support networks, as well as the possibilities of institutional power, are but a few of the intersecting dynamics of the world of *homo academicus* that Bourdieu (1990a) – and, following him, Wyn Jones (this volume, 93) – points to as crucial in the operation of the academic field. For an intriguingly different treatment, see Bauman (1987).

3 We are now beginning to get detailed evaluations of precisely how this process took place; see particularly Guilhot (2010a and forthcoming) for an examination of rationalism.

4 As in the debate between Wallace (1996), Booth (1997) and Smith (1997).

5 See Wheatland (2009: 281–5); as he reports, another realist John Herz (whose legacy is also undergoing reassessment today) quipped at the time that 'the left Hegelian Weltgeist has found its temporary abode there in the Central European section of the OSS' (Wheatland 2009: 281). For a wider overview, see Katz (1989).

6 See Bourdieu (1987); and, for his critique of critical sociologists hostility toward statistics, see Bourdieu (1990b).

7 For an argument in favour of engagement, see Hanssen (2000: 97–157, especially).

8 On Hook, see Phelps (1992).

9 Interestingly, and significantly, Hook's critique was aimed in large part at figures such as Reinhold Niebuhr – a fact that complicates even further the story of American realism. For a wider treatment, see Guilhot (2010a).

10 Again, see Wheatland (2009: Chapter Four); for a wider treatment of the New York intellectuals see Jumonville (1991) and Wadd (1987).

11 I have tried to sketch some of these in Williams (2007a); for a pointed and insightful treatment see Drolet (2011).

12 For different appraisals, see particularly Linklater (1982) and Booth (2007).

13 As, for instance, in the engagement between Schmitt and Walter Benjamin; for one rendering, see Bredekamp (1999).

14 Interestingly, this passage is also cited in Neufeld's (1995: 122) early contribution to critical IR theory, though its implications are not taken up.

Bibliography

Bauman, Z. (1987) *Legislators and Interpreters: On Modernity, Post-Modernity, and Intellectuals*, Ithaca: Cornell University Press.

Booth, K. (1997) 'A Reply to Wallace', *Review of International Studies* 23(3): 371–7.

_____ (2007) *Theory of World Security*, Cambridge: Cambridge University Press.

Bourdieu, P. (1987) *Distinction: A Social Critique of the Judgment of Taste*, Cambridge, MA: Harvard University Press.

_____ (1990a) *Homo Academicus*, Stanford: Stanford University Press.

_____ (1990b) *In Other Words*, Stanford: Stanford University Press.

Bredekamp, H. (1999) 'From Walter Benjamin to Carl Schmitt, via Thomas Hobbes', *Critical Inquiry* 25(2): 247–66.

Drolet, J-F. (2011) *American Neoconservatism*, New York: Hurst.

Guilhot, N. (2010a) *Inventing International Relations*, New York: Columbia University Press.

—— (2010b) 'American Katechon: When Political Theology Became International Relations', *Constellations* 17(2): 224–53.

—— (forthcoming) 'Cyborg Pantocrator: International Relations Theory from Decisionism to Rational Choice', *Journal of the History of Behavioural Sciences*.

Hanssen, B. (2000) *Critique of Violence,* London: Routledge.

Jumonville, N. (1991) *Critical Crossings: The New York Intellectuals in Post-War America*, Berkeley: University of California Press.

Jütersonke, O. (2010) *Morgenthau, Law and Realism*, Cambridge: Cambridge University Press.

Katz, B.M. (1989) *Foreign Intelligence: Research and Analysis in the Office of Strategic Services, 1942–45*, Cambridge, MA: Harvard University Press.

Koskenniemi, M. (2002) *The Gentle Civilizer of Nations*, Cambridge: Cambridge University Press.

Linklater, A. (1982) *Men and Citizens in the Theory of International Relations*, London: MacMillan.

Morgenthau, H. (1959) 'The Nature and Limits of a Theory of International Relations', in W.T.R. Fox (ed.) *Theoretical Aspects of International Relations*, Notre Dame: Notre Dame University Press.

Neufeld, M. (1995) *The Restructuring of International Relations Theory*, Cambridge: Cambridge University Press.

Phelps, C. (1992) *Young Sidney Hook: Marxist and Pragmatist*, Ithaca: Cornell University Press.

Scheuerman, W. (2007) *Frankfurt School Perspectives on Globalization, Democracy, and the Law*, London: Routledge.

—— (2009) *Morgenthau*, Cambridge: Polity Press.

—— (2011) *The Realist Case for Global Reform,* Cambridge: Polity Press.

Smith, S. (1997) 'Power and Truth: A Reply to William Wallace', *Review of International Studies* 23(4): 507–16.

Wadd, A. (1987) *The New York Intellectuals: The Rise and Decline of the Anti-Stalinist Left*, Chapel Hill: University of North Carolina Press.

Wallace, W. (1996) 'Truth and Power, Monks and Technocrats: Theory and Practice in International Relations', *Review of International Studies* 22(3): 301–21.

Wheatland, T. (2009) *The Frankfurt School in Exile*, Minneapolis: University of Minnesota Press.

Williams, M.C. (2007a) *Culture and Security: Symbolic Power and the Politics of International Security,* London: Routledge.

—— (ed.) (2007b) *Realism Reconsidered: The Legacy of Hans Morgenthau in International Relations*, Oxford: Oxford University Press.

15

TURNING TOWARDS THE WORLD

Practicing critique in IR

Kimberly Hutchings

Introduction

> When the complex dynamics of the politics of critique are fully appreciated, the critique of politics which follows will combine prescriptive ambition with vulnerability.
>
> *(Hutchings 1996: 190)*

My initial engagement with International Relations (IR) theory was provoked by its explicitly 'critical' turn in the 1980s. At that time I was writing on Kantian critique and its legacy in the work of selected twentieth-century thinkers: Habermas, Arendt, Foucault and Lyotard. IR critical theories provided a kind of 'case study', which, I argued, illustrated persistent patterns in critical thinking that could be traced back to Kant's original formulation of a critical project for philosophy. The reflections on critical theory in IR in all four of the interviews at the beginning of this volume raise perennial questions about the meaning and purpose of critique. And, in this respect, they constitute a set of temptations to re-tread familiar pathways of thought. At the same time, certain themes in the four critical theorists' accounts of themselves point to the futility of constantly rehearsing old arguments.

In this contribution, my aim is to resist the temptation to explore old ground and to take inspiration from the ways that all four of the theorists interviewed refuse to be held down by the impossibilities inherent in any genuinely critical position. To be a critic is to be prescriptively ambitious without authoritative ground. Critical claims cannot be redeemed *a priori* but only, and then always only, provisionally, through intersubjective engagement. In spite of the differences in substance, methodology and tone between the accounts of Cox, Linklater, Booth and Wyn Jones, all of them link the past and future of critical theory in IR with a turn towards the world. In what follows, I first look at the ways in which this turn is manifested in the comments of the four thinkers and then, in the second section, move on to set out my own stall as to what a turn towards the world in critical IR theory should mean.

'Critique is a way of life'

Booth's comment (this volume, 71) could serve as a motto for all four theorists under consideration here. In their autobiographical stories, as well as in their accounts of their intellectual and political work, we can see that critique is not a settled set of propositions, but an ongoing practice and ethos. Cox, it turns out, is influenced by conservatism and syndicalism as well as Gramsci. Linklater has turned from Habermas to Elias. Booth finds classical realism a helpful resource. Wyn Jones has re-thought his attitude to quantitative methods. Though certain names recur, in particular those of Gramsci and the Frankfurt School, the interviews tell a story of eclecticism and shifting sources of inspiration. The theorists problematize the clear-cut lines customarily drawn between IR Critical Theory (capitalized), mainstream theories such as realism or the English School and poststructuralism or postcolonialism. Out of the four thinkers, only Booth is firmly of the view that poststructuralism is antithetical to critique, citing both its identification of emancipation with eurocentrism and cultural imperialism, and its 'self-marginalizing' character. By and large, however, the other thinkers are not interested in opening up the wars of reason between different critical theories in IR or different strands of critical thinking in ethical, political and social theory. Instead they turn towards the world, and focus on the future agenda of critique.

> Critical theory is a mode of thought that exposes the common current doctrines as inadequate in dealing with global problems, and that tries to find other elements that could be thought of, either separately or collectively, as an alternative.
>
> *(Cox, this volume, 20)*

Cox has a normative commitment to ideals of global equity and peace. He argues, however, that, in a plural world, these ideals cannot be adequately formulated in an intra-civilizational discourse. Critical theory, for Cox, now needs to focus on how transcivilizational ways of thinking might be developed. There are, of course, many objections that could be made to the use of the term 'civilization' here. But whatever difficulties there might be with Cox's project, it exemplifies the importance of a turn to the world to redeem the authority of critique. Across all of his work, Cox has been clear that critique is always historically conditioned, but in his earlier work there was an assumption that world historical conditions had a unified meaning and that there was no need for any work of translation between the critical theorist's diagnosis of the present and that of those to whom he was speaking (Cox 1981; 1996). But in his more recent work, this authoritative reading of history is made open to challenge by having to be put in the terms of others.

> For critical theorists, the aim is not to side with contemporary political movements necessarily, but rather to take the long-term view by thinking about alternative forms of political organization and the prospects for realizing them.
>
> *(Linklater, this volume, 54)*

Linklater's characterization of critical theory fits with the concerns of his own work in its various manifestations. The vision of a post-Westphalian political community in *The Transformation of Political Community* (1998) was one example of a 'long-term view' of how cosmopolitan ideals might be realizable in history. As with Cox, a particular reading of history has been central to Linklater's version of critical IR theory. In his more recent work, this is joined by an explicit philosophical anthropology, centred on the potential generalizability of the 'harm principle'. As he points out in his interview, Linklater's work has in the past been criticised for its over-reliance on Habermas and has been charged with utopianism and eurocentrism. In this respect, his critics have suggested that the way in which Linklater practices critical theory comes too close to reifying the grounds of its (that practice's) own authority. These are the grounds of a singular interpretation both of modernity and of the nature of moral reason (Hutchings 2008).

While it is clearly still the case that Linklater is looking to find ways of realizing what he sees as the progressive side of the legacy of Enlightenment, the move from Habermas to Elias can also be seen as a shift in orientation, from the authority of reason and history to the authority of the world as a precarious and shifting process of becoming. In his earlier work, Linklater adapted Habermasian notions of 'collective learning', but without giving any substantive account of how such learning occurred and how it could be sustained. Elias's comparative sociology of civilizing processes provides a way into understanding the sociology of moral life, and how relations of identification and empathy may or may not be extended across the boundaries of existing political communities. In moving from cosmopolitanism as the logical implication of counterfactually evident universal values, to cosmopolitanism as feeling, the critical theorist's attention is directed away from the conditions of his own judgement to the world of sensibility. The redemption of the claims made as to contemporary civilizing processes is ultimately in the hands of others.

> Our duty as critical theorists is to change the collective consciousness of society, to challenge the ideas that made us.
>
> *(Booth, this volume, 78)*

Of the four theorists under consideration here, Booth is the one that states his prescriptive vision most strongly and with most certainty. He is also the one that makes the most explicit claim for the idea of common humanity as sameness. He wants to defend the possibility of grand theory, while acknowledging that there are no blueprints for the future and that the task of critique will always be ongoing. For this reason, as noted above, he is the only one of the theorists that seems inclined to re-fight the wars of reason, in particular against post-structuralist arguments. For this reason also, it is in Booth's work that the turn to the world implicit in the idea of critique is most threatened. Booth's insistence on learning and understanding as much as possible about what is actually going on, on the ground, in the world, his recognition of the limitations of theoretical prescription and his willingness to engage with the risks of political action are at odds with his preoccupation with the ground of critical judgement. When the critic becomes convinced of the need to claim the high ground for the authority of their judgement, then discussion becomes oriented towards that ground. In the case of Booth, to the extent that critique is a priori grounded in the identity of emancipation with autonomy (or in Darwin's account of the human species) it shifts from the register of critique to that of speculation. When this happens, then critique ceases to be critical, that is, it ceases to acknowledge the vulnerability of its own prescriptive claims and to look to the world for their redemption.

> To me there are two reasons why we should be concerned about the question of emancipation. It is a matter of ethical responsibility and, in the case of anyone who views themselves as producing work that is in any way critical, it is also a matter of internal coherence.
>
> *(Wyn Jones, this volume, 96)*

As with the other theorists, Wyn Jones argues that critique is necessarily oriented towards emancipatory values. In his account of critical theory in general and critical security studies in particular, he stresses the importance of having an alternative vision. And even though he does not give 'emancipation' any particular content, the implication is that in any given political context, it is the responsibility of the critical theorist to be able to articulate and defend an account of how the world should be. In this respect, like Booth, he is impatient with the post-structuralist suspicion of emancipatory theory. Unlike Booth, however, he argues that the division between different strands of critical theory in IR is misleading and that it should be possible within critical security studies to forge a 'meaningful synthesis' of different 'critical strands'.

In terms of shifts in his thinking, even though he is no longer working within critical IR theory, Wyn Jones's comments about the political origins of his intellectual concerns, about his current work, about the lack of authorial control over the reception of his work, and about the potential agenda of critical security studies, all direct attention away from debates about the critic's authority towards engagement with the world. This is evident in the reassessment of positivist research methods, in the revaluation of realism, and in the importance given to bridging the gap between the academy and the realm of policy and practice. The title of Wyn Jones's contribution highlights the idea of an external validation for critical theory. The 'test of practice', as with Cox's transcivilizational dialogue and Linklater's harm principle, puts the redemption of the claims of critical theory firmly in the hand of the audience to whom they are addressed.

There are clearly many different themes and claims in the work of the four thinkers interviewed. What I have tried to pick up in my comments are the ways in which the critical register of these theorists is sustained in their accounts of their own critical practice. Ultimately, I argue, it is sustained by the combination of prescriptive ambition and vulnerability that characterizes theorizing that looks towards the world for its authorization: epistemically, ethically and politically. It would be possible, as I sketched out in the case of Booth, to offer a deconstruction of all of the thinkers to show how their critical credentials are not always sustained in the ways in which they formulate their argument and make their claims. But I am more interested in thinking constructively about different ways of taking critical theory forward. The values of equity, peace, emancipation and solidarity, to which all the theorists featured in this volume subscribe, are not only valued by critical theorists. What distinguishes critical theorists from other theorists with similar normative aspirations is the way in which those values are understood to be meaningful and universalizable. From the critical theorist's point of view, how the world is understood matters for how the values of equity, peace, emancipation and solidarity have meaning and traction in any given context, whether as a premise of argument or a requirement for action. The claims of critical theory are authoritative only in so far as the audience of those claims recognizes and endorses them. In this respect, the critical theorist is always in a political relation to his or her audience that is implicitly democratic. This makes the assumptions of critical theorists about the world crucial to the practice of critique and to the possibilities of its success or failure. I am, therefore, interested in how the turn to the world that constitutes critical theory is best accomplished when addressing questions of equity, peace, emancipation and solidarity in world politics.

Thinking the world

Critical theory in IR has been associated with various versions of moral and political cosmopolitanism. But it has not always treated the question of 'who are the people?' that make up the implicit cosmopolis particularly critically. In other words, there has been a tendency to assume that the nature of the world is knowable a priori. Cox speaks of civilizations, Linklater of a common humanity and civilizing processes, and Booth of a common humanity forcibly and falsely divided by capitalist, racist and patriarchal structures. In all cases, these accounts of the world are framed in the language of western philosophy and ideology, and the world is treated as spatially and temporally unified. This means that the world of the critical theorist is one in which he is at home, centred in familiar theoretical and historical ground. Only Wyn Jones is cautious about offering a generalized account of his audience, and locates it much more specifically in particular contexts (Wales, the UK, Norway). And only Wyn Jones identifies the phenomenon of existential friction and displacement as the key spur to critique, in his experience of being a member of a stateless nation in a world of states. Following Wyn Jones's lead, I want to suggest that the turn to the world that makes theory critical requires an openness to displacing a priori assumptions about the world. And that this in turn requires a re-cognition of the critical IR theorist's place within, and relation to, the world of international politics. William Connolly describes the process of this re-cognition in terms of the risky endeavour of keeping your place as a critical theorist whilst at the same time being open to your own displacement (Connolly 2008).

All critical theory starts from an identification with, and a diagnosis of, the *present*. The critical theorist is immanent to the present with which he or she engages, and which he or she aims to challenge and change as a way of thinking, a set of structures, practices or institutions. For the critical IR theorist, the 'present' encompasses the world as a whole, which creates particular challenges for the spatio-temporal location of the critic's judgement, which is required to open itself up to a world in which the notion of the 'present' cannot be taken for granted. Where critical theory remains too close to home in its construal of the world's 'present', the aspiration towards global ethical and political engagement is taken to be inherent in the resources for thought opened up by western modernity. But there are real problems with the idea that the world can be identified with the present of western modernity, its successes and its failures. As I have argued elsewhere, the idea that there is a singular world political present relies on heroic and untenable assumptions about both history and theory (Hutchings 2008). Instead we should recognize that the world is made up of multiple and cross-cutting presents, which cannot be subsumed under any overarching account of world political time without an uncritical retreat into metaphysics. The present with which the critic identifies interacts and overlaps, but does not coincide neatly, with that of large swathes of the audience of his or her claims.

If we inhabit a world of plural temporalities, of 'multiple modernities' (Mitchell 2000) or 'heterotemporality' (Chakrabarty 2000), then how is the critical theorist to turn to the world for the redemption of his or her claims? Negotiating 'presents' makes the work of the critical theorist much harder, since it requires the painful, political effort of cross-temporal engagement without the shortcuts enabled by the taken for granted fusion of his or her particular present with the world political present as such. I suggest that this can only be done if the critic is willing to risk going rather further from home than critical theorists have often been willing to do.

In his interview, Booth talks about a future cosmopolitan community as our original home, the one from which we are displaced by the workings of power and exploitation. In contrast, it seems to me that there is no original home for humanity in critical theory. At best there is a wager on the embrace of homelessness in an effort to make a world in which equity, peace, emancipation and solidarity are at home. In only ever being at best partially at home, heterotemporally oriented critique partakes of the partiality and revisability of the presents to which it is immanent. The extent to which the critic's interventions are, or are not, timely will depend on the ways in which his or her 'present' interlocks with the 'presents' of his audience. This means that making the home/s of equity, peace, emancipation and solidarity will necessarily be a collaborative enterprise.

Critical theory always has radical implications. It is no coincidence that the practice of critique foreshadows, or even, as in the case of Habermas's counterfactual logic of communicative action, appears actually to *require* a radically democratized world. The democratization of critique itself is part and parcel of the pursuit of equity, peace, emancipation and solidarity. And it requires an element of self-surrender in the critic, not in the sense that the critic's orientation to certain prescriptive goals is given up, but in the sense that the critic abandons any claim to monopoly of the meaning of critique and turns to the world to develop and clarify his or her critical project.

In this respect, the accounts given of the practice of critique by the four thinkers interviewed seem to me to under-emphasize the ways in which feminist, postcolonial and green critical thinking take the critical project in IR forward. The ongoing debate and/or synthesis between the Frankfurt School and post-structuralist thinking is touched on by all of the theorists. This is not a trivial debate, but a focus on it, whether from the point of view of seeing complementarities or antitheses, which pulls critique back to a preoccupation with critique's groundlessness, and risks burying the critic in the history of western philosophy rather than enabling him or her to turn to the world. In the meantime, a tendency towards *listing* axes of power and hierarchy in the world pervades accounts of critical theory in a way that fails to do justice to the specificity of the ways in which such axes drive the re-working of critical practice and of the substantive aspirations of critique. In this respect, feminist, postcolonial and green critical theories do not just add 'issues' to the agenda of critical theory, but involve fundamental reorientations of critical practice, which become matters of difficult theoretical and practical negotiation around the meanings of critical theory's prescriptive ambition for a world of equity, peace, emancipation and solidarity.

Feminist critical interventions challenge the practice and substantive aspirations of critical theory. They challenge the practice by demonstrating how modes of thinking inherent in the philosophical and ideological traditions on which critical theory draws are bound up with gendered relations of power. As the audience of the claims of critique, feminists are wary of arguments cast in a language of binary oppositions, which privileges the heroic position of the critic, of reason over emotion, or takes male as norm and identifies progress with equity as sameness. In these respects, feminists have taken issue in various ways with Marxist and Frankfurt School arguments, not to dismiss their value but to reorient them towards the role of gender as a structuring principle of thought as well as of social and political relations (Hutchings 2003).

In substantive terms, feminism throws back the ideals of equity and peace at the critic and requires critical theorists to grapple with what it might mean to re-shape these ideals to take account of gendered power. This opens up debates about whether equity requires a wholesale challenge to existing modes of organizing reproductive and caring work, a complete revaluation of prevalent values, or perhaps whether it needs to be premised on *difference* rather than the *sameness* (Robinson 1999; Mohanty 2003). In relation to peace, feminist arguments deepen the critique of direct and structural violence and offer new accounts of the conditions that would need to be in place to take the world beyond war and the war system. In so doing, feminism challenges the complicity of all modern ideological traditions, including revolutionary traditions, with violent practices that sustain, and are sustained by, gendered hierarchies (Parpart and Zalewski 2008).

As with feminism, postcolonial critical interventions are not about the dismissal of critical theory, but about the reception and redemption of claims about peace, equity, emancipation and solidarity. In terms of the practice of critical theory, postcolonialism raises the question of the meaning of the universal reach of the critic's claims, and the accounts of truth and history on which they rest. Is the meaning of modernity always the same? Is it possible to read any singular trajectory into the workings of history? Whose imagination is shaping the contours of utopia (Chakrabarty 2000; Nandy 2002, 2009)? Postcolonial thinking reorients the practice of critical theory by challenging it to take its identification with the subaltern seriously, and not to assume that the meaning of subalternity is known in advance. Substantively, postcolonialism invites the critic to provincialize his or her commitments to post-national constellations, human rights or cosmopolitan democracy. It forces the critic to address issues of cultural imperialism and paternalism in emancipatory projects. And it radicalizes thinking about how historical injustices may be addressed, not only for people imagined as the global poor, but for the imaginations of those produced and 'othered' by modernity as backward, indigenous, or nomadic (Inayatullah and Blaney 2004; Nayak and Selbin 2010).

Traditionally, critical theory of the Frankfurt School type subsumed issues relating to gender and imperialism under a broader story of capitalist subordination. In contrast, as Wyn Jones points out, issues of technology, production and relations to nature were central to Adorno and Horkheimer and their reading of the 'dark' side of modernity. In the take up of critical theory in IR, these are themes that have been less central than those relating to intra-human relations, the historically immanent possibilities of transcendence of borders, peace, human rights, distributive justice, global civil society and transnational democracy. Yet, if the redemption of the claims of critical theory is taken seriously by the putatively universal audience to whom those claims are addressed, a focus on relations between species and the relation between the human species and the global environment necessarily transforms the practice and agenda of critical theory in important ways. When it comes to practice, the critical theorist is obliged to think in terms of intrinsic limitation and dependence as the *sine qua non* of world imagining and making. And in terms of the agenda of critical theory, ecological issues take on a much greater priority in the project of making a world of equality and freedom (Vogler and Imber 1996; Stevis and Assetto 2001; Newell and Paterson 2010).

Conclusion

Feminist, postcolonial and green arguments exemplify critical theory as both a mode of theoretical practice and a set of normative aspirations. Critical theory is not about capturing the high ground of critical authority nor designing global blueprints for the future, it is the ongoing attempt to render the goals of equity, peace, emancipation and solidarity real and realizable for those who suffer from their absence, and for those in more privileged positions who are nevertheless committed to those ends. The audience of critical theory is the constituency of those who are exploited and oppressed, including the victims of patriarchy, imperialism and environmental degradation, and it is that audience who finds that the work of critical theory does or does not resonate with their own understandings of equity, peace, emancipation and solidarity.

The ongoing process of disorientation and reorientation of judgement that doing critique involves does not limit the prescriptive ambitions of the critic. Without a commitment to conditions that transcend the inequity, violence, domination and alienation that currently characterize the world, then there is no critique. However, in decentring the critic's representation of the world and his or her place in it, the practice of critique always also confirms the transfer of authoritative judgement from the critic to the world.

Bibliography

Chakrabarty, D. (2000) *Provincializing Europe: postcolonial thought and historical difference*, Princeton: Princeton University Press.

Connolly, W. (2008) 'The Power of Assemblages and the Fragility of Things', *British Journal of Politics and International Relations* 10(2): 241–50.

Cox, R.W. (1981) 'Social Forces, State and World Orders: beyond international relations theory', *Millennium* 10(2): 126–55.

____ (1996) *Approaches to World Order*, Cambridge: Cambridge University Press.

Hutchings, K. (1996) *Kant, Critique and Politics*, London: Routledge.

____ (2003) *Hegel and Feminist Philosophy*, Cambridge: Polity Press.

____ (2008) *Time and World Politics: thinking the present*, Manchester: Manchester University Press.

Inayatullah, N. and Blaney, D (2004) *International Relations and the Problem of Difference*, New York: Routledge.

Linklater, A. (1998) *The Transformation of Political Community: ethical foundations of the post-Westphalian era*, Cambridge: Polity Press.

Mitchell, T. (ed.) (2000) *Questions of Modernity*, Minneapolis and London: University of Minnesota Press.

Mohanty, C.T. (2003) *Feminism Without Borders: decolonising theory, practicing solidarity*, Durham and London: Duke University Press.

Nandy, A. (2002) *Time Warps: silent and evasive pasts in Indian politics and religion*, New Brunswick: Rutgers University Press.

____ (2009) *The Intimate Enemy: loss and recovery of self under colonialism*, 2nd edn, New Delhi: Oxford University Press.

Nayak, M and Selbin, E. (2010) *Decentering International Relations*, London: Zed Books.

Newell, P. and Paterson, M. (2010) *Climate Capitalism*, Cambridge: Cambridge University Press.

Parpart, J. and Zalewski, M. (eds) (2008) *Rethinking the Man Question: sex, gender and violence in international relations*, London: Zed Books.

Robinson, F. (1999) *Globalizing Care*, Boulder: Westview Press.

Stevis, D. and Assetto, V. (eds) (2001) *The International Political Economy of the Environment: critical perspectives*, Boulder: Lynne Rienner.

Vogler, J. and Imber, M. (eds) (1996) *The Environment and International Relations*, London: Routledge.

INDEX

Bold = extended discussion; n = occurring in notes

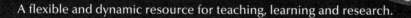